PERFOR

To Bernhard Giesen

PERFORMANCE AND POWER

JEFFREY C. ALEXANDER

polity

First published in 2011 by Polity Press

Polity Press
65 Bridge Street
Cambridge CB2 1UR, UK

Polity Press
350 Main Street
Malden, MA 02148, USA

ISBN-13: 978-0-7456-4817-0
ISBN-13: 978-0-7456-4818-7 (pb)

A catalog record for this book is available from the British Library.

Typeset in 10.5 on 12 pt Sabon
by Servis Filmsetting Ltd, Stockport, Cheshire
Printed and bound in Great Britain by MPG Books Group Limited, Bodmin, Cornwall

The publisher has used its best endeavors to ensure that the URLs for external websites referred to in this book are correct and active at the time of going to press. However, the publisher has no responsibility for the websites and can make no guarantee that a site will remain live or that the content is or will remain appropriate.

For further information on Polity, visit our website: www.politybooks.com

CONTENTS

CONTENTS

PREFACE AND ACKNOWLEDGMENTS

This book brings together my essayistic efforts to create cultural pragmatics. Some of them are more theoretical; others apply the new perspective to controversial empirical topics of the day. Between philosophically oriented metatheory and purely factual investigation is a productive place that Robert Merton called sociological theory in the middle range. That is the sweet spot towards which cultural pragmatics aims, even as it gestures to the philosophical and the factual environments on either of its sides.

This project has occupied me for much of the last decade. It developed in the course of graduate and undergraduate seminars at Yale; in weekly workshops of the Yale Center for Cultural Sociology, which I direct with Ron Eyerman and Philip Smith; and in a series of Yale-Konstanz seminars organized with Bernhard Giesen, which culminated in the volume we edited with Jason Mast, *Social Performance: Symbolic Action, Cultural Pragmatics, and Ritual* (Cambridge 2006).

Graduate students and colleagues on both sides of the Atlantic have been significant for the development of cultural pragmatics, as responsive audiences, interpreting critics, fellow actors and co-writers of the emerging theoretical script. I owe a great deal to my collaboration with Bernhard Giesen, with whom I have been working for three decades in the creation of cultural-sociological theory. I am indebted also to Jason Mast, whose theoretical dissatisfaction provided a decisive early stimulus and whose insights and friendship provided energy all along the way. I would like also to thank John Thompson, a founder and publisher of Polity Press, for his encouragement, and Nadine Amalfi for her editorial assistance.

These essays appeared over a four-year period and have been revised in small and sometimes in larger ways for their publication here. Two are published here for the first time. I thank the following journals and presses for permission to publish the others.

Chapters 1, 2, and 8: Cambridge University Press for "Introduction: symbolic action in theory and practice: the cultural pragmatics of symbolic action," "Cultural pragmatics: social performance between ritual and strategy," and "From the depths of despair: performance, counter performance and September 11" in Alexander, J. C., Giesen, B. and Mast, J. (eds.), *Social Performance: Symbolic Action, Cultural Pragmatics, and Ritual* (2006).

Chapters 3 and 7: *Culture, Newsletter of the Sociology of Culture Section of the American Sociological Association* for "Performance and Power" and "Performance and Counter-Power (1 and 2): The Civil Rights Movement and the Civil Sphere" (Autumn 2005, Winter and Spring 2006).

Chapter 4: Oxford University Press for "Note on Concept and Method" in my book-length effort to apply cultural pragmatics to domestic power struggle in a democratic society, *The Performance of Politics: Obama's Victory and the Democratic Struggle for Power* (2010).*

Chapter 5: *The Journal of Power* for "The Democratic Struggle for Power: The 2008 Presidential Campaign in the United States" (vol. 2(1), pp. 65–88; 2009).

Chapter 9: European University Institute for "Power and Performance: The War on Terror between the Sacred and the Profane," in *RSCAS Distinguished Lectures Working Paper Series* (vol. 1; 2007).

Chapter 10: Ashgate for "Public Intellectuals and Civil Society," in Fleck, C., Hess, A. and Stina Lyon, E. (eds.), *Intellectuals and their Publics: Perspectives from the Social Sciences* (2009).

---

* For another book-length application of cultural pragmatics, this one to power struggles in a non-Western setting, see Jeffrey C. Alexander, *Performative Revolution in Egypt: An Essay in Cultural Power* (London and New York: Bloomsbury Academic, 2011).

Men cherish something that seems like the real thing as much as they do the real thing itself.

Machiavelli, *Discourses*

That which taken away the reputation of Sincerity, is the doing or saying of such things, as appear to be signes, that what they require other men to believe, is not believed by themselves.

Hobbes, *Leviathan*

A lot of this is theater. How do you communicate to 38 million people? You're not sitting down talking to them. So it's gesture, symbol, the narrative, the drama. Who's the protagonist? Who's the antagonist?

Jerry Brown, Governor of California

INTRODUCTION

Culture and power usually find themselves face to face at the far ends of social theory as well as in the black-and-white stereotypes of social life. Culture is internal, power external. Culture is about subjectivity, power about objectivity. Culture is will and enthusiasm, power coercion and force. Culture involves emotion; power is all calculation and choice.

In reality, culture and power are everywhere intertwined. Politicians win power by convincing voters to believe, becoming symbolic representations of the hopes and fears and dreams of collective life. After they take hold of the reins of power and gain control of administration in the state, the new rulers cannot just order people about, expecting them to obey or else. They need to make government meaningful, to align administration with the stories citizens tell each other about what they hope and what they do and where the best of society should be. So the powerful couch their commands as requests and frame their administration as the last, best hope of humankind. If they cannot, and end up just issuing commands, the people will not see government as a symbol of their values and, in a democracy, they will take the rulers' power away. Not in a dictatorship, but even an emperor wants to rule with the mandate of heaven. When authoritarian rulers lose the mandate, when they fail to make even the effort to embody culture and symbolize collective meanings, they need to employ more force and coercion. This is a lot less efficient and much more time consuming, and it arouses more resistance. Even for those who have authoritarian power the hatred of their subjects is a terrible thing.

We owe to Max Weber the conceptual separation of power from meaning and also, paradoxically, the first elusive step toward bringing

1

them together. For Weber, power is the ability to carry out one's wishes against the will of others. This structural definition is without recourse to voluntary compliance; in fact, it is dead set against it. Here we have the tradition of power politics, *realpolitik*, statism, naked force. No wonder Weber famously defines the modern state by its ability to monopolize the means of violence. Under the influence of this Weber, the Weber of domination (*Herrschaft*), political sociology emerges as the hard-headed study of how forceful imposition is distributed and whether it is visible or hidden in plain sight.

This is a dead end, not just hard but thick-headed. Weber's minimalist definition is too much. It does not allow us to understand what power really is and how it works, or not, in meaningful ways.

Weber implicitly acknowledges this inadequacy when he places on top of his working theory of power the concept of legitimacy. Power is usually exercised in reference to some belief, which transforms power into authority. Beyond this recognition, however, Weber does not have a lot to say. His ideal-types of legitimate authority – charismatic, traditional, and rational-legal – parse broad historical transformations of power but tell us precious little about how legitimacy actually works. Despite occasional charismatic eruptions, modern authority is seen as something that is generally rational-legal, as all about following procedures and fine print, about calculating and impersonal bureaucrats and responsible, goal-oriented politicians. But neither modern organizations nor politics works in this way. Power cannot legitimate itself simply by citing its rational-legal authority. The concept of rational-legal legitimacy is a straitjacket, a hindrance to creative thinking about how modern power is, and is not, meaningfully defined.

Weber's century-old typology makes historical sense, but it turns the process of making power meaningful into a black box from which there protrudes little intellectual light. It suffers from a crimped understanding of modernity as deracinated, as bound to mechanical causality and stripped of myth and telos. How can power be made meaningful if modernity itself is conceived as having shed the very idea of meaning along the way?

To get power closer to meaning we need a more cultural sociology. Strong programs in cultural sociology take off from the notion that between traditional and modern societies there is not a radical epistemological break. Moderns still have their myths and meanings; they are still sustained by narratives that move toward an idealized telos, that motivate rather than simply determine, that inspire and not only cause. In modern societies, culture structures remain strong

2

and binding. They are not subject to scientific scrutiny and discarded if they falsified in this way. Cultural truth is moral and aesthetic. In the world of meaning, as Robert Bellah long ago suggested, symbolic realism, not social reduction, reigns supreme.

We can move beyond Weber by linking power more directly with culture, but "culture" per se is too big, too structural, too inert. Power comes into being when social actors exercise their agency. It is subtle and complex, often of exquisite indirection, a process that is not all that different from how dramatic actors project the power of their characters in a play. In a theatrical performance, the script is set, the viewers have tickets and are in their seats, the scenery is designed and the lighting is cast. But everything, at least all the really most important things, still remain. It is up to the actors to play the scene, to convince those watching that they really are the characters they say they are, that the pretend life on stage is truthful, that, being a simulation, it is the real thing all right.

Culture structures are powerful, but they provide only the background representations for active social life. Real living people, whether as individuals or in groups, move about in practical situations of multiple possibility. Even in theatrical set pieces, when actors share the same culture structures and the same stage, it is difficult for audiences to be certain what the actors mean to say. It is that much more difficult for social actors. Because they must bring meaning to bear pragmatically, in situations of multiple possibility, they try to carve fluid, action-specific scripts from the background of broad cultural meanings. In modern and even more so in postmodern societies, scripts are not written in stone but continuously revised. And, while some members of the contemporary audience have tickets, some cannot afford them, others choose not to show up, and many mill around during the performance, refusing to take their seats. In contemporary societies, the props and stagings of action are always shifting, and it is difficult for actors and audiences to know where and when to put themselves into the scene. Critics – reviewers, journalists, intellectuals, and everyday wise guys – provide running evaluations of performances as they are unfolding, often thrusting vituperative and contentious interpretations into the *mise-en-scène*. The upshot is that the power to mount a play is often abruptly taken away.

The difference between tradition and modernity is not that meaning is there, in earlier societies, and not here today. It is rather that the context for making meaning has changed. It is not only that, with modernity, "the social, political, and cultural" must be distinguished but, as I argue in chapter 4, the "performative" must be separated out, analytically and empirically, as well. When societies were small and compact and their collective identities sturdy and homogeneous, when social organization seemed closely to reflect metaphysical meanings rooted in the certainties of an other-worldly life, it was not nearly so hard to make oneself understood or one's power believed. Under these conditions, symbolic action was more often ritualized, more easily generating shared feelings and expectations, sustaining community, and frequently repeated in familiar ways. As societies become more complex, more divided vertically and more fragmented horizontally, and as they lose their metaphysical anchoring, the ability for performances to create fusion between actors, texts, and audiences breaks down. Authenticity becomes problematic and criticism becomes the order of the day. Political opponents strive to separate the other's actions from meaning, to make them seem artificial. Modernity not only invents the very idea of performance, but gives it a bad name. When the meaning of symbolic action is misapprehended, the actor seems awkward and wooden, as if she is putting on an act. Successful performance seems natural, not contrived, not a performance but an effortless expression, true to life.

The first and second chapters of this book elaborate a theory of cultural pragmatics. I separate out the elements that compose a social performance, define them, explain how they have become separated from one another in the face of historical complexity, and describe the implications of this transforming for meaning-making, especially in modern and postmodern social life. Power contributes to the construction of social performance, and as it becomes separated from other elements it initiates a new form of social performance.

When cultural-pragmatic theory is applied to the "challenge of power," I suggest in chapter 3, it bring light into the black box, illuminating the process of legitimacy in a deeper, post-Weberian way. If we are to understand how power is exercised, we need not only cultural theory from the late Durkheim, hermeneutics, semiotics and post-structuralism, but the tools of theater, film, television, and performance studies, of media research, of reception theory, and ideas about emotion and materiality.

Power is performative in every one of its hydra-headed forms. Wars are won not only on battlefields but in hearts and minds, on both the home and the enemy side. Staging and dramaturgy are critical, and when they fail – as I show in chapter 9, "War and performance: Afghanistan and Iraq" – counter-performances emerge that can undermine confidence and shatter legitimacy. Terrorism is the steel edge of the knife blade, seemingly pure coercion, but its exercise is likewise enmeshed in binary coding and narration, and carefully choreographed, as chapter 8, "Performing terror on September 11," documents in a depressing way.

It would seem a whole lot easier – a theoretical slam dunk – to conceptualize the exercise of democratic power as symbolically meaningful and performatively enacted. That this has not been the case is not only the fault of Max Weber. It is also because of the "cynical reason" that so often masquerades as the common sense of modern life. Rather than seeing money as the mother's milk of politics, and strategy as the key to political organization, in chapter 5 – "Democratic power and political performance" – I demonstrate how symbol and staging, narrative and coding, performance and counter-performance defined the epochal power struggle between Barack Obama and John McCain in the American presidential contest of 2008. In winning that historic election, Barack Obama brought the de-fused elements of performance together in a masterful, apparently seamless way, but he has not been nearly as successful in his symbolic efforts since he has held the actual fundaments of state power in his hands. The often-told adage that one campaigns in poetry but governs in prose is wrong. Without poetry, governing cannot succeed, as Obama in power – at least for the first two years – has learned to his deep regret. Obama's failure to symbolize, and the consequences of his evacuation of the public stage, are the topic of chapter 6.

Even when the cultural character of mainstream politics is acknowledged, theorists and researchers are inclined to view mass protest movements as deliberative actions of rational resistance. In chapter 7, "Performing counter-power: The civil rights movement," I examine dramatic moments in the African-American freedom struggle and show that the performance of meaning was actually at the core of that great mid-century movement for civil rights.

In the final chapters of this book, I turn from political to cultural power. Even for those who, like Pierre Bourdieu, acknowledge the significance of power in the cultural domain, its exercise is conceived as structured by the distribution of material resources, its motivation as ingrained habit, and its reception pretty much as a sure thing. My understanding of cultural power could not be more different. As I suggest in chapter 10, "Intellectuals and public performance," intellectuals become important, not by virtue of their credentials and status, but because of how dramatically they attack the civil deficits of their national societies and inspire its civil repair. In chapter 11, I move from morality to aesthetics. The impact of even the most prestigious aesthetic objects is uneven and precarious. Such variation in "iconic power" can be conceptualized as a matter of aesthetic performativity, which is mediated by the interpretive power of critics. Without attending to the fiercely independent judgment of critics, it is impossible to gauge the exercise of cultural power in modern social life.

Michel Foucault turned Weber's separation of power and meaning on its head. He knotted them into the couplet power/knowledge, treating each as if it were the *sine qua non*, the very condition for operation of the other side. If it were only that easy to make oneself understood, to assure that one's power were accepted and obeyed! Foucault describes persons inside systems of knowledge/power as occupying subject positions. But people are not subjects; they are actors. People anchor their actions in culture structures, but they continuously script their lines of actions in pragmatic and meaningfully distinctive ways. Sometimes these scripts are believed, and they give power legitimacy. Often, however, the justifications that power evocatively proffers are questioned. Its knowledge is not acknowledged, its supposed expertise fervently resisted, and sometimes counter-performances are mounted in its place. One does not simply speak truth to power. One must perform it as well.

— 1 —

THE CULTURAL PRAGMATICS OF SYMBOLIC ACTION

with Jason Mast

The question of theory and practice permeates not only politics but culture, where the analogue for theory is the social-symbolic text, the bundle of everyday codes, narratives, and rhetorical configurings that are the objects of hermeneutic reconstruction. Emphasizing action over its theory, praxis theorists have blinded themselves to the deeply imbedded textuality of every social action (Bourdieu 1984; Swidler 1986; Turner 1969). But a no less distorting myopia has affected the vision from the other side. The pure hermeneut (e.g., Dilthey 1976; Ricoeur 1976) tends to ignore the material problem of instantiating ideals in the real world. The truth, as Marx (1972: 145) wrote in his Xth thesis on Feuerbach, is that, while theory and practice are different, they are always necessarily intertwined.

Theory and practice are interwoven in everyday life, not only in social theory and social science. In the following chapters, we will see that powerful social actors understand the conceptual issues of performance in an intuitive, ethnographic, and practical way. Individuals, organizations, and parties moved "instinctively" to hook their actions into the background culture in a lively and compelling manner, working to create an impression of sincerity and authenticity rather than one of calculation and artificiality, to achieve verisimilitude. Social movements' public demonstrations display a similar performative logic. Movement organizers, intensely aware of media organizations' control over the means of symbolic distribution, direct their participants to perform in ways that will communicate that they are worthy, committed, and determined to achieve acceptance and inclusion from the larger political community. Social actors, embedded in collective representations and working through symbolic and material means, implicitly orient towards others as if they were actors

7

on a stage seeking identification with their experiences and understandings from their audiences.

Towards a cultural pragmatics

Kenneth Burke (1957 [1941]) introduced the notion of symbolic action; Clifford Geertz (1973a) made it famous. These thinkers wanted to draw attention to the specifically cultural character of activities, the manner in which they are expressive rather than instrumental, irrational rather than rational, more like theatrical performance than economic exchange. Drawing also from Burke, Erving Goffman (1956) introduced his own dramaturgical theory at about the same time. Because of the one-sidedly pragmatic emphases of symbolic interactionism, however, the specifically cultural dimension of this Goffmanian approach (Alexander 1987a) to drama made hardly any dent on the sociological tradition, though it later entered into the emerging discipline of performance studies.

In the decades that have ensued since the enunciation of these seminal ideas, those who have taken the cultural turn have followed a different path. It has been meaning, not action, that has occupied central attention, and deservedly so. To show the importance of meaning, as compared to such traditional sociological ciphers as power, money, and status, it has been necessary to show that meaning is a structure, just as powerful as these others (Rambo and Chan 1999; Somers 1995). To take meaning seriously, not to dismiss it as an epiphenomenon, has been the challenge. Strong programs in contemporary cultural sociology (Alexander and Sherwood 2002; Alexander and Smith 1998, 2010; Edles 1998; Emirbayer and Goodwin 1996; Jacobs 1996; Kane 1997; Sewell 1985; Smith 1998; Somers 1995) have followed Ricoeur's philosophical demonstration that meaningful actions can be considered as texts, exploring codes and narratives, metaphors, metathemes, values, and rituals in such diverse institutional domains as religion, nation, class, race, family, gender, and sexuality. It has been vital to establish what makes meaning important, what makes some social facts meaningful at all.

In terms of Charles Morris's (1938) classic distinction, strong programs have focused on the syntactics and semantics of meaning, on the relations of signs to one another and to their referents. Ideas about symbolic action and dramaturgy gesture, by contrast, to the pragmatics of the cultural process, to the relations between cultural texts and the actors in everyday life. While the latter considerations

8

have by no means been entirely ignored by those who have sought to sustain a meaning-centered program in cultural sociology (e.g., Wagner-Pacifici 1986), they have largely been addressed either through relatively ad hoc empirical studies or in terms of the metatheoretical debate over structure and agency (Alexander 1988a, 2003a; Hays 1994; Kane 1991; Sahlins 1976; Sewell 1992). Metatheory is indispensable as an orienting device. It thinks out problems in a general manner and, in doing so, provides more specific, explanatory thinking with a direction to go. The challenge is to move downward on the scientific continuum, from the presuppositions of metatheory to the models and empirical generalizations upon which explanation depends. Metatheoretical thinking about structure and agency has provided hunches about how this should be done, and creative empirical studies show that it can be, but there remains a gaping hole between general concepts and empirical facts. Without providing systematic mediating concepts – a middle range theoretical model – even the most fruitful efforts to bridge semantics and pragmatics (e.g., Kane 1997; Sahlins 1981; Wagner-Pacifici 1986) have an ad hoc, "one off" character, and the more purely metatheoretical often produce awkward, even oxymoronic circumlocutions.[1] Cultural practices are not simply speech acts. Around the same time Goffman was developing a pragmatic dramaturgy in sociology, John Austin (1957) introduced ordinary language philosophy to the idea that language could have a performative function and not only a constative one. Speaking aims to get things done, Austin denoted, not merely to make assertions and provide descriptions. In contrast to simply describing, the performative speech act has the capacity to realize its semantic contents; it is capable of constituting a social reality through its utterance. On the other hand, it can fail. Because a performative may or may not work – it may or may not succeed in realizing its stated intention – Austin keenly observes, its appropriate evaluative standard is not truth and accuracy, but "felicitous" and "infelicitous."

When Austin turned to investigating felicity's conditions, however, like Goffman he stressed only the speech act's interactional context, and failed to account for the cultural context out of which particular signs are drawn forth by a speaker. This philosophical innovation could have marked a turn to the aesthetic and to considerations of what makes actions exemplary (Arendt 1958; Ferrara 2001); instead, it led to an increasing focus on the interactional, the situational, and the practical (e.g., Goffman 1956; Habermas 1984; Schegloff 1987; Searle 1961). Austin's innovation, like Goffman's dramaturgy, had the effect of cutting off the practice of language from its texts.

Saussure would have agreed with Austin that *parole* (speech) must be studied independently of *langue* (language). However, he would have insisted on the "arbitrary nature of the sign" – that, to consider its effectiveness, spoken language must be considered in its totality, as both *langue* and *parole*. A sign's meaning is arbitrary, Saussure demonstrated, in that "it actually has no natural connection with the signified" (1985: 38), that is, the object it is understood to represent.[2] Its meaning is arbitrary in relation to its referent in the real world, but it is also arbitrary in the sense that it is not determined by the intention or will of any individual speaker or listener. Rather, a sign's meaning derives from its relations – metaphorical, metonymic, synec-dochic – to other signs in a system of sign relations, or language. The relations between signs in a cultural system are fixed by social conven-tion; they are structures that social actors experience as natural, and unreflexively depend on to constitute their daily lives. Consequently, an accounting of felicity's conditions must attend to the cultural structures that render a performative intelligible, meaningful, and capable of being interpreted as felicitous or infelicitous, in addition to the mode and context in which the performative is enacted.

In this respect, Saussure's sometimes errant disciple, Jacques Derrida, was a faithful son, and it is in Derrida's (1982a [1972]) response to Austin's speech act theory that post-structuralism begins to demonstrate a deep affinity with contemporary cultural pragmat-ics. Derrida criticizes Austin for submerging the contribution of the cultural text to performative outcome. Austin "appears to consider solely the conventionality constituting the *circumstance* of the utter-ance (*énoncé*), its contextual surroundings," Derrida admonishes, "and not a certain conventionality intrinsic to what constitutes the speech act (locution) itself, all that might be summarized rapidly under the problematic rubric of 'the arbitrary nature of the sign'" (1988: 15). In this way, Derrida sharply admonishes Austin for ignor-ing the "citational" quality of even the most pragmatic writing and speech. What he means is that all words cite the seemingly absent background cultural texts from which they derive their meanings. "Could a performative utterance succeed," Derrida asks, "if its for-mulation did not repeat a 'coded' or iterable utterance, or in other words, if the formula I pronounce in order to open a meeting, launch a ship or a marriage were not identifiable as conforming with an itera-ble model, if it were not then identifiable in some way as a 'citation'?" (1988: 18).

10

Because there can be no determinate, trans-contextual relation of signifier and referent, difference always involves *différance* (Derrida 1982b). Interpreting symbolic practice – culture in its "presence" – always entails a reference to culture in its "absence," that is, to an implied semiotic text. In other words, to be practical and effective in action – to have a successful performance – actors must be able to make the meanings of culture structures stick. Since meaning is the product of relations between signs in a discursive code or text, a dramaturgy that intends to take meaning seriously must account for the cultural codes and texts that structure the cognitive environments in which speech is given form.

Dramaturgy emerges from the confluence of hermeneutic, post-structural, and pragmatic theories of meaning's relation to social action. Cultural pragmatics grows out of this confluence, maintaining that cultural practice must be theorized independently of cultural symbolics, even as it remains fundamentally interrelated with it. Cultural action puts texts into practice, but it cannot do so directly, without passing "go." A theory of practice must respect the relative autonomy of structures of meaning. Pragmatics and semantics are analytical, not concrete distinctions.

The real and the artificial

One of the challenges in theorizing contemporary cultural practice is the manner in which it seems to slide between artifice and authenticity. There is the deep pathos of Princess Diana's death and funeral, mediated, even in a certain sense generated by, highly constructed, commercially targeted televised productions, yet so genuine and compelling that the business of a great national collectivity came almost fully to rest. There are the Pentagon's faked anti-ballistic missile tests and its doctored action photographs of smart missiles during the Iraq war, both of which were taken as genuine in their respective times. There is the continuous and often nauseating flow of staged-for-camera pseudo-events, which Daniel Boorstin (1961) had already flushed out in the 1960s. Right along beside them, there is the undeniable moral power generated by the equally "artificial" media events studied by Daniel Dayan and Elihu Katz (1992) – Sadat's arrival in Jerusalem, the Pope's first visit to Poland, and John F. Kennedy's funeral.

Plays, movies, and television shows are staged "as if" they occur in real life, and in real time. To seem as if they are "live," to seem

11

real, they are increasingly shot "on location." National armies intimidate one another by staging war games, completely artificial events whose intention – not to produce a "real" effect – is announced well before they occur, but which often alter real balances of power. Revolutionary guerrilla groups, such as the Zapatista rebels from Chiapas, Mexico, represent powerful grassroots movements that aim to displace vast material interests and often have the effect of getting real people killed. Yet the masses in such movements present their collective force via highly staged photo-marches, and their leaders, like subcommander Marcos, enter figuratively into the public sphere, as iconic representations of established cultural forms.

The effort at artificially creating the impression of liveness is not new. The Impressionist painters wanted to trump the artificiality of the French Academy by moving outside, to be closer to the nature they were representing, to paint "*en plein air.*" The Lincoln–Douglas debates were highly staged, and their "real influence" would have been extremely narrow were it not for the hyperbolic expansiveness of the print media (Schudson 1998). The aristocracies and emerging middle classes of the Renaissance, the period marking the very birth of modernity, were highly style conscious, employing facial make-up and hair shaping on both sides of the gender divide, and engaging, more generally, in strenuous efforts at "self-fashioning" (Greenblatt 1980). It was the greatest writer of the Renaissance, after all, who introduced into Western literature the very notion that "the whole world's a stage, and we merely actors upon it."

Despite a history of reflexive awareness of artificiality and constructedness, such postmodern commentators as Baudrillard (1983) announce, and denounce, the contemporary interplaying of reality with fiction as demarcating a new age, one in which pragmatics has displaced semantics, social referents have disappeared, and only signifiers powered by the interests and powers of the day remain. Such arguments represent a temptation, fueled by a kind of nostalgia, to treat the distinction between the real and artificial in an essentialist way. Cultural pragmatics holds that this vision of simulated hypertextuality is not true, that the signified, no matter what its position in the manipulated field of cultural production, can never be separated from some set of signifiers (see also Sherwood 1994).

The relation between authenticity and modes of presentation are, after all, historically and culturally specific.[3] During the Renaissance, for instance, the theater, traditionally understood to be a house of spectacle, seduction, and idolatry, began to assume degrees of authenticity traditionally reserved for the dramatic text, which was

12

honored for its purity and incorruptibility. The relation between authenticity and the senses shifted during this time as well. Its close association with the aural eroding, authenticity became an attribute of the visual. The visual displaced the aural as the sense most closely associated with apprehending and discerning the authentic, the real, and the true. The aural, on the other hand, was increasingly presumed to "displace 'sense'" and language to "dissolve into pure sound and leave reason behind" (Peters 2000: 163).

It is difficult to imagine a starker example of authenticity's cultural specificity than Donald Frischmann's (1994) description of the Tzotzil people's reaction to a live theatrical performance staged in their village of San Juan Chamula, in Chiapas, Mexico in 1991. Frischmann describes how, during the reenactment of an occurrence of domestic violence, the audience was taken by "a physical wave of emotion [that] swept through the entire crowd," nearly knocking audience members "down onto the floor." During a scene in which a confession is flogged out of two accused murderers the line separating theatrical production and audience completely disintegrated: "By this point in the play, the stage itself was full of curious and excited onlookers – children and men, surrounding the actors in an attempt to get a closer look at the stage events, which so curiously resembled episodes of *real life* out in the central plaza" (Frischmann 1994: 223, italics in original).

For cultural pragmatics, authenticity is an interpretive category rather than an ontological state. The status of authenticity is arrived at, is contingent, and results from processes of social construction; its accomplishment is separated from any transcendental, ontological referent. If there is a normative repulsion to the fake or inauthentic, cultural pragmatics suggests this must be treated in an analytical way, as a structuring code in the symbolic fabric actors depend on to interpret their lived realities.

Yes, we are "condemned" to live out our lives in an age of artifice, a world of mirrored, manipulated, and mediated representation. But the constructed character of symbols does not make them less real. A talented anthropologist and a clinical psychologist published a lengthy empirical account (Marvin and Ingle 1999) describing the flag of the United States, the "stars and stripes," as a totem for the American nation, a tribe whose members periodically engage in blood sacrifice so that the totem may continue to thrive. Such a direct equation of contemporary sacrality with pre-literate tribal life has its dangers, as we are about to suggest, yet there is much in this account that rings powerfully true.

13

Nostalgia and counter-nostalgia: Sacrality then and now

For those who continue to insist on the centrality of meaning in contemporary societies, and who see these meanings as in some necessary
manner refractions of culture structures, the challenge is to incorporate the distinctiveness of "modernity," an historical designation that
now includes postmodernity as well. Why does it remain so difficult
to conceptualize the cultural implications of the vast historical difference between earlier times and our own? One reason is that so much
of contemporary theorizing about culture has seemed determined to
elide it. The power–knowledge fusion that Foucault postulates at the
center of the modern episteme is, in fact, much less characteristic of
contemporary societies than it was of earlier, more traditional ones,
where social structure and culture were relatively fused. The same is
true for Bourdieu's habitus, a self that is mere nexus, the emotional
residue of group position and social structure that much more clearly
reflects the emotional situation of early societies than the autonomiz-
ing, reflexive, deeply ambivalent psychological processes of today.

Culture still remains powerful in an a priori manner, even in the
most contemporary societies. Powers are still infused with sacralizing discourses, and modern and postmodern actors can strategize
only by typifying in terms of institutionally segmented binary codes.
Secularization does not mean the loss of cultural meaning, the emergence of completely free-floating institutions, or the creation of purely
self-referential individual actors (see also Emirbayer and Mische
1998). There remains, in Ken Thompson's (1990) inimitable phrase,
the "dialectic between sacralization and secularization." But action
does not relate to culture in an unfolding sort of way. Secularization
does mean differentiation rather than fusion, not only between
culture, self, and social structure, but also within culture itself.

Mannheim (1971 [1927]) pointed out that it has been the unwillingness to accept the implications of such differentiation that
characterizes conservative political theory, which from Burke (1987
[1790]) to Oakeshott (1981 [1962]) to contemporary communitarians
has given short shrift to cultural diversity and individual autonomy.
Such an unwillingness has also undermined the genuine and important insights of interpretively oriented cultural social science.

For the relatively small group of modern social thinkers who have
maintained that, despite modernization, meaning still matters, the
tools developed for analyzing meaning in traditional and simple
societies have often seemed sufficient. For instance, late in his
career Durkheim used descriptions of Australian aboriginal clans'

ceremonial rites to theorize that rituals and "dramatic performances" embed and reproduce the cultural system in collective and individual actions (1996: 378). The Warramunga's ceremonial rites that honor a common ancestor, Durkheim argued, "serve no purpose other than to make the clan's mythical past present in people's minds" and thus to "revitalize the most essential elements of the collective consciousness" (p. 379). Almost a decade after the close of World War II, Shils and Young (1953) argued that Queen Elizabeth II's coronation signified nothing less than "an act of national communion," and W. Lloyd Warner (1959) argued Memorial Day represented an annual ritual that reaffirmed collective sentiments and permitted organizations in conflict to "subordinate their ordinary opposition and cooperate in collectively expressing the larger unity of the total community" (p. 279).

These latter arguments demonstrate a stunning symmetry with Durkheim's descriptions of the ritual process in comparatively simple and homogeneous aboriginal clans. They reveal how modern cultural thinkers often jump, each in their own creative way, directly from late Durkheim to late modernity, without making the necessary conceptual adjustments along the way. The effect is to treat the characteristics that distinguish modern from traditional societies as residual categories. It was in reaction to such insistence on social-cum-cultural integration that conflict theory made claims, long before postmodern constructivism, that public cultural performances were not affective but merely cognitive (Lukes 1977), that they sprang not from cultural texts but from artificial scripts (Benjamin 1968 [1936]), that they were less rituals in which audiences voluntarily if vicariously participated than symbolic effects controlled and manipulated by elites (Birnbaum 1955).

The old-fashioned Durkheimians, while not political conservatives, were often motivated by the same nostalgia for an earlier, simpler, and more cohesive age. Yet their critics have been moved by feelings of a not altogether different kind, by an anti-nostalgia that barely conceals their own deep yearning for the sacred life. In confronting the fragmentations of modern and postmodern life, political radicals have often been motivated by cultural conservatism. From Marx and Weber to the Frankfurt school (Horkheimer and Adorno 1972), from Arendt's (1951) mass society theory to Selznick's (1951, 1952), from Jameson (1991) to Baudrillard, left cultural critics have lodged the nostalgic claim that nothing can ever be the same again, that capitalism or industrial society or mass society or postmodernity has destroyed the possibility for meaning. The result has been that cultural history has been understood allegorically (see also Clifford 1986, 1988). It is narrated as a process of disenchantment, as a fall from Eden, as declension from a once golden age of wholeness and holiness (Sherwood 1994). The assertion is that once representation is encased in some artificial substance, whether it is substantively or only formally rational, it becomes mechanical and unmeaningful.

The classical theoretical statement of this allegory remains Walter Benjamin's (1968 [1936]) "The Work of Art in the Age of Mechanical Reproduction," veneration (!) for which has only grown among postmodern critics bent on exposing the artificiality of the present age. Benjamin holds that the auratic quality of art, the aura that surrounded it and gave it a sacred and holy social status, is inherently diminished by art's reproducibility. Sacred aura is a function of distance. It cannot be maintained once mechanical reproduction allows contact to become intimate, frequent, and, as a result, mundane. Baudrillard's simulacrum marks merely one more installment in the theoretical allegory of disenchantment. A more recent postmodern theorist, Peggy Phelan (1993: 146), has applied this allegory in suggesting that, because the "only life" of performance is "in the present," it "cannot be saved, recorded, documented, or otherwise participate in the circulation of representations of representations." Once performance is mechanically mediated, its meaningfulness is depleted. The argument here is pessimistic and Heideggerian. If ontology is defined in terms of *Dasein*, as "being there," then any artificial mediation will wipe it away. "To the degree that performance attempts to enter the economy of reproduction," Phelan predictably writes, "it betrays and lessens the promise of its own ontology."

We can escape from such critical and misleading nostalgia only by developing a more complex sociological theory of performance. It was Burke (1957, 1965) who first proposed to transform the straightforward action theory of Weber and Parsons, the schema of means-ends-norms-conditions that critiqued, yet simultaneously mimicked, economic man. Burke proposed taking "act" in a theatrical rather than a nominalist and mundane manner. For example, the "conditions" of action should be conceptualized as a "scene" upon which an action could be played out and displayed. With analytical transformations such as these, cultural traditions can be viewed not merely as regulating actions but as informing dramas, the performance of which displays exemplary motives, inspires catharsis, and allows working through (Burke 1959).

The implications of this extraordinary innovation were limited by the literary nature of Burke's ambitions and by the fact that he, too, betrayed nostalgia for a simpler society. Burke suggests (1965: 449, italics added), on the one hand, that "a drama is a mode of symbolic action so designed that an audience *might* be induced to 'act symbolically' in sympathy with it." Yet, he insists that "insofar as the drama *serves* this function it may be studied as a 'perfect mechanism' composed of parts moving in mutual adjustment to one another like clockwork." The idea is that, if audience sympathy is gained, then society really has functioned as a dramatic text, with true synchrony among its various parts. In other words, this theory of dramaturgy functions, not only as an analytical device, but also as an allegory for re-enchantment. The implication is that, if the theory is properly deployed, it will demonstrate for contemporaries how sacrality can be recaptured, that perhaps it has never disappeared, that the center will hold.

Such nostalgia for re-enchantment affected the most significant line of dramaturgical thinking to follow out from Burke. More than any other thinker, it was Victor Turner who demonstrated the most profound interest in modernizing ritual theory, with notions of ritual process, social dramas, liminality, and communitas being the most famous result (Turner 1969; see also Edles 1998). When he turned to dramaturgy, Turner (1974a, 1982) was able to carry this interest forward in a profoundly innovative manner, creating a theory of social dramas that deeply marked the social science of his day (Abrahams 1995; Wagner-Pacifici 1986). At the same time, however, Turner's intellectual evolution revealed a deep personal yearning for the more sacred life, demonstrated most forcefully in his identification of how ritual participation with liminal moments and communitas (1969).

Turner used these terms to describe social relations and forms of symbolic action that are unique to the ritual process. Derived from the term *limen*, which is Latin for "threshold," Turner defines liminality as representing "the midpoint of transition in a status-sequence between two positions" (1974a: 237). All rituals include liminal phases, Turner argued, in which traditional status distinctions dissolve, normative social constraints abate, and a unique form of solidarity, or communitas, takes hold:

> Communitas breaks in through the interstices of structure, in liminality; at the edges of structure . . . and from beneath structure . . . It is almost everywhere held to be sacred or "holy," possibly because it transgresses or dissolves the norms that govern structured and institutionalized relationships and is accompanied by experiences of unprecedented potency. (Turner 1969: 128)

17

During liminal moments, Turner maintains, social distinctions are leveled and an egalitarian order, or "open society" (1974a: 112), is momentarily created among ritual participants. Liminal social conditions foster an atmosphere of communitas, in which ritual participants are brought closer to the existential and primordial, and distanced from dependence on the cognitive, which Turner associates with the structured, normative social order. In such moments, the "unused evolutionary potential in mankind which has not yet been externalized and fixed in structure" is released, and ritual participants are free to "enter into vital relations with other men" (1974a: 127–8). Turner's re-enchantment imagery is unmistakable. It combines Marxist, utopian formulations of post-revolutionary, radical equality on the one hand, with Nietzschean (1956 [1872]) formulations of Dionysian social action on the other. Through liminality we may return to an idealized state of simple humanity, a community of equals; the dissolution of structure will initiate the erosion of our socially constructed selves, thus allowing us to explore the potency of our "unused evolutionary potential."

When Turner turned explicitly to theorizing about highly differentiated societies, he moved from an analytical model based on ritual to one based on performance. The concept of liminality weathered this transition, but Turner modified it. He recognized that relationships between ritual producers and audiences in post-industrial contexts are more complicated and contingent than those in tribal settings. Post-industrial actors demonstrate greater degrees of interpretive autonomy and more control over their solidary affiliations than the tribal members among whom Turner's fieldwork had been carried out. Thus, Turner introduces the concept "liminoid" to represent liminal-*like* moments and communitas-*like* sentiments that post-industrial actors experience in (ritual-*like*) social dramas that are more individualized and entered into more freely, "more a matter of choice, not obligation" (1982: 55). Despite these insightful modifications, the spirit of liminality, and the nostalgic sentiments that shaped it, continued to permeate every Turner's later work, exerting powerful sway in contemporary performance studies, as will be shown below.

If Turner moved from ritual to theater, his colleague, drama theorist and avant-garde theater producer Richard Schechner (1977a, 1977b, 1985, 1988), moved from theater to ritual and back again. Turner's theoretical cofounder of contemporary performance studies, Schechner provided the first systematic insight into the "mutual positive feedback relationship of social dramas and aesthetic performances" (2002: 68). His theorizing also provides a path for understanding failed cultural productions, yet he himself hankered for the wholeness that Peter Brook (1969) called "Holy Theatre." Schechner, even more than Turner, was animated as much by existential as analytical ambition, and his vision of performance studies is deeply shaped by the nostalgia for re-enchantment embedded in Turner's theorizing. Liminality, in Turner's theorizing, represented the pathway to re-enchantment. Liminality, for Schechner, is the cornerstone of performance studies:

> Performance Studies is "inter" – in between. It is intergenric, interdisciplinary, intercultural – and therefore inherently unstable. Performance studies resists or rejects definition. As a discipline, PS [sic] cannot be mapped effectively because it transgresses boundaries, it goes where it is not expected to be. It is inherently "in between" and therefore cannot be pinned down or located exactly. (Schechner 1998: 360)

For Schechner, performance studies is a set of performative acts that, if properly deployed, will catalyze liminality in the broader social arena, destabilize the normative structure, inspire criticism, and reacquaint mundane social actors with the primordial, vital, and existential dimensions of life. Put another way, for Schechner, performance studies is a vehicle for re-enchantment.

Clifford Geertz made a similar move from anthropology to theatricality, employing notions of staging and looking at symbolic action as dramatic representation. Yet it is striking how Geertz confined himself to studying performances inside firmly established and articulated ritual containers, from the Balinese cockfight (1973b), where "nothing happens" but an aesthetic affirmation of status structures, to the "theatre state" of nineteenth-century Bali (1980), where highly rigid authority structures were continuously reaffirmed in a priori, choreographed ways. In Geertz's dramaturgy, background collective representations and myths steal each scene. In the Balinese case, cultural scripts of masculinity, bloodlust, and status distinctions seem to literally exercise themselves through the social actions that constitute the cockfight event, leaving precious little room for the contingencies that accompany social actors' varying degrees of competency and complicity. The structural rigidity in Geertz's dramaturgy is doubly striking when juxtaposed to Turner and Schechner's emphasis on liminality and the social and cultural dynamism that liminal social actors may initiate.

What characterizes this entire line of thinking – which has been so central to the development of contemporary cultural-sociological thought – is the failure to take up the theoretical possibilities created by seeing symbolic action as performance. Fully intertwining semantics and pragmatics can allow for the openness and contingency that is blocked by theoretical nostalgia for simpler and more coherent societies.

In an influential volume that capped the "Turner era," and segued to performance theory, John MacAloon (1984: 1) offered a description of cultural performance that exemplified both the achievements and the limitations to which we are pointing here. Turner's and Geertz's influence cannot be missed: MacAloon defined performance as an "occasion in which as a culture or society we reflect upon and define ourselves, dramatize our collective myths and history, present ourselves with alternatives, and eventually change in some ways while remaining the same in others." Through social performances we tell a story about ourselves to ourselves (Geertz 1973b), and, because performances precipitate degrees of liminality, they are capable of transforming social relations. The communitarian emphasis on holism, on cultural, social, and psychological integration, is palpable.

Taking off from Burke in a different direction, Goffman initiated a second, decidedly less nostalgic line of dramaturgical theory. Half persuaded by game theory and rational choice, Goffman adopted a more detached, purely analytical approach to the actor's theatrical preoccupations. He insisted on complete separation of cultural performance from cultural text, of actor from script. Rejecting out of hand the possibility that any genuine sympathy was on offer, either from actor or from audience, Goffman described performance as a "front" behind which actors gathered their egotistical resources and upon which they displayed the "standardized expressive equipment" necessary to gain results. Idealization was a performative, but not an affective, moral, or cognitive fact. In modern societies, according to Goffman, the aim was to convincingly portray one's own ideal values as isomorphic with those of another, despite the fact that such complementarity is rarely the case.

Goffman's cool conceptual creativity contributed signally to understanding social performance, but the instrumental tone of his thinking severed, not only analytically but in principle – that is ontologically – the possibility of strong ties between psychological motivation, social performance, and cultural text. In linguistics, this opening toward a pure pragmatics of performance was taken up by Del Hymes. Following Austin's emphasis on the performative, Hymes (1964) stressed the need for "highlighting the way in which communication is carried out, above and beyond its referential content."

In anthropology, this line was elaborated in Milton Singer's (1959) explorations of cultural performances in South Asian societies, which he described as the "most concrete observable units of the cultural structure," and which he broke down into such standard features as performers, audience, time span, beginnings, endings, place, and occasion. This form of Goffmanian, analytical deconstruction has combined with nostalgic theories of liminality to feed forcefully into one of the two broad currents of contemporary performance studies. Explicitly praxis-oriented, this strain of performance theory emphasizes exclusively the pragmatic dimensions of resistance and subversion, focusing in an exaggerated manner on questions of commodification, power, and the politics of representation (Auslander 1997, 1999; Conquergood 2002; Diamond 1996; McKenzie 2001). Raising the ghost of Marx's Thesis X and giving it a Foucaultian twist, this strand argues that an epistemology centered on thickly describing the world represents ethnocentric, "epistemic violence" (Conquergood 2002: 146; cf. Ricoeur 1971; Geertz 1973c). The point of practicing performance studies is to *change* the world. Liminality, which represents ideal sites for contestation, and pragmatism, which romanticizes actor autonomy and individual self-determination, are natural theoretical bedfellows.

This praxis approach is attracted to sites of contestation where performances of resistance and subversion are understood to flourish in the ceremonial and interactional practices of the marginalized, the enslaved, and the subaltern (Conquergood 1995, 2002). Rejecting the "culture as text" model, this approach argues that subaltern groups "create a culture of resistance," a "subjugated knowledge" that must be conceptualized not as a discourse but as "a repertoire of performance practices" (Conquergood 2002: 150). As a repertoire of practices, culture is theorized as embodied and experiential, and thus wholly unrecognizable to members of the dominant culture.[4] Citationality in these works is limited to representing strategies that "reclaim, short-circuit, and resignify" the hegemonic code's "signed imperatives" (p. 151). While members of the dominant culture are incapable of recognizing subaltern cultures, savvy agents of resistance are described as capable of creatively citing hegemonic codes in order to play upon and subvert them.

This theoretical constraining of citationality to intra-group representational processes has the effect of conceptualizing subaltern groups as radically culturally autonomous. This leads ineluctably to the conclusion that such groups' identities are constituted wholly from within; that they share no symbolic codes with the dominant culture. Yet if subaltern performances are to creatively play upon and subvert dominant culture, subversive performers must already have

21

internalized the hegemonic code. To play upon it creatively and felicitously, they must be able to *cite* the code in a deeply intuitive manner. One must communicate *through* the code, not merely *against* it. Homi Bhabha expressed this succinctly: "mimicry is at once resemblance and menace" (1994: 86). Foucault is not simply a theorist of subjugated knowledges, Turner a theorist of subversion,[5] and Butler a philosopher of the Goffmanian world. One must not generalize from empirical examples of resistance to a full-blown, purely pragmatic and cognitivist view of the world.

Whether Marxist or Heideggerian, conservative or postmodern, Turnerian or Goffmanian, this line of dramaturgical thinking – while enormously instructive – has placed blinders on dramaturgical theory and cultural social science. To develop a satisfying theory of cultural practice, we must separate ourselves from both nostalgia and anti-nostalgia. Not only disenchantment but re-enchantment characterizes post-traditional societies (Bauman 1993; Sherwood 1994). If social action can continue to be understood by social actors and social interpreters as a meaningful text – and empirical evidence suggests overwhelmingly that this continues to be the case – then cultural practice must continue to be capable of capturing sacrality and of displaying it in successful symbolic performance. Disenchantment must be understood, in other words, not as the denial of some romanticized ontology, much less as proof that, in the post-metaphysical world of modernity, social actors live only in a de-ontological way (Habermas 1993). What disenchantment indicates, rather, is unconvincing cultural practice, failed symbolic performance.

An alternative form of dramaturgical theorizing is beginning to emerge. In contrast to the anti-nostalgic, praxis-oriented strand, some performance studies scholars have resisted the allure of pragmatic promises of uber-agency and retained an interest in liminality and identity more aligned with Geertzian dramaturgy and Derridean citationality; this approach emphasizes culturally structured scripts even if actors subvert their normative power (Roach 1996, 2007; Taylor 1995). Such arguments show that even performances of resistance depend on and redeploy dominant, hegemonic codes.

Citationality is foregrounded when these empirical investigations hermeneutically reconstruct how past performances, performers, and imagined cultural identities manifest themselves in, or "ghost," performances in the present (Carlson 2001; Roach 1996, 2000; Taylor 1995). Alterity takes place within, not simply against, historically produced cultural contexts (Roach 1996; Taylor 1995). Performers in the present innovate, create, and struggle for social change through small but significant revisions of familiar scripts, which are themselves carved from deeply rooted cultural texts – as actors in a production of *Macbeth* (Carlson 2001: 9), mourning musicians and pallbearers in a New Orleans jazz funeral (Roach 2000), or protesting mothers of Argentina's "disappeared" children (Taylor 1995). In these studies, the imagined past weighs heavily on the present, but actors are shown to be capable of lacing the coded past with significant, at times profoundly dramatic, revisions.[6]

In her analysis of Argentina's "Dirty War," for instance, Diane Taylor concludes that rather than simply a repertoire of practices, culture must be understood as a relatively autonomous system of "*pretexts*" (1995: 300, original italics) from which scripts for practice emerge. Once embodied in actors, she argues, scripts become objects of cognition that are open to circumscribed, coded revisions. To protest the military Junta's "disappearing" of the nation's young men, and the sexual violence it visited upon women, Argentine "mothers of the disappeared" – "*Los Madres*" – staged dramatic performances of resistance in the Plaza de Mayo, the political, financial, and symbolic center of Buenos Aires (Taylor 1995: 286). In their performances, the women of Los Madres enacted a script of Motherhood. Taylor views such self-casting as "highly problematic," suggesting it obscured differences among women and "limited the [Resistance's] arena of confrontation" (1995: 300). Why did the *madres* make the "conscious political choice" to assume the motherhood role, she asks? Why did they perform according to a script that relegated them to "the subordinate position of mediators between fathers and sons," when they could have "performed as women, wives, sisters, or human rights activists?" Her answer rejects the epistemology of pragmatic choice, liminality as existential freedom, and cognitive performativity:

> I have to conclude that the military and the Madres reenacted a collective fantasy [in which their] positions were, in a sense, already there as *pre*text or script. Their participation in the national tragedy depended little on their individual position as subjects. On the contrary: their very subjectivity was a product of their position in the drama. (Taylor 1995: 301, original italics)

The performative turn in sociology today

Since the late 1980s, strong programs in cultural sociology have been demonstrating culture's determinative power and its relative autonomy from the social structure. These studies have challenged tendencies to treat culture as epiphenomenal, as a "tool kit" (Swidler 1986), as a reflection of material domination (Bourdieu 1984), or as homologous with social power (Foucault 1972). As the new century gets under way, cultural sociology now takes a performative turn. The theory of cultural pragmatics interweaves meaning and action in a nonreductive way, pointing toward culture structures while recognizing that only through the actions of concrete social actors is meaning's influence realized. Cultural pragmatics is a social scientific response to the conditions of a post-metaphysical world in which institutional and cultural differentiation makes successful symbolic performance difficult to achieve. To develop a theory of cultural practice, we must take these historical limitations seriously. Cultural life has radically shifted, both internally and in its relation to action and social structure. Yet, despite these changes, culture can still be powerfully meaningful; it can possess and display coherence, and it can exert immense social effect. To understand how culture can be meaningful, but may not be, we must accept history but reject radical historicism. Life is different but not completely so. Rather than sweeping allegorical theory, we need allegorical deconstruction and analytic precision. We need to break the "whole" of symbolic action down into its component parts. Once we do so, we will see that cultural performance covers the same ground that it always has, but in a radically different way.

— 2 —

SOCIAL PERFORMANCE BETWEEN RITUAL AND STRATEGY

Rituals are episodes of repeated and simplified cultural communication in which the direct partners to a social interaction, and those observing it, share a mutual belief in the descriptive and prescriptive validity of the communication's symbolic contents and accept the authenticity of one another's intentions. It is because of this shared understanding of intention and content, and of the intrinsic validity of the interaction, that rituals have their effect and affect. Ritual effectiveness energizes the participants and attaches them to each other, increases their identification with the symbolic objects of communication, and intensifies the connection of the participants and the symbolic objects with the observing audience, the relevant "community" at large.

If there is one cultural quality that marks the earliest forms of human social organization, it is the centrality of rituals. From births to conjugal relationships, from peaceful foreign relations to the preparation for war, from the healing of the sick to the celebration of collective well-being, from transitions through the age structure to the assumption of new occupational and political roles, the affirmation of leadership and the celebration of anniversaries – in earlier forms of society such social processes tended to be marked by ritualized symbolic communication. If there is one cultural quality that differentiates more contemporary, large-scale, and complex social organizations from earlier forms, it is that the centrality of such ritual processes has been displaced. Contemporary societies revolve around open-ended conflicts between parties who do not necessarily share beliefs, frequently do not accept the validity of one another's intention, and often disagree even about the descriptions that people offer for acts.

Social observers, whether they are more scientific or more philosophical, have found innumerable ways to conceptualize this historical transformation, starting with such thoroughly discredited evolutionary contrasts as primitive/advanced or barbarian/civilized, and moving on to more legitimate but still overly binary distinctions such as traditional/modern, oral/literate, or simple/complex. One does not have to be an evolutionist or accept the simplifying dichotomies of meta-history to see that a broad change has occurred. Max Weber pitted his contingent historical approach against every shred of evolutionary thinking, yet the decentering of ritual was precisely what he meant by the movement from charisma to routinization and from traditional to value and goal-rational society. Rather than being organized primarily through rituals that affirm metaphysical and consensual beliefs, contemporary societies have opened themselves to processes of negotiations and reflexivity about means and ends, with the result that conflict, disappointment, and feelings of bad faith are at least as common as integration, affirmation, and the energizing of the collective spirit.

Still, most of us who live in these more reflexive and fragmented societies are also aware that, for better and for worse, such processes of rationalization in fact have not completely won the day (Alexander 2003c). There is a continuing symbolic intensity based on repeated and simplified cognitive and moral frames (Goffman 1967, 1974) that continues to mark all sorts of individual and private relationships. More public and collective processes – from social movements (Eyerman and Jamison 1991) to wars (Smith 2005), revolutions (Apter and Saich 1994; Hunt 1984; Sewell 1980), political transitions (Edles 1998; Giesen 2006; Goodman 2007), and scandals (Mast 2006) and even to the construction of scientific communities (Hagstrom 1965) – continue to depend on the simplifying structures of symbolic communications and on cultural interactions that rely on, and to some degree can generate, intuitive and unreflective trust (Barber 1983; Sztompka 1999). It might even be said that, in a differentiated, stratified, and reflexive society, a strategy's success depends on belief in the validity of the cultural contents of the strategist's symbolic communication and on accepting the authenticity and even the sincerity of another's strategic intentions. Virtually every kind of modern collectivity, moreover, seems to depend at one time or another on integrative processes that create some sense of shared identity (Giesen 1998; Ringmar 1996; Spillman 1997), even if these are forged, as they all too often are, in opposition to simplistic constructions of those who are putatively on the other side (Chan 1999; Jacobs 2000; Ku 1999).

26

At both the micro and the macro levels, both among individuals and between and within collectivities, our societies still seem to be permeated by symbolic, ritual-like activities. It is precisely this notion of "ritual-like," however, that indicates the puzzle we face. We are aware that very central processes in complex societies are symbolic, and that sometimes they are also integrative, at the group, intergroup, and even societal level. But we also clearly sense that these processes are not rituals in the traditional sense (see also Lukes 1977). Even when they affirm validity and authenticity and produce integration, their effervescence is short lived. If they have achieved simplicity, it is unlikely they will be repeated. If they are repeated, it is unlikely that the symbolic communication can ever be so simplified in the same way again.

This is the puzzle to which the present chapter is addressed. Is it possible to develop a theory that can explain how the integration of particular groups and sometimes even whole collectivities can be achieved through symbolic communications, while continuing to account for cultural complexity and contradiction, for institutional differentiation, contending social power, and segmentation? Can a theory give full credence to the continuing role of belief while acknowledging that unbelief and criticism are also the central hallmarks of our time?

In order to solve this puzzle, I will develop a systematic, macrosociological model of social action as cultural performance. In so doing, I will enter not only into the historical origins of theatrical performance and dramaturgical theory (e.g., Auslander 1997; Austin 1957; Burke 1965; Carlson 1996; Geertz 1980; Goffman 1974; Schechner 2002; Turner 2002) but also into the history and theories of social performance. This means looking at how, and why, symbolic action moved from ritual to theater (Turner 1982) and why it so often moves back to "ritual-like" processes again (Schechner 1976).

The gist of my argument can be briefly stated. The more simple the collective organization, the less its social and cultural parts are segmented and differentiated, the more the elements of social performances are *fused*. The more complex, segmented, and differentiated the collectivity, the more these elements of social performance become *de-fused*. To be effective in a society of increasing complexity, social performances must engage in a project of *re-fusion*. To the degree they achieve re-fusion, social performances become convincing and effective – more ritual-like. To the degree that social performances remain de-fused, they seem artificial and contrived, less like rituals than like performances in the pejorative sense. They are less effective as a result. Failed performances are those in which the actor, whether individual or collective, has been unable to sew back together the

27

elements of performance to make them appear seamlessly connected. This performative failure makes it much more difficult for the actor to realize his or her intentions in a practical way.

This argument points immediately to the question of just what the elements of social performance are. I will elucidate these in the section immediately following. Then, with this analytical model of social performance safely in hand, I will turn back to the historical questions of what allowed earlier societies to more frequently make their performances into rituals and how later social developments created the ambiguous and slippery contexts for performative action in which we find ourselves today. Once this historical argument is established, I will come back to the model of performative success and failure and will elaborate its interdependent elements in more detail.

The elements of cultural performance

Cultural performance is the social process by which actors, individually or in concert, display for others the meaning of their social situation. This meaning may or may not be one to which they themselves subjectively adhere; it is the meaning that they, as social actors, consciously or unconsciously wish to have others believe. In order for their display to be effective, actors must offer a plausible performance, one that leads those to whom their actions and gestures are directed to accept their motives and explanations as a reasonable account (Garfinkel 1967; Scott and Lyman 1968). As Gerth and Mills (1964: 55) once put it, "Our gestures do not necessarily 'express' our prior feelings," but rather "they make available to others a sign." Successful performance depends on the ability to convince others that one's performance is true, with all the ambiguities that the notion of aesthetic truth implies. Once we understand cultural performance in this way, we can easily make out the basic elements that compose it.

Systems of collective representation: Background symbols and foreground scripts

Marx ([1852] 1962: 247) observed that "just when they seem engaged in revolutionizing themselves and things, in creating something that has never yet existed," social actors "anxiously conjure up the spirits of the past to their service and borrow from them names, battle cries, and costumes in order to present the new scene of world history in this time-honored disguise and this borrowed language."

Marx is describing here the systems of collective representations that background every performative act.

Actors present themselves as being motivated by and toward existential, emotional, and moral concerns, the meanings of which are defined by patterns of signifiers whose referents are the social, physical, natural, and cosmological worlds within which actors and audiences live. One part of this symbolic reference provides the deep background of collective representations for social performance; another part composes the foreground, the scripts that are the immediate referent for action. These latter can be understood as constituting the performance's immediate referential text. As constructed by the performative imagination, background and foreground symbols are structured by codes that provide analogies and antipathies and by narratives that provide chronologies. In symbolizing actors' and audiences' worlds, these narratives and codes simultaneously condense and elaborate, and they employ a wide range of rhetorical devices, from metaphor to synecdoche, to configure social and emotional life in compelling and coherent ways. Systems of collective representations range from "time immemorial" myths to invented traditions created right on the spot, from oral traditions to scripts prepared by such specialists as playwrights, journalists, and speech writers.

Like any other text, these collective representations, whether background or foreground, can be evaluated for their dramatic effectiveness. I will say more about this later, but what is important at this point is to see that no matter how intrinsically effective, collective representations do not speak themselves. Boulton (1960: 3) once described theater as "literature that walks and talks before our eyes." It is this need for walking and talking – and seeing and listening to the walking and talking – that makes the practical pragmatics of performance different from the cultural logic of texts. It is at this conjuncture that cultural pragmatics is born.

Actors

These patterned representations are put into practice, or are encoded (Hall 1980), by flesh-and-blood people. As Reiss (1971: 138) suggests in his study of the relation between theatrical technique and meaning in seventeenth-century French theater, "the actor is as real as the spectator; he is in fact present in their midst." Whether or not they are consciously aware of the distinction between collective representations and their walking and talking, the actor's aim is to make this distinction disappear. As Reiss (1971: 142) puts it, the actor's desire

29

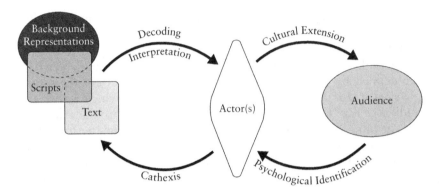

Figure 2.1. Successful performance: re-fusion.

is "to cause the spectator to confuse his emotions with those of the stage character." While performers must be oriented to background and foreground representations, their motivations vis-à-vis these patterns are contingent. In psychological terms, the relation between actor and text depends on cathexis. The relation between actor and audience, in turn, depends on the ability to project these emotions and textual patterns as moral evaluations. If those who perform cultural scripts do not possess the requisite skills (Bauman 1989), then they may fail miserably in the effort to project their meanings effectively. See Figure 2.1.

Observers/audience

Cultural texts are performed so that meanings can be displayed to others. "Others" constitutes the audience of observers for cultural performance. They decode what actors have encoded (Hall 1980), but they do so in variable ways. If cultural texts are to be communicated convincingly, there needs to be a process of cultural extension that expands from script and actor to audience. Cultural extension must be accompanied by a process of psychological identification, such that the members of the audience project themselves into the characters they see onstage. Empirically, cultural extension and psychological identification are variable. Audiences may be focused or distracted, attentive or uninterested (Berezin 1997: 28, 35, 250; Verdery 1991: 6). Even if actors cathect to cultural texts, and even if they themselves possess high levels of cultural proficiency, their projections still may not be persuasive to the audience/observers. Observation can be merely cognitive. An audience can see and can

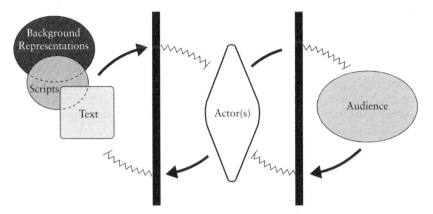

Figure 2.2. Performance failure: de-fusion.

understand without experiencing emotional or moral signification. As we will see in the following section, there are often "social" explanations of this variability. Audiences may represent social statuses orthogonal to the status of performers. Audience attendance may not be required, or it may be merely compelled. Critics can intervene between performance and audience. There might not be an audience in the contemporary sense at all, but only participants observing themselves and their fellow performers. This latter condition facilitates cultural identification and psychological extension, though it is a condition much less frequently encountered in the complex societies of the present day. See Figure 2.2.

Means of symbolic production

In order to perform a cultural text before an audience, actors need access to the mundane material things that allow symbolic projections to be made. They need objects that can serve as iconic representations to help them dramatize and make vivid the invisible motives and morals they are trying to represent. This material ranges from clothing to every other sort of "standardized expressive equipment" (Goffman 1956: 34–51). Actors also require a physical place to perform and the means to assure the transmission of their performance to an audience.

Mise-en-scène

With texts and means in hand, and audience(s) before them, social actors engage in dramatic social action, entering into and projecting

31

the ensemble of physical and verbal gestures that constitutes performance. This ensemble of gestures involves more than the symbolic
devices that structure a nonperformed symbolic text. If a text is to
walk and talk, it must be sequenced temporally and choreographed
spatially (e.g., Berezin 1997: 156). The exigencies of time and space
create specific aesthetic demands; at some historical juncture new,
social roles such as director and producer emerge that specialize in
this task of putting text "into the scene."

Social power

The distribution of power in society – the nature of its political,
economic, and status hierarchies, and the relations among its elites
– profoundly affects the performance process. Power establishes an
external boundary for cultural pragmatics that parallels the internal
boundary established by a performance's background representations. Not all texts are equally legitimate in the eyes of the powers
that be, whether possessors of material or interpretive power. Not
all performances, and not all parts of a particular performance, are
allowed to proceed. Will social power (Mann 1986) seek to eliminate
certain parts of a cultural text? Who will be allowed to act in a performance, and with what means? Who will be allowed attendance?
What kinds of responses will be permitted from audience/observer?
Are there powers that have the authority to interpret performances
independently of those that have the authority to produce them? Are
these interpretive powers also independent of the actors and the audience itself, or are social power, symbolic knowledge, and interpretive
authority much more closely linked?

Every social performance, whether individual or collective, is affected
fundamentally by each of the elements presented here. In the language
of hermeneutics, this sketch of interdependent elements provides a
framework for the interpretive reconstruction of the meanings of performative action. In the language of explanation, it provides a model
of causality. One can say that every social performance is determined
partly by each of the elements I have laid out – that each is a necessary
but not sufficient cause of every performative act. While empirically
interrelated, each element has some autonomy, not only analytically
but empirically vis-à-vis the others. Taken together, they determine,
and measure, whether and how a performance occurs, and the degree
to which it succeeds or fails in its effect. Two pathways lead out from
the discussion thus far. The analytic model can be developed further,

elaborating the nature of each factor and its interrelations with the others. I will take up this task in a later section. Before doing so, I will engage in a historical discussion. I wish to explore how the analytical model I have just laid out, despite the fact it is so far only presented very simply, already provides significant insight into the central puzzle of ritual and rationalization with which I introduced this essay and that defines its central question.

The conditions for performativity: Historical transformations

The model of performance I am developing here provides a new way of looking at cultural and organizational change over broad spans of historical time. We can see differently how and why rituals were once so central to band and tribal societies and why the nature of symbolic action changed so remarkably with the rise of states, empires, and churches. We can understand why both the theater and the democratic polis arose for the first time in ancient Greece and why theater emerged once again during the early modern period at the same time as open-ended social dramas became central to determining the nature of social and political authority. We can understand why Romanticism, secularization, and industrial society made the authenticity of symbolic action such a central question for modern times.

Old-fashioned rituals: Symbolic performances in early societies

Colonial and modernist thinkers were deeply impressed by the ritualistic processes that explorers and anthropologists observed when they encountered societies that had not experienced "civilization" or "modernity." Some associated the frequency of rituals with the putative purity of early societies (Huizinga 1950 [1938]) and others with some sort of distinctively primitive, nonrational mentality (Levy-Bruhl 1923). Huizinga (1950 [1938]: 14), for example, stressed that rituals create not a "sham reality" but "a mystical one," in which "something invisible and in actual takes beautiful, actual, holy form." Less romantic observers still emphasized the automatic, predictable, engulfing, and spontaneous qualities of ritual life. Weber exemplified this understanding in a sociological manner. It also marked the modern anthropological approach to ritual that became paradigmatic. Turner (1977: 183) defined rituals as "stereotyped" and as "sequestered"; Goody (1986: 21) called them "homeostatic";

and Leach (1972: 334), insisting also on "repetition," expresses his wonderment at how, in the rituals he observed, "everything in fact happened just as predicted" (1972: 199).

Against these arguments for the essential and fundamental difference of symbolic interactions in earlier societies, critical and postmodern anthropologists have argued for their more "conjunctural" (Clifford 1988: 11) quality. Those mysterious rituals that aroused such intense admiration and curiosity among earlier observers, it is argued, should be seen not as expressions of some distinctive essence but simply as a different kind of practice (Conquergood 1992). The model I am developing here allows us to frame this important insight in a more nuanced, less polemical, and more empirically oriented way. Rituals in early societies, I wish to suggest, were not so much practices as performances, and in this they indeed are made of the same stuff as social actions in more complex societies. In an introduction to his edition of Turner's posthumous essays, Schechner (1987: 7) suggested that "all performance has at its core a ritual action." Actually, this statement must be reversed. All ritual has at its core a performative act.

This is not to deny the differences between rituals and performances of a less affecting kind. What it does suggest, however, is that they exist on the same continuum and that the difference between them is a matter of variation, not fundamental type. Early ritual performances reflect the social structures and cultures of their historically situated societies. They are distinctive in that they are fused. Fusion is much more likely to be achieved in the conditions of less complex societies, but it occurs in complex societies as well.

To see why performances in simpler societies more frequently became rituals, we must examine how early social structure and culture defined the elements of performance and related them to one another in a distinctive way. The explanation can be found in their much smaller size and scale; in the more mythical and metaphysical nature of their beliefs; and in the more integrated and overlapping nature of their institutions, culture, and social structures. Membership in the earliest human societies (Service 1962, 1979) was organized around the axes of kinship, age, and gender. Forming collectivities of 60 to 80 members, people supported themselves by hunting and gathering and participated in a small set of social roles with which every person was thoroughly familiar. By all accounts, the subjectivity that corresponded with this kind of social organization resembled what Stanner (1972), when speaking of the Australian Aboriginals, called "dream time." Such consciousness merged mundane and practical dimensions with the sacred and metaphysical to the extent that religion did not exist as a separate form. In such societies, as Service (1962: 109) once remarked, "there is no religious organization" that is "separated from family and band."

The structural and cultural organization of such early forms of societies suggests differences in the kinds of social performance they can produce. The collective representations to which these social performances refer are not texts composed by specialists for segmented subgroups in complex and contentious social orders. Nor do these collective representations form a critical "metacommentary" (Geertz 1973d) on social life, for there does not yet exist deep tension between mundane and transcendental spheres (Bellah 1970; Eisenstadt 1982; Goody 1986; Habermas 1984). The early anthropologists Spencer and Gillen (1927) were right at least in this, for they suggested that the Engwura ritual cycle of the Australian Arunta recapitulated the actual lifestyle of the Arunta males. A century later, when Schechner (1976: 197) observed the Tsembaga dance of the Kaiko, he confirmed that "all the basic moves and sounds – even the charge into the central space – are adaptations and direct lifts from battle."

The tight intertwining of cultural text and social structure that marks social performances in early societies provides a contextual frame for Durkheim's theoretical argument about religion as simply society writ large. While claiming to propose a paradigm for studying every religion at all times, Durkheim might better be understood as describing the context for social performances in early societies. Durkheim insists that culture is identical with religion, that any "proper" religious belief is shared by every member of the group, and that these shared beliefs are always translated into the practices he calls rituals, or rites. "Not only are they individually accepted by *all members* of that group, but they also belong *to* the group and *unify* it . . . A society whose members are united because they imagine the sacred world and its relation with the profane world *in the same way*, and because they *translate* this common representation into identical practices, is called a Church" (Durkheim [1912] 1996: 41, italics added).[1]

In such ritualized performances, the belief dimension is experienced as personal, immediate, and iconographic. Through the painting, masking, and reconfiguring of the physical body, the actors in these performances seek not only metaphorically but also literally to become the text, their goal being to project the fusion of human and totem, "man and God," sacred and mundane. The symbolic roles that define participation in such ritualized performances emerge directly, and without mediation, from the other social roles actors play. In the Engwura ritual (Spencer and Gillen 1927), the Arunta males performed the parts they actually held in everyday Arunta life. When social actors perform such roles, they do not have a sense of separation from them; they have little self-consciousness about themselves as actors. For participants and observers, rituals are not considered to be a performance in the contemporary sense at all, but rather to be a natural and necessary dimension of ongoing social life. As for the means of symbolic production, while not always immediately available, they generally are near at hand – a ditch dug with the sharp bones of animals, a line drawn from the red coloring of wild flowers, a headdress made from bird feathers, an amulet fashioned from a parrot's beak (Turner 1969: 23–37).

In this type of social organization, participation in ritual performance is not contingent, either for the actors or the observers. Participation is determined by the established and accepted hierarchies of gender and age, not by individual choices that respond to the sanctions and rewards of social powers or segmented social groups. Every relevant party in the band or tribe must attend to ritual performances. Many ceremonies involve the entire community, for they "regard their collective well-being to be dependent upon a common body of ritual performances" (Rappaport 1968, in Schechner 1976: 211). Turner (1982: 31, original italics) attested that "the *whole* community goes through the *entire* ritual round." Durkheim (1996 [1912]) also emphasized obligation, connecting it with the internal coherence of the audience. In the ritual phase of Aboriginal society, he wrote, "the population comes together, concentrating itself at specific places . . . The concentration takes place when a clan or a portion of the tribe is summoned to come together" (Durkheim 1996 [1912]: 217).

Nor are attendees only observers. At various points in the ritual, those merely watching the ritual performance are called upon to participate – sometimes as principals and at other times as members of an attentive chorus providing remonstrations of approval through such demonstrative acts as shouting, crying, and applause. At key phases in male initiation ceremonies, for example, women attend closely and, at particular moments, play significant ritual roles (Schechner 2002). They express indifference and rejection early in the performance and display physical signs of welcome and admiration in order to mark its end. Even when they do not participate, ritual audiences are hardly strangers. They are linked to performers by direct or indirect family ties.

In terms of the elementary model I have laid out already, it may be said that such ritualized social actions fuse the various components of

36

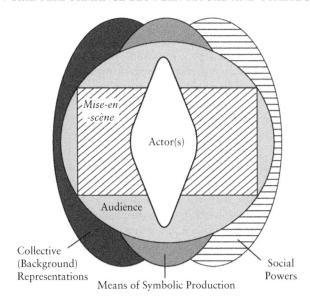

Figure 2.3. The fused elements of performance inside simple social organization.

performance – actors, audiences, representations, means of symbolic production, social power, and *mise-en-scène*. See Figure 2.3.

Symbolic production

It is the actor/audience part of this fusion to which Service (1962: 109) referred when he wrote that "the congregation is the camp itself." Levi-Strauss (1963: 179) meant to emphasize the same fusing when he spoke of the "fabulation" of ritual as a "threefold experience." It consists "first of the shaman himself, who, if his calling is a true one . . . undergoes specific states of a psychosomatic nature; second, that of the sick person, who may or may not experience an improvement of his condition; and, finally, that of the public, who also participates in the cure, experiencing an enthusiasm and an intellectual and emotional satisfaction which produce collective support." In the studies of shamanistic rituals offered by postmodern performance theorists, we can read their ethnographic accounts as suggesting fusion in much the same way. "They derive their power from listening to the others and absorbing daily realities. While they cure, they take into them their patients' possessions and obsessions and let the latter's illnesses become theirs . . . The very close relationship these healers maintain

37

with their patients remains the determining factor of the cure" (Trinh 1989, in Conquergood 1992: 44).

With sacred texts tied to mundane society, actors' roles tied to social roles, performance directly expressing symbolic text and social life, obligatory participation, and homogeneous and attentive audiences, it is hardly surprising that the effects of ritual performances tend to be immediate and only infrequently depart from the expectations of actors and scripts (see also Schechner 1976: 205, 1981: 92–4). As Levi-Strauss attested (1963: 168, italics added), "There is . . . no reason to doubt the efficacy of certain magical practices" precisely because "the efficacy of magic implies *a belief in* magic." Rites not only mark transitions but also create them, such that the participants become something or somebody else as a result. Ritual performance not only symbolizes a social relationship or change; it also actualizes it. There is a direct effect, without mediation.

Anthropologists who have studied rituals in earlier forms of society reported that the tricks of ritual specialists rarely were scrutinized. Levi-Strauss (1963: 179) emphasized the role of "group consensus" when he began his famous retelling of Boas's ethnography of Quesalid. The Kwakiutl Indian was so unusually curious as to insist (at first) that the sorcerer's rituals indeed were tricks. Yet after persuading ritual specialists to teach him the tricks of their trade, Quesalid himself went on to become a great shaman. "Quesalid did not become a great shaman because he cured his patients," Levi-Strauss assures us; rather, "he cured his patients because he had *become* a great shaman" (1963: 180, italics added). Shamans effect cures, individual and social, because participants and observers of their performances believe they have the force to which they lay claim. Shamans, in other words, are institutionalized masters of ritual performance. The success of this performance depends, in the first place, on their dramatic skills, but these skills are intertwined with the other dimensions that allow performances to be fused in simple social organizations.

Social complexity and post-ritual performances

Fused performances creating ritual-like effects remain important in more complex societies. There are two senses in which this is true. First, and less importantly for the argument I am developing here, in primary groups such as families, gangs, and intergenerationally stable ethnic communities, role performances often seem to reproduce the macrocosm in the microcosm (Slater 1966). Even inside of complex

societies, audiences in such primary groups are relatively homogeneous, actors are familiar, situations are repeated, and texts and
traditions, if once invented, eventually take on a time immemorial
quality. The second sense in which ritual-like effects remain central
– and this is most important for my argument here – is that fusion
remains the goal of performances even in complex societies. It is the
context for performative success that has changed.

As I noted earlier, historians, anthropologists, and sociologists have
analyzed the sporadic and uneven processes that created larger-scale
societies in innumerably different ways. There is sharply contrasting
theorizing about the causes and pathways of the movement away
from simpler social organization in which ritual played a central role
to more complex social forms, which feature more strategic, reflexive, and managed forms of symbolic communication. But there is
wide consensus that such a transformation did occur, that the processes of "complexification," "rationalization," or "differentiation"
(Alexander and Colomy 1990; Champagne 1992; Eisenstadt 1963;
Habermas 1984; Luhmann 1995; Thrift 1999) produce new and different kinds of symbolic communications. Even Goody (1986: 22)
spoke confidently of the transition "from worldview to ideology."

This emphasis on ideology is telling, and it leads directly to the
argument about changes in the conditions for performativity that I
am making here. Earlier sociological and anthropological investigations into the social causes of the transition from simple forms of
social organization emphasized the determining role of economic
change. Technological shifts created more productivity, which led
to surplus and the class system, and finally to the first distinctive
political institutions, whose task was to organize the newly stratified
society and to administer material and organizational needs. By the
end of the 1950s, however, anthropologists already had begun to
speak less of technological changes than shifts in economic orientations and regimes. When Fried (1971: 103) explained "the move from
egalitarian to rank society," he described a shift "from an economy
dominated by reciprocity to one having redistribution as a major
device." In the same kind of anti-determinist vein, when Service
(1962: 171) explained movement beyond the monolithic structures of
early societies to the "twin forms of authority" that sustained distinctive economic and political elites, he described it as "made *possible* by
greater productivity" (1962: 143, italics added). Sahlins (1972) built
on such arguments to suggest that it was not the economic inability
to create surplus that prevented growth but the ideological desire to
maintain a less productivity-driven, more leisurely style of life. Nolan

and Lenski (1995) made the point of this conceptual-cum-empirical development impossible to overlook: "Technological advance created the possibility of a surplus, but to transform that possibility into a reality required an ideology that *motivated* farmers to produce more than they needed to stay alive and productive, and *persuaded* them to turn that surplus over to someone else" (1995: 157, italics added). As the last comment makes clear, this whole historiographic transition in the anthropology of early transitions points to the critical role of ideological projects. The creation of surplus depended on new motivations, which could come about only through the creation of symbolic performances to persuade others, not through their material necessity or direct coercion.

The most striking social innovation that crystallized such a cultural shift to ideology was the emergence of written texts. According to Goody (1986: 12), the emergence of text-based culture allowed and demanded "the decontextualization or generalization" of collective representations, which in oral societies were intertwined more tightly with local social structures and meanings. With writing, the "communicative context has changed dramatically both as regards the emitter and as regards the receivers" (Goody 1986: 13): "In their very nature written statements of the law, of norms, of rules, have had to be abstracted from particular situations in order to be addressed to a universal audience out there, rather than delivered face-to-face to a specific group of people at a particular time and place" (p. 13). Only symbolic projection beyond the local would allow groups to use economic surplus to create more segmented, unequal, and differentiated societies. Without the capacity for such ideological projection, how else would these kinds of more fragmented social orders ever be coordinated, much less integrated in an asymmetrical way?

These structural and ideological processes suggest a decisive shift in actors' relation to the means of symbolic production. In text-based societies, literacy is essential if the symbolic processes that legitimate social structure are to be carried out successfully. Because literacy is difficult and expensive, priests "have privileged access to the sacred texts." This allows "the effective control of the means of literate communication," concentrating interpretative authority in elite hands (Goody 1986: 16–17). Alongside this new emergence of monopoly power, indeed because of it, there emerges the necessity for exercising tight control over performance in order to project ideological control over distantiated and subordinate groups. Evans-Pritchard (1940: 172, italics added) once wrote that, in order to "allow him to *play the part he plays* in feuds and quarrels," the Nuer chief needs only "ritual

40

qualifications." Because the Nuer "have no law or government," or any significant social stratification, obeying their chief follows from the perception that "they are sacred persons" (1940: 173). In his study of the origins of political empires, Eisenstadt (1963: 65) demonstrated, by contrast, how with the "relative autonomy of the religious sphere and its 'disembeddedness' from the total community and from the other institutional spheres," everything about political legitimation has changed. The sacredness of the economic, political, and ideological elites has to be achieved, not assigned. As Eisenstadt put it, these elites now "*tried* to maintain dominance" (1963: 65, italics added); it was not given automatically to them. "In all societies studied here, the rulers *attempted to portray* themselves and the political systems they established as the bearers of special cultural symbols and missions. They *tried to depict* themselves as transmitting distinct civilizations . . . The rulers of these societies invariably *tried to be perceived* as the propagators and upholders of [their] traditions [and they] desire[d] to minimize any group's pretensions to having the right *to judge and evaluate* the rulers or to sanction their legitimation" (Eisenstadt 1963: 141, italics added).

An ambitious recent investigation into pharonic Egypt finds the same processes at work. "A state imposed by force and coercing its subjects to pay taxes and perform civil and military service," Assmann (2002: 74) writes, "could hardly have maintained itself if it had not rested on a core semiology that was as persuasive as the state itself was demanding." Reconstructing "the semantics that underlie the establishment of the state" (2002: 75), Assmann finds that in the Old Kingdom Egyptians "clung to the graphic realism of hieroglyphic writing" with an "astounding tenacity." This "aspiration to permanence" meant that state rituals involved "maximum care . . . to prevent deviation and improvisation." Only the lector priest's "knowledge of the script and his ability to recite accurately" could "ensure that precisely the same text was repeated at precisely the same time in the context of the same ritual event, thus bringing meaning, duration, and action into precise alignment" (Assmann 2002: 70–71). By the time of the Middle Kingdom, Assmann reports (2002: 118–119), "the kings of the Twelfth Dynasty were in a fundamentally different position." Social and cultural complexity had proceeded to such an extent that the pharonic rulers "had to assert themselves against a largely literate and economically and militarily powerful aristocracy . . . and win over the lower strata." These objectives "could not be achieved by force alone," Assmann observes, "but only by the power of eloquence and explanation."

41

The assertion of political power was no longer a matter of apodictic self-glorification, but was accomplished by the power of the word. "Be an artist in speech," recommends one text, "then you will be victorious. For behold: the sword-arm of a king is his tongue. Stronger is the word than all fighting." The kings of the Twelfth Dynasty understood the close links between politics and the instantiation of meaning (Assmann 2002: 118–19).

In terms of the model I am developing here, these empirical accounts suggest de-fusion among the elements of performance: (1) the separation of written foreground texts from background collective representations; (2) the estrangement of the means of symbolic production from the mass of social actors; and (3) the separation of the elites who carrying out central symbolic actions from their mass audiences. The appearance of seamlessness that made symbolic

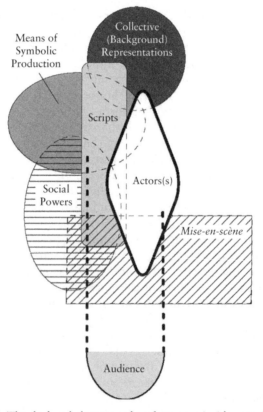

Figure 2.4. The de-fused elements of performance inside complex social organization.

action seem ritualistic gives way to the appearance of greater artifice and planning. Performative action becomes more achieved and less automatic. See Figure 2.4.

The emergence of theatrical from ritual performance

To this point in our historical discussion, my references to performance have been generated analytically, which is to say they have been warranted by the theoretical considerations presented in the first section. While it seems clear that the emergence of more segmented, complex, and stratified societies created the conditions – and even the necessity – for transforming rituals into performances, the latter, more contingent processes of symbolic communication were not understood by their creators or their audiences as contrived or theatrical in the contemporary sense. There was social and cultural differentiation, and the compulsion to project and not merely to assume the effects of symbolic action, but the elements of performance were still not de-fused enough to create self-consciousness about the artificiality of that process.

Thus, when Frankfort (1948: 135–6) insists on the "absence of drama" in ancient Egypt, he emphasizes both the continuing fusion of sacred texts and actors and the relative inflexibility, or resistance to change, of ancient societies (see also Kemp 1989: 1–16). "It is true," Frankfort concedes, "that within the Egyptian ritual the gods were sometimes represented by actors." For example, an embalming priest might be "wearing a jackal mask" to impersonate the god Anubis. In fact, one of the best-preserved Egyptian texts, the *Mystery Play of the Succession*, "was performed when a new king came to the throne." Nonetheless, Frankfort insists, such performances "do not represent a new art form." He calls them "simply the 'books' of rituals." They may be "dramatic," but "they certainly are not drama." In drama, the meaning and consequences of action unfold, and in this sense are caused by, the theatrical challenge of *mise-en-scène*: "In drama, language is integrated with action and a change is shown to be a consequence of that action." In Egyptian rites, by contrast, as in Durkheim's Aboriginal ones, the "purpose is to *translate* actuality in the unchanging form of myth . . . The gods appear and speak once more the words they spoke 'the first time'" (Frankfort 1948: 135–136, italics added). It is the actuality of myth that marks ritual.

Only in the Greek city-states did drama in the contemporary sense emerge. The social organizational and cultural background for these developments was crucial, of course, even as the emergence of dramatic performance fed back into social and cultural organization in turn. As compared to the fused and ascriptive hierarchies that ruled urban societies in the Asian empires, in Greece there emerged urban structures of a new, more republican kind. They were organized and ruled by elites, to be sure, but these elites were internally democratic. As Schachermeyr (1971 [1953]: 201) emphasized in his widely cited essay, the historically unprecedented "autonomy of the citizen body" in the Greek cities was accompanied by the equally distinctive "emancipation of intellectual life from Greek mythology." These new forms of organizational and culture differentiation fostered, according to Schachermeyr, a "revolutionary spirit" that engaged in "a constant fight against the monarchical, dictatorial, or oligarchic forms of government."

This marked opening up of social and cultural space focused attention on the projective, performative dimension of social action, subjecting the ritualized performances of more traditional life to increased scrutiny and strain (e.g., Plato 1980). In Greek society, we can observe the transition from ritual to performance literally and not just metaphorically. We actually see the de-fusion of the elements of performance in concrete terms. They became more than analytically identifiable: their empirical separation became institutionalized in specialized forms of social structure and available to commonsense reflection in cultural life.

Greek theater emerged from within religious rituals organized around Dionysus, the god of wine (Hartnoll 1968: 7–31). In the ritual's traditional form, a dithyramb, or unison hymn, was performed around the altar of Dionysus by a chorus of 50 men drawn from the entire ethnos. In terms of the present discussion, this meant continuing fusion: actors, collective representations, audiences, and society were united in a putatively homogeneous, still mythical way. In expressing his nostalgia for those earlier, pre-Socratic days, Nietzsche (1956 [1872]: 51–55, 78–79) put it this way: "In the dithyramb we see a community of unconscious actors all of whom see one another as enchanted . . . Audience and chorus were never fundamentally set over against each other . . . An audience of spectators, such as we know it, was unknown . . . Each spectator could quite literally imagine himself, in the fullness of seeing, as a chorist [sic]."

As Greek society entered its period of intense and unprecedented social and cultural differentiation (Gouldner 1965), the content of the dithyramb gradually widened to include tales of the demi-gods and fully secular heroes whom contemporary Greeks considered their ancestors. The background representational system, in other words, began to symbolize – to code and to narrate – human and not only sacred life. This interjection of the mundane into the sacred introduced symbolic dynamics directly into everyday life, and vice versa. During communal festivals dedicated to performing these new cultural texts, the good and bad deeds of secular heroes were recounted along with their feuds, marriages and adulteries, the wars they started, the ethnic and religious ties they betrayed, and the sufferings they brought on their parents and successors. Such social conflicts now provided sources of dramatic tension that religious performers could link to sacred conflicts and could perform on ritual occasions.

As the background representations became reconfigured in a more socially oriented and dramaturgical way – as everyday life became subject to such symbolic reconstruction – the other elements of performance were affected as well. The most extraordinary development was that the social role of actor emerged. Thespius, for whom the very art of theatrical performance eventually came to be named, stepped out of the dithyramb chorus to become its leader. During ritual performance, he would assume the role of protagonist, either god or hero, and carry on a dialog with the chorus. Thespius formed a traveling troupe of professional actors. Collecting the means of symbolic production in a cart whose floor and tailboard could serve also as a stage, Thespius traveled from his birthplace, Icaria, to one communal festival after another, eventually landing in Athens where, in 492 BC, he won the acting prize just then established by the City Dionysus festival.

During this same critical period of social development, systems of collective representations began for the first time not only to be written down – becoming actual texts – but also to separate themselves concretely from religious life. In fifth-century Athens, theater writing became a specialty; prestigious writing contests were held, and prizes were awarded to such figures as Aeschylus and Sophocles. Such secular imagists soon became more renowned than temple priests. At first, playwrights chose and trained their own actors, but eventually officials of the Athenian festival assigned actors to playwrights by lot. In our terms, this can be seen as having the effect of emphasizing and highlighting the autonomy of the dramatic script vis-à-vis the intentions or charisma of its creators (cf. Gouldner 1965: 114).

As such an innovation suggests, the independent institution of performance criticism also had emerged, mediating and pluralizing social power in a new way (see also McCormick 2009). Rather than being absorbed by the performance, as on ritual occasions, interpretation now confronted actors and writers in the guise of judges, who represented aesthetic criteria separated from religious and even moral considerations. At the same time, judges also represented the city that sponsored the performance, and members of the polis attended performances as a detached audience of potentially critical observers. Huizinga (1950 [1938]: 145) emphasized that, because the state did not organize theatrical competitions, "audience criticism was extremely pointed." He also suggested that the public audience shared "the tension of the contest like a crowd at a football match"; yet it seems clear that they were not there simply to be entertained. The masked performers of Greek tragedies remained larger than life, and their texts talked and walked with compelling emotional and aesthetic force, linking performance to the most serious and morally weighted civic issues of the day. From Aeschylus to Sophocles to Euripedes, Greek tragic drama (Jaeger 1945: 232–381) addressed civic virtue and corruption, exploring whether there existed a natural moral order more powerful than the fatally flawed order of human society. These questions were critical for sustaining the rule of law and an independent and democratic civil life.

Nietzsche (1956 [1872]: 78–9) complained that, with the birth of tragedy, "the poet who writes dramatized narrative can no more become one with his images" and that he "transfigures the most horrible deeds before our eyes by the charm of illusion." In fact, however, the de-fusion of performative elements that instigated the emergence of theater did not necessarily eliminate performative power; it just made this power more difficult to achieve. This increased difficulty might well have provided the social stimulus for Aristotle's aesthetic philosophy. In terms of the theoretical framework I am developing here, Aristotle's poetics can be understood in a new way. It aimed to crystallize, in abstract theoretical terms, the empirical differentiation among the elements of performance that pushed ritual to theater. What ritual performers once had known in their guts – without having to be told, much less having to read – Aristotle (1987) now felt compelled to write down. His *Poetics* makes the natural artificial. It provides a kind of philosophical cookbook, instructions for meaning-making and effective performance for a society that has moved from fusion to conscious artifice. Aristotle explained that performances consisted of plots and that effective plotting demanded narratives with a beginning, middle, and end. In his theory of catharsis, he explained, not teleologically but empirically, how dramas could affect an audience: tragedies have to evoke sensations of "terror and pity" if emotional effect is to be achieved.

This sketch of how theater emerged from ritual is not teleological or evolutionary. What I have proposed, rather, is a universally shared form of social development, one that responds to growing complexity in social and cultural structure. Ritual moved toward theater throughout the world's civilizations in response to similar social and cultural developments – the emergence of cities and states, of religious specialists, of intellectuals, and of needs for political legitimation. "There were religious and ritual origins of the Jewish drama, the Chinese drama, all European Christian drama and probably the Indian drama," Boulton (1960: 194) informs us, and "in South America the conquering Spaniards brought Miracle Plays to Indians who already had a dramatic tradition that had development out of their primitive cults."

Social complexity waxes and wanes, and with it the development of theater from ritual. Rome continued Greek theatricality, but with the decline of the empire and the rise of European feudalism the ritual forms of religious performance dominated once again. What happened in ancient Greece was reiterated later in medieval Europe, when secular drama developed from the Easter passion plays. In twelfth-century Autun, a center of Burgundian religious activity, an astute observer named Honorius actually made an analogy between the effects of the Easter Mass and the efforts of the ancient tragedians (Hardison 1965: 40; Schechner 1976: 210). "It is known," Honorius wrote, "that those who recited tragedies in theaters presented the actions of opponents by gestures before the people." He went on to suggest that "in the theatre of the Church before the Christian people," the struggle of Christ against his persecutors is presented by a similar set of "gestures" that "teaches to them the victory of his redemption." Honorius compared each movement of the Mass to an equivalent movement in tragic drama and described what he believed were similar – tightly bound and fused, in our terms – audience effects. "When the sacrifice has been completed, peace and communion are given by the celebrant to the people," he wrote, and "then, by the *Ite, missaest*, they are ordered to return to their homes [and] they shout *Deogratias* and return home rejoicing." It is no wonder that Boulton (1960) equates such early religious pageants with acting. Suggesting that "the earliest acting was done by priests and their assistants," she notes that "one of the causes of the increasing secularization of the drama was that laymen had soon to be called in to fill in parts in the expanding 'cast'" (1960: 195).

By the early seventeenth century in Europe, after the rise of city-states, absolutist regimes, the scientific revolution, and internal religious reforms, the institution of criticism was already fully formed: "Nearly every play had a prologue asking for the goodwill of the critics" (Boulton 1960: 195). Long before the rise of the novel and the newspaper, theatrical performances became arenas for articulating powerful social criticisms. Playwrights wove texts from the fabric of contemporary social life, but they employed their imagination to do so in a sharply accented, stimulating, and provocative manner. The performance of these scripted representations were furnaces forging metaphors that circulated back to society, marking a figure-eight movement (Schechner 1977a; Turner 1982: 73–4) from society to theater and back to society again. Secular criticism did not emerge only from rationalist philosophy or from the idealized arguments in urban cafes (Habermas 1989 [1962]) but also from theatrical performances that projected moral valuation even while they entertained. While providing sophisticated amusement, Molière pilloried not only the rising bourgeois but also the Catholic Church, both of which returned his vituperation in kind. Shakespeare wrote such amusing plays that he was patronized as low brow by the more intellectual playwrights and critics of his day. Yet Shakespeare satirized every sort of conventional authority and dramatized the immorality of every sort of social power. Reviled by the Puritan divines, such Elizabethan drama was subject to strenuous efforts at censorship. The Restoration comedies that followed were no less caustic in their social ambitions or stinging in their effects. In his study of seventeenth-century drama, Reiss (1971: 122) observes that "the loss of illusion follows when the *mise-en-scène* is designed with no attempt at *vraisemblance*," and he concludes that "the theater relied . . . on the unreality of the theatrical situation itself . . . to maintain a distance" (1971: 144). Taking advantage of performative de-fusion, these playwrights used stagecraft to emphasize artificiality rather than to make it invisible, producing a critical and ironic space between the audience and the mores of their day.

The emergence of social drama

The historical story I am telling here addresses the puzzle at the core of this chapter: Why do ritually organized societies give way, not to social orders regulated simply by instrumentally rational action, but instead to those in which ritual-like processes remain vital in a central way?

It is vital for this story to see that the emergence of theater was more or less simultaneous with the emergence of the public sphere as a compelling social stage. For it was, in fact, roughly during the same period as theatrical drama emerged that social drama became a major form of social organization – and for reasons that are much the same.

When society becomes more complex, culture more critical, and authority less ascriptive, social spaces open up that organizations must negotiate if they are to succeed in getting their way. Rather than responding to authoritative commands and prescriptions, social processes become more contingent, more subject to conflict and argumentation. Rationalist philosophers (Habermas 1989 [1962]) speak of the rise of the public sphere as a forum for deliberative and considered debate. A more sociological formulation would point to the rise of a public stage, a symbolic forum in which actors have increasing freedom to create and to project performances of their reasons, dramas tailored to audiences whose voices have become more legitimate references in political and social conflicts. Responding to the same historical changes that denaturalized ritual performance, collective action in the wider society comes increasingly to take on an overtly performative cast.

In earlier, more archaic forms of complex societies, such as the imperial orders of Egypt or Yucatan, social hierarchies simply could issue commands, and ritualized ideological performances would provide symbolic mystification. In more loosely knit forms of complex social organization, authority becomes more open to challenge, the distribution of ideal and material resources more subject to contention, and contests for social power more open-ended and contingent. Often, these dramatic contests unfold without any settled script. Through their success at prosecuting such dramas, individual and collective actors gain legitimacy as authoritative interpreters of social texts.

It is a commonplace not only of philosophical but also of political history (e.g., Bendix 1964) that during the early modern period the masses of powerless persons gradually became transformed into citizens. With the model of social performance now firmly in hand, it seems more accurate to say that non-elites also were transformed from passive receptacles to more active, interpreting audiences.[2] With the constitution of citizen-audiences, even such strategic actors as organizations and class fractions were compelled to develop effective forms of expressive communication. In order to preserve their social power and their ability to exercise social control, elites had to transform their interest conflicts into widely available performances that could project persuasive symbolic forms. As peripheries gradually became incorporated into centers, pretenders to social power strove to frame their conflicts as dramas. They portrayed themselves as protagonists in simplified narratives, projecting their positions, arguments, and actions as exemplifications of sacred religious and secular texts. In turn, they "cast" their opponents as narrative antagonists, as insincere and artificial actors who were only role playing to advance their interests.

These are, of course, broad historical generalizations. My aim here is not to provide empirical explanations but to sketch out theoretical alternatives, to show how a performative dimension should be added to more traditional political and sociological perspectives. But while my ambition is mainly theoretical, it certainly can be amplified with illustrations that are empirical in a more straightforward way. What follows are examples of how social processes that are well known both to historical and lay students of this period can be reconstructed with the model of performance in mind.

Thomas Becket

When Thomas Becket opposed the effort of Henry II to exercise political control over the English Church, he felt compelled to create a grand social drama that personalized and amplified his plight (Turner 1974b). He employed as background representation the dramatic paradigm of Christ's martyrdom to legitimate his contemporary script of antagonism to the king. While Henry defeated Sir Thomas in instrumental political terms, the drama Becket enacted captured the English imagination and provided a new background text of moral action for centuries after.

Savanorola

In the Renaissance city-states (Brucker 1969), conflicts between Church and state were played out graphically in the great public squares, not only figuratively but often also literally before the eyes of the increasingly enfranchised *populo*. Heteronomy of social power was neither merely doctrine nor institutional structure. It was also public performance. Savanorola began his mass popular movement to cleanse the Florentine Republic with a dramatic announcement in the Piazza della Signoria, where open meetings had taken place already. Savanorola's public hanging, and the burning of his corpse that followed, were staged in the same civil space. Observed by an overflowing audience of citizens and semi-citizens – some horrified, others grimly satisfied (Brucker 1969: 271) – the performance instigated by

Savanorola's arrest, confession, and execution graphically drew the curtain on the reformer's spiritual renewal campaign. It is hardly coincidental that, during this same period, Machiavelli gave advice to Italian princes not only about how to muster dispersed administrative power but also about how to display power of a more symbolic kind. He wished to instruct the prince about how to perform like one so that he could appear, no matter what the actual circumstances, to exercise power in a ruthlessly efficient and supremely confident way.

The American Revolution

In 1773, small bands of anti-British American colonialists boarded three merchant ships in the Boston harbor and threw 90,000 tons of Indian tea into the sea. The immediate, material effect of what immediately became represented in the popular imagination as "the Boston tea party" was negligible, but its expressive power was so powerful that it created great political effects (Labaree 1979: 246ff). The collective performance successfully dramatized colonial opposition to the British crown, and mobilized fervent public support.

> The undertaking had all the signs of a well-planned operation . . . The rain had stopped, and some people showed up with lanterns to supplement the bright moonlight that now illuminated the scene . . . As work progressed, a large crowd gathered at the wharf to watch the proceedings in silent approval. It was so quiet that a witness standing at some distance could hear the steady whack-whack of the hatchets . . . "This is the most magnificent Movement of all," wrote John Adams in his diary the next day. "There is a Dignity, a Majesty, a Sublimity in this last Effort of the Patriots that I great admire . . . This Destruction of the Tea," he concluded, "is so bold, so daring to form, intrepid, and inflexible, and it must have so important Consequences and so lasting, that I cannot but consider it as an Epocha [sic] in History." (Labaree 1979: 144–5)

Later, the inaugural military battle of the American Revolution, in Lexington, Massachusetts, was represented in terms of theatrical metaphor as "the shot heard 'round the world'." In contemporary memorials of the event, social-dramatic exigencies exercised powerful sway. American and British soldiers were portrayed in the brightly colored uniforms of opposed performers. Paul Revere was portrayed as performing prolog, riding through the streets and shouting, "The Redcoats are coming, the Redcoats are coming," though he probably did not. The long lines of soldiers on both sides often were depicted as accompanied by fifes and drums. Bloody and often confusing battles of the War for Independence were narrated retrospectively as fateful and dramatic contests, their victors transformed into icons by stamps and etchings.

The French Revolution

A similar staging of radical collective action as social drama also deeply affected the revolution in France. During its early days, *sans coulottes* women sought to enlist a promise of regular bread from King Louis. They staged the "momentous march of women to Versailles," an extravagantly theatrical pilgrimage that one leading feminist historian has described as "the recasting of traditional female behavior within a republican mode" (Landes 1988: 109–11). As the revolution unfolded, heroes and villains switched places according to the agonistic logic of dramatic discourse (Furet 1981) and theatrical configuring (Hunt 1984), not only in response to political calculation. No matter how violent or bloodthirsty in reality, the victors and martyrs were painted, retrospectively, in classical Republican poses and togas, as in David's celebrated portrait of Marat Sade (Nochlin 1993).

It was Turner (1974a, 1982) who introduced the concept of social drama into the vocabulary of social science more than 30 years ago. For a time, this idea promised to open macro-sociology to the symbolic dynamics of public life (e.g., Moore and Myerhoff 1975, 1977), but with a few significant exceptions (e.g., Alexander 1988b; Edles 1998; Wagner-Pacifici 1986) the concept has largely faded from view, even in the field of performance studies. One reason has to do with the triumph of instrumental reason in rational-choice and critical theories of postmodern life. There were also, however, basic weaknesses in the original conceptualization itself. Turner simplified and moralized social performance in a manner that obscured the autonomy of the elements that composed it. Searching for a kind of natural history of social drama, on the one hand, and for a gateway to ideological communitas, on the other, Turner spoke (1982: 75) of the "full formal development" of social dramas; of their "full phase structure." While acknowledging that social complexity created the conditions for social drama, he insisted that it "remains to the last simple and ineradicable," locating it in "the developmental cycle of all groups" (1982: 78). He believed that the "values and ends" of performances were "distributed over a range of actors" and were projected "into a system . . . of shared or consensual meaning" (1982: 75). Social dramas can take place, Turner (1987) insisted, only "among those

members of a given group . . . who feel strongly about their membership [and] are impelled to enter into relationships with others which
become fully 'meaningful', in the sense that the beliefs, values, norms,
and symbolism "carried" in the group's culture become . . . a major
part of what s/he might regard as his/her identity" (1987: 46; for
similar emphases, see Myerhoff 1978: 32; Schechner 1987).

From the perspective on social dramas I am developing here, this
is exactly what does not take place. The elements of social-dramatic
performances are de-fused, not automatically hung together, which is
precisely why the organizational form of social drama first emerged.
Social drama is a successor to ritual, not its continuation in another
form.

We are now in a position to elaborate the propositions about
performative success and failure set forth in the first section.

Re-fusion and authenticity: The criteria for performative success and failure

The goal of secular performances, whether on stage or in society,
remains the same as the ambition of sacred ritual. They stand or fall
on their ability to produce psychological identification and cultural
extension. The aim is to create, via skillful and affecting performance, the emotional connection of audience with actor and text and
thereby to create the conditions for projecting cultural meaning from
performance to audience. To the extent these two conditions have
been achieved, one can say that the elements of performance have
become fused.

Nietzsche (1956 [1872]) elegized the "bringing to life [of] the plastic
world of myth" (p. 126) as one of those "moments of paroxysm that
lift man beyond the confines of space, time, and individuation" (1956
[1872]: 125). He was right to be mournful. As society becomes more
complex, such moments of fusion become much more difficult to
achieve. The elements of performance become separated and independently variable, and it becomes ever more challenging to bring
texts into life.

The challenge confronting individual and collective symbolic
action in complex contemporary societies, whether on stage or in
society at large, is to infuse meaning by re-fusing performance. Since
Romanticism, this modern challenge has been articulated existentially
and philosophically as the problem of authenticity (Taylor 1989).
While the discourse about authenticity is parochial, in the sense that

it is specifically European, it provides a familiar nomenclature for communicating the sense of what performative success and failure mean. On the level of everyday life, authenticity is thematized by such questions as whether a person is "real"– straightforward, truthful, and sincere. Action will be viewed as real if it appears *sui generis*, the product of a self-generating actor who is not pulled like a puppet by the strings of society. An authentic person seems to act without artifice, without undue self-consciousness, without reference to some laboriously thought-out plan or text, without concern for manipulating the context of her actions, and without worries about that action's audience or its effects. The attribution of authenticity, in other words, depends on an actor's ability to sew the disparate elements of performance back into a seamless and convincing whole. If authenticity marks success, then failure suggests that a performance will seem insincere and faked: the actor seems out of role, merely to be reading from an impersonal script, pushed and pulled by the forces of society, acting not from sincere motives but to manipulate the audience.

Such an understanding allows us to move beyond the simplistic polarities of ritual versus rationality or, more broadly, of cultural versus practical action. We can say, instead, that re-fusion allows ritual-like behavior, a kind of temporary recovery of the ritual process. It allows contemporaries to experience ritual because it stitches seamlessly together the disconnected elements of cultural performance. In her performative approach to gender, Butler (1999: 179) insists that gender identity is merely "the stylized repetition of acts through time" and "not a seemingly seamless identity." Yet seamless is exactly what the successful performance of gender in everyday life appears to be. "In what sense," Butler (1999: 178) then asks, "is gender an act?" In the same sense, she answers, "as in other ritual social dramas . . . The action of gender requires a performance that is repeated. This repetition is at once a reenactment and reexperiencing of a set of meanings already socially established; and it is the mundane and ritualized form of their legitimation."

In psychological terms, it is this seamless re-fusion that Csikszentmihalyi (1975) described as "flow" (see also Schechner 1976) in his innovative research on virtuoso performance in art, sport, and games. In the terms I am developing here, what Csikszentmihalyi (1975) discovered in these widely varying activities was the merging of text, context, and actor, a merging that resulted in the loss of self-consciousness and a lack of concern for – even awareness of – the scrutiny of observers outside the action itself. Because of "the merging of action and awareness," Csikszentmihalyi (1975: 38)

54

writes, "a person in flow has no dualistic perspective." The fusion of the elements of performance allows not only actors but also audiences to experience flow, which means they focus their attention on the performed text to the exclusion of any other possible interpretive reference: "The steps for experiencing flow . . . involve the . . . process of delimiting reality, controlling some aspect of it, and responding to the feedback with a concentration that excludes anything else as irrelevant" (Csikszentmihalyi 1975: 53–4).

Performances in complex societies seek to overcome fragmentation by creating flow and achieving authenticity. They try to recover a momentary experience of ritual, to eliminate or to negate the effects of social and cultural de-fusion. Speaking epigrammatically, one might say that successful performances re-fuse history. They break down the barriers that history has erected – the divisions between background culture and scripted text, between scripted text and actors, between audience and *mise-en-scène*. Successful performances overcome the deferral of meaning that Derrida (1991) recognized as *différance*. In a successful performance, the signifiers seem actually to become what they signify. Symbols and referents are one. Script, direction, actor, background culture, *mise-en-scène*, audience, means of symbolic production – all these separate elements of performance become indivisible and invisible. The mere action of performing accomplishes the performance's intended effect (see also Austin 1957). The actor seems to be Hamlet; the man who takes the oath of office seems to be the president.

While re-fusion is made possible only by the deposition of social power, the very success of a performance masks its existence. When performance is successful, social powers manifest themselves not as external or hegemonic forces that facilitate or oppose the unfolding performance but merely as sign-vehicles, as means of representation, as conveyors of the intended meaning. This is very much what Bourdieu (1990 [1968]: 211) had in mind when he spoke of the exercise of graceful artistic taste as culture "becoming natural." The connoisseur's poised display of aesthetic judgment might be thought of as a successful performance in the sense that it thoroughly conceals the manner in which this gracefulness is "artificial and artificially acquired," the result of a lengthy socialization resting upon class privilege. "The virtuosi of the judgment of taste," Bourdieu writes, present their knowledge of art casually, as if it were natural. Their aim is to present "an experience of aesthetic grace" that appears "completely freed from the constraints of culture," a performance "little marked by the long, patient training of which it is the product."

Attacking the hegemonic exercise of sexual rather than class power, Butler (1999) makes a similar argument. The successful performance of gender, she claims, makes invisible the patriarchal power behind it. The difference is that, by drawing upon the theories of Austin and Turner, Butler (1999) can explicitly employ the language of performance. "Gender is . . . a construction that regularly conceals its genesis; the tacit collective agreement to perform, produce, and sustain discrete and polar genders as cultural fictions is obscured by the credibility of those productions . . . The appearance of substance is precisely that, a constructed identity, a performative accomplishment which the mundane social audience, including the actors themselves, come to believe and to perform in the mode of belief" (1999: 179).

When post-ritual drama emerged in ancient Greece, Aristotle (1987) explained that a play is "an imitation of action, not the action itself." When re-fusion occurs, this cautionary note goes unheeded. The performance achieves verisimilitude – the appearance of reality. It seems to be action, not its imitation. This achievement of the appearance of reality via skillful performance and flow is what Barthes (1972a [1957]) described in his celebrated essay on "true wrestling." He insisted that the "public spontaneously attunes itself to the spectacular nature of the contest, like the audience at a sub-urban cinema . . . The public is completely uninterested in knowing whether the context is rigged or not, and rightly so; it abandons itself to the primary virtue of the spectacle, which is to abolish all motives and all consequences: what matters is not what it thinks but what it sees" (1972a [1957]: 15).

How does cultural pragmatics work? The inner structures of social performance

Having elaborated the criteria of performative failure and success, I now turn to a more detailed discussion of the elements and relations that sustain it. I will draw upon the insights of drama theory to decompose the basic elements of performance into their more complex component parts, and I will link these insights to the social dramas that compose the public sphere. To be able to move back and forth between theatrical and social drama enriches both sides of the argument; it also helps document my core empirical claim. Social action in complex societies so often is ritual-like because it remains performative. The social conditions that gave rise to theater also gave rise to post-ritual forms of symbolic action.

The challenge of the script: Re-fusing background representations with contingent performance

Behind every actor's social and theatrical performance lies the already established skein of collective representations that compose culture – the universe of basic narratives and codes and the cookbook of rhetorical configurations from which every performance draws. In a theatrical performance, the actor strives to realize "individual character," as Turner (1982: 94) put it, but he or she can do so only by taking "partly for granted the culturally defined roles supposedly played by that character: father, businessman, friend, lover, fiancé, trade union leader, farmer, poet" (1982: 94). For Turner, "these roles are made up of collective representations shared by actors and audience, who are usually members of the same culture" (Turner 1982), but we do not have to accept his consensual assumptions to get his point. The ability to understand the most elementary contours of a performance depends on an audience knowing already, without thinking about it, the categories within which actors behave. In a complex social order, this knowledge is always a matter of degree. In contrast with Turner (1982), I do not presume that social performance is ritualistic; I wish to explain whether and how and to what degree.

It is precisely at this joint of contingency or possible friction between background representations and the categorical assumptions of actors and audience that scripts enter into the scene. The emergence of the script as an independent element reflects the relative freedom of performance from background representations. From within a broader universe of meanings, performers make conscious and unconscious choices about the paths they wish to take and the specific set of meanings they wish to project. These choices are the scripts – the action-oriented subset of background understandings. If script is meaning primed to performance, in theatrical drama this priming is usually, though not always, sketched out beforehand. In social drama, by contrast, scripts more often are inferred by actors. In a meaning-searching process that stretches from the more intuitive to the more witting, actors and audiences reflect on performance in the process of its unfolding, gleaning a script upon which the performance "must have" been based.

In such social-dramatic scripting, actors and audiences actively engage in drawing the hermeneutical circle (Dilthey 1976). Performances become the foreground parts upon which wholes are constructed, the latter being understood as the scripts that allow the sense of an action to be ascertained. These scripts become, in turn, the parts of future wholes. It seems only sensible to suggest that an

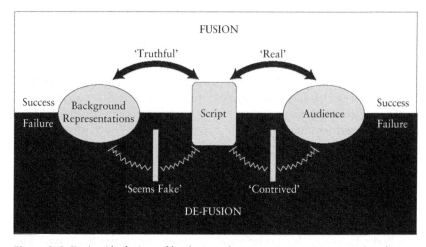

Figure 2.5. Fusion/de-fusion of background representation, script, and audience.

authentic script is one that rings true to the background culture. Thus, as one critic of rock music suggests, "authenticity is often located in current music's relationship to an earlier, 'purer' moment in a mythic history of the music" (Auslander 1999: 71). Yet, while this seems sensible, it would be misleading, since it suggests the naturalistic fallacy. It is actually the illusory circularity of hermeneutic interpretation that creates the sense of authenticity, and not the other way around. A script seems to ring true to the background culture precisely because it has an audience-fusing effect. This effectiveness has to do with the manner in which it articulates the relationship among culture, situation, and audience. Another music critic (Margolick 2000: 56) argues against the claim that Billie Holiday's recording of "Strange Fruit" – the now almost-mythical, hypnotic ballad about black lynching – succeeded because lynching was "already a conspicuous theme in black fiction, theater, and art." Holiday's singing was successful because "it was really the first time that anyone had so . . . poetically transmitted the message." The existence of the background theme is a given; what is contingent is the actor's dramatic technique, which is designed to elicit an effective audience response. In our terms, this is a matter of fusing the script in two directions, with background culture on the one side and with audience on the other. If the script creates such fusion, it seems truthful to background representations and real to the audience. The former allows cultural extension; the latter psychological identification. See Figure 2.5.

The craft of script-writing addresses these possibilities. The writer

58

aims to "achieve concentration" (Boulton 1960: 12–13) of background meaning. Effective scripts compress the background meanings of culture by changing proportion and by increasing intensity. They provide such condensation (see also Freud 1950 [1900]) through dramatic techniques.

Cognitive simplification

"In a play," Boulton (1960: 12–13) wrote, "there are often repetitions even of quite simple facts, careful explanations, addressing of people by their names more frequently than in real conversation and various oversimplifications which to the reader of a play in a study may seem almost infantile." The same sort of simplifying condensation affects the less consciously formed scripts of successful social dramas. As they strive to become protagonists in their chosen narrative, such social performers as politicians, activists, teachers, therapists, or ministers go over time and time again the basic story line they wish to project. They provide not complex but stereotyped accounts of their positive qualities as heroes or victims, and they melodramatically exaggerate (Brooks 1976) the malevolent motives of the actors they wish to identify as their antagonists, depicting them as evildoers or fools.

Professional speechwriters plotting social dramas are as sensitive to this technical exigency as screenwriters and playwrights plotting theatrical ones. In Peggy Noonan's (1998) manual *On Speaking Well*, the much-heralded speechwriter for presidents Ronald Reagan and George H. W. Bush emphasized time and time again that simplification is the key to achieving the fusion among speaker, audience, and background culture (see also Flesch 1946). "You should treat the members of the audience as if they're friends," Noonan (1998: 23) instructs, which means "that you're going to talk to them the way you talk to your friends, with the same candor and trust and respect." Noting the "often unadorned quality to sections of great speeches, a directness and simplicity of expression," Noonan (1998: 48) attributes this to the fact that "the speaker is so committed to making his point, to being understood and capturing the truth." Sentences "must be short and sayable," she warns, because "your listeners [are] trying to absorb what you say" (1998: 35). Noonan praised Bush's acceptance speech at the 1988 Republican Convention in terms of this two-way fusion. On the one hand, her script allowed Bush to connect his own life to the background representations of American society. Bush "was not only telling about his life in a way that was truthful and specific [but] was also connecting his life to history – the history of those who'd fought

World War II and then come home to the cities, and married, and gone on to invent the suburbs of America, the Levittowns and Hempsteads and Midlands." On the other hand, the script allowed Bush to fuse speaker with audience: "He was also connecting his life to yours, to everyone who's had a child and lived the life that children bring with them . . . You were part of the saga" (Noonan 1998: 28–9).

Time–space compression

Responding to the emergence of theater from ritual, Aristotle (1987) theorized that every successful drama contains the temporal sequence of beginning, middle, and end. In early modern Europe, when ritual was secularized and de-fused once again, the demand for narrative coherence became a stricture that dramatists must stress "three unities"– of action, place, and time (Boulton 1960: 13ff). Given the material and behavioral constraints on performance, the classic dramatists argued, theatrical action must be clearly of one piece. If the background culture is to be articulated clearly and if the audience is to absorb it, then performance must take place in the confines of one dramatic scene – in one narrative place – and must unfold in continuous time.

Such social dramas as congressional hearings or televised investigations strive strenuously to compress time and space in the same way. With large visual charts, lead investigators display time lines for critical events, retrospective plottings whose aim is to suggest continuous action punctuated by clearly interlinked causes and effects. Daytime television is interrupted so that the representations of these investigations themselves can unfold in continuous and real, and thus forcefully dramatic time. Ordinary parliamentary business is suspended so that such political-cultural performances, whether grandiose or grandiloquent, can achieve the unity of action, place, and time.

Moral agonism

The fusion achieved by successful scripting does not suggest harmonious plots. To be effective, in fact, scripts must structure meaning in an agonistic way (Arendt 1958; Benhabib 1996). Agonism implies a dynamic movement that hinges on a conflict pitting good against evil (Bataille 1985), creating a wave-like dialectic that highlights the existential and metaphysical contrast between sacred and profane. "Performing the binaries" (Alexander 2003b) creates the basic codes and propels narratives to pass through them. The drama's protagonists are aligned forcefully with the sacred themes and figures of

60

cultural myth and, through this embodiment, become new icons and create new texts themselves. Signaling their antipathy to the profane, to the evil themes and figures that threaten to pollute and to overwhelm the good, one group of actors casts doubt on the sincerity and verisimilitude of another. If a protagonist successfully performs the binaries, audiences will pronounce the performer to be an "honest man," the movement to be "truly democratic," an action to be the "very epitome of the Christian spirit." If the performance is energetically and skillfully implanted in moral binaries, in other words, psychological identification can be achieved and elements from the background culture can be dramatically extended.

Agonistic scripting is exhibited most clearly in grandiloquent performance. Geertz (1973b: 420–1) portrayed the Balinese cockfight as "a blood sacrifice offered . . . to the demons," in which "man and beast, good and evil, ego and id, the creative power of aroused masculinity and the destructive power of loosened animality fuse in a bloody drama." Barthes (1972a [1957]: 17) recounted how the wrestler's "treacheries, cruelties, and acts of cowardice" are based in an "image of ignobility" portrayed by "an obese and sagging body" whose "asexual hideousness always inspires . . . a particularly repulsive quality." But performing the binaries is also fundamental to the emergent scripts of everyday political life. In 1980, in the debate among Republican and Democratic candidates for vice president of the United States, the Republican contender from Indiana, Senator Dan Quayle, sought to gain credibility by citing the martyred former president John F. Kennedy. Quayle's opponent, Texas Senator Lloyd Benton, responded with a remark that not merely scored major debating points but also achieved folkloric status in the years following: "Senator, I had the honor of knowing Jack Kennedy, and you're no Jack Kennedy." Speaking directly to his political opponent, but implicitly to the television audiences adjudicating the authenticity of the candidates, Senator Benton wished to separate his opponent's script from the nation's sacred background representations. To prove they were not aligned would block Senator Quayle from assuming an iconic role. As it turned out, while Senator Quayle's debate performance failed, he was elected anyway.

Explicating "the general artistic laws of plot development," Boulton (1960: 41ff) observed that "a play must have twists and turns to keep interest until the end." To keep the audience attentive and engaged, staged dramas "must develop from one crisis to another." After an initial clarification, in which "we learn who the chief characters are, what they are there for and what are the problems with which they start," there must be "some startling development giving rise to new problems." This first crisis will be followed by others, which "succeed one another as causes and effects."

Turner (1974a) found almost exactly the same plot structure at work in social drama. He conceptualized it as involving successive phase movements, from breach to crisis, redress, and reintegration or schism. The initial breach that triggers a drama "may be deliberately, even calculatedly, contrived by a person or party disposed to demonstrate or challenge entrenched authority." But a breach also "may emerge [simply] from a scene of heated feelings" (Turner 1982: 70), in which case the initiation of a social drama is imputed, or scripted, by the audience, even when it is not intended by the actors themselves.

The naturalism underlying Turner's dramaturgical theory prevents him from seeing twisting and turning as a contingent effort to refuse background culture and audience with performative text. In her revisions of Turner's scheme, Wagner-Pacifici (1986, 1994, 2000) demonstrated just how difficult it is for even the most powerful social actors to plot the kind of dramatic sequencing that an effective script demands. Her study of the 1978 kidnapping and assassination of the Italian prime minister Aldo Moro (Wagner-Pacifici 1986) can be read as a case study of failed performance. Despite Moro's status as the most influential Italian political figure of his day, the popular prime minister could not convince other influential collective actors to interpret his kidnapping in terms of his own projected script. He wished to portray himself as still a hero, as the risk-taking and powerful protagonist in a performance that would continue to demonstrate the need for a historic "opening to the Left" and, thus, the necessity to negotiate with his terrorist kidnappers to save his life. Against this projected script, other social interpreters, who turned out to be more influential, insisted that Moro's kidnapping illuminated a script not of romantic heroism but of a tragic martyrdom, which pointed to a narrative not of reconciliation but of revenge against a terrorist Left. Wagner-Pacifici herself attributes the failure of Moro's performance primarily to unequal social power and the control that anti-Moro forces exercised over the means of symbolic production. The more multidimensional model I am elaborating here would suggest other critically important causes of the failed performance as well.

The challenge of mise-en-scène: Re-fusing script, action, and performative space

Even after a script has been constructed that allows background culture to walk and talk, the "action" of the performance must begin in real time and at a particular place. This can be conceptualized as the challenge of instantiating a scripted text, in theatrical terms as *mise-en-scène*, which translates literally as "putting into the scene." Defining *mise-en-scène* as the "confrontation of text and performance," Pavis (1988: 87) spoke of it as "bringing together or confrontation, in a given space and time, of different signifying systems, for an audience." This potential confrontation has developed because of the segmentation that social complexity rends among the elements of performance. It is a challenge to put them back together in a particular scene.

Rouse (1992: 146) saw the "relationship between dramatic text and theatrical performance" as "a central element in the Occidental theatre." Acknowledging that "most productions here continue to be productions 'of' a preexisting play text," he insists that "exactly what the word 'of' means in terms of [actual] practices is, however, far from clear," and he suggests that "the 'of' of theatrical activity is subject to a fair degree of oscillation." It seems clear that the specialized dramatic role of director has emerged to control this potential oscillation. In Western societies, theatrical performances long had been sponsored financially by producers and had been organized, in their dramatic specifics, by playwrights and actors. As society became more complex, and the elements of performance more differentiated, the coordinating tasks became more demanding. By the late nineteenth century, according to Chinoy (1963: 3, in McConachie 1992: 176), there was "so pressing a need" that the new role of director "quickly preempted the hegemony that had rested for centuries with playwrights and actors." Chinoy (1963) believes that "the appearance of the director ushered in a new theatrical epoch," such that "his experiments, his failures, and his triumphs set and sustained the stage" (1963: 3).

When Boulton (1960: 182–3) warned that "overdirected scripts leave the producer no discretion," she meant to suggest that, because writers cannot know the particular challenges of *mise-en-scène*, they should not write specific stage directions into their script. Writers must leave directors "plenty of scope for inventions." Given the contingency of performance, those staging it will need a large space within which to exercise their theatrical imagination. They will need to coach actors on the right tone of voice, to choreograph the space and timing among actors, to design costumes, to construct props, and to arrange lights. When Barthes (1972a [1957]: 15) argued that "what makes the circus or the arena what they are is not the sky [but] the drenching and vertical quality of the flood of light," he points to such directorial effect. If the script demands grandiloquence, Barthes observes, it must contrast darkness with light, for "a light without shadow generates an emotion without reserve" (1972a [1957]: 15).

For social dramas, in which scripts are attributed in a more contemporaneous and often retrospective way, *mise-en-scène* more likely is initiated within the act of performance itself. This coordination is triggered by the witting or unwitting sensibilities of collective actors, by the observing ego of the individual – in Mead's terms, her "I" as compared with her "me"– or by suggestions from an actor's agents, advisors, "advance men," or event planners. This task of instantiating scripts and representations in an actual scene underscores, once again, the relative autonomy of symbolic action from its so-called social base. The underlying strains or interest conflicts in a social situation do not simply "express" themselves. Social problems not only must be symbolically plotted, or framed (Eyerman and Jamison 1990; Snow et al. 1986), but also must be performed on the scene. In analyzing "how social movements move," Eyerman (2006) highlights "the physical, geographical aspects of staging and managing collective actions." In theorizing the standoff, Wagner-Pacifici (2000: 192–3) distinguishes between "ur-texts" and "texts-in-action," explaining how the often deadly standoffs between armed legal authorities and their quarries are triggered by "rules of engagement" (2000: 157) that establish "set points" (2000: 47) in a physical scene, such as barricades. Temporal deadlines also are established, so that the "rhythm of siege" becomes structured by the "clock ticking" (2000: 64). Standoffs are ended by violent assault only when dramatic violations occur vis-à-vis these specific spatial and temporal markers in a particular scene.

The challenge of the material base: Social power and the means of symbolic production

While *mise-en-scène* has its own independent requirements, it remains interdependent with the other performative elements. One thing on which its success clearly depends is access to the appropriate means of symbolic production. Goffman's (1956) early admonishment has not been sufficiently taken to heart: "We have given insufficient attention to the assemblages of sign-equipment which large numbers of performers can call their own" (1956: 22–3). Of course, in the more typically fused performances of small-scale societies, access to such means was not usually problematic. Yet even for such naturalistic and fused performances, the varied elements of symbolic production did not appear from nowhere. In his study of the Tsembaga, for example,

Schechner (1976) found that peace could be established among the warring tribes when they performed the *konjkaiko* ritual. While the ritual centered on an extended feast of wild pig, it took "years to allow the raising of sufficient pigs to stage a *konjkaiko*" (1976: 198). War and peace thus depended on a ritual process that was "tied to the fortunes of the pig population" (p. 198).

One can easily imagine just how much more difficult and consequential access to the means of symbolic production becomes in large-scale complex societies. Most basic of all is the acquisition of a venue. Without a theater or simply some makeshift stage, there can be no performance, much less an audience. Likewise, without some functional equivalent of the venerable soapbox, there can be no social drama. The American presidency is called "the bully pulpit" because the office provides its occupant with extraordinary access to the means for projecting dramatic messages to citizens of the United States.

Once a performative space is attained, moreover, it must be shaped materially. Aston and Savona (1991: 114) remarked that "the shape of a playing space can be altered by means of set construction." There is, in the literal and not the figurative or metaphysical sense, a material "base" for every symbolic production. While the latter are not simply shaky superstructures in the vulgar Marxist manner, neither can cultural performances stand up all by themselves. *Le Robert Micro* (2006) defines *mise-en-scène* as "*l'organization matérielle de la représentation*," and the means of symbolic production refers to the first half of this definition, the material organization. Still, even the physical platforms of performance must be given symbolic shape. Every theater is marked by "the style in which it is designed and built," write Aston and Savona (1991: 112), and social dramas are affected equally by the design of their place. During the 1998 Clinton impeachment, it was noted widely that the hearings were being held in the old Senate office building, an ornate setting whose symbolic gravitas had been reinforced by the civil theatrics of Watergate decades before.

Yet the design of theatrical space depends, in part, on technological means. In the preindustrial age, according to Aston and Savona (1991), the "confines" of the "large and inflexible venue" (1991: 114) of open-air theaters placed dramatic limits on the intimacy that performers could communicate, whatever the director's theatrical powers or the artistry of the script. Later, the introduction of lighting "established the convention of the darkened auditorium" and "limited the spectator's spatial awareness to the stage area" (1991: 114). Once attention is focused in this manner – as Barthes (1972b

65

[1957]) also suggests in his observations on spectacle – a "space can be created within a space" (Aston and Savona 1991: 114), and greater communicative intimacy is possible.

Equally significant dramatic effects have followed from other technical innovations in the means of symbolic production. The small size of the television as compared with the movie screen limited the use of long-distance and ensemble shots, demanded more close-up camera work, and required more editing cuts to create a scene. Greater possibilities for dramatic intimacy and agonistic dialog entered into televised performance as a result. The availability of amplification pushed the symbolic content of performance in the opposite way. With the new technological means for electronically recording and projecting the human voice, recordings proliferated and large-scale commercial musicals became amplified electronically through microphones. Such developments changed the criteria of authenticity. Soon, not only concerts but also most nonmusical plays needed to be amplified as well, "because the results sound more 'natural' to an audience whose ears have been conditioned by stereo television, high fidelity LPs, and compact disks" (Copeland 1990, in Auslander 1999: 34).

It is here that social power enters into performance in particular ways. Certainly, censorship and intimidation have always been employed to prevent the production and distribution of symbolic communication and, thus, to prevent or control political dissent. What is more interesting theoretically and empirically, however, and perhaps more normatively relevant in complex semi-democratic and even democratic societies, is the manner in which social power affects performance by mediating access to the means of symbolic production (e.g., Berezin 1991, 1994). The use of powerful arc lights, for example, was essential to Leni Riefenstahl's *mise-en-scène* in her infamous propaganda film, *Triumph of the Will*, which reconstructed Adolph Hitler's triumphant evening arrival at the Nuremberg rally in 1933. Whether Riefenstahl had the opportunity to put her imagination into place, however, was determined by the distribution of German political and economic power. Because Hitler's party had triumphed at the level of the state, Nazis controlled the means of symbolic production. As an artist, Reifenstahl herself was infatuated by the Nazi cause, and she wrote a script that cast Hitler in a heroic light. But the tools for making her drama were controlled by others. It was Goebbels who could hire the brilliant young filmmaker and could provide her with the means for staging her widely influential work.

In most social-dramatic performances, the effect of social power is even less direct. To continue with our lachrymose example, when the Nazi concentration camps remained under control of the Third Reich, their genocidal purpose could not be dramatized. Performative access to the camps – the critical "props" for any story – was denied to all but the most sympathetic, pro-Nazi journalists, still photographers, and producers of newsreels and films. On the few occasions when independent and potentially critical observers were brought to the camps, moreover, they were presented with falsified displays and props that presented the treatment of Jewish prisoners in a fundamentally misleading way. This control over the means of symbolic production shifted through force of arms (Alexander 2003a, 2009). Only after allied troops liberated the western camps did it become possible to produce the horrifying newsreels of dead and emaciated Jewish prisoners and to distribute them worldwide (Zelizer 1998). It would be hard to think of a better example of performance having a material base and of this base depending on power in turn.

As this last example suggests, in complex societies social power provides not only the means of symbolic production but of symbolic distribution as well. The more dependent a dramatic form is on technology, the more these two performative phases become temporally distinct. It is one thing to perform a drama, and even to film it, and it is quite another to make it available to audiences throughout the land. In the movie industry, distribution deals develop only after films are made, for those who represent theater syndicates insist on first examining the performances under which they intend to draw their bottom line. Similarly, video technology has separated the distribution of social dramas from live-action transmission. Media events (Boorstin 1961; Dayan and Katz 1992) are social performances whose contents are shaped by writers and photographers and whose distribution is decided by corporate or state organization. If the former represent "hermeneutical power" and the latter social power in the more traditional sense, then there is a double mediation between performance and audience. As we will see, there are, in fact, many more mediations than that. See Figure 2.6.

Whether those who "report" media effects are employed by institutions whose interests are separated from – and possibly even opposed to – those of the performers is a critical issue for whether or not social power affects performance in a democratic way. Because control over media is so vital for connecting performances with audience publics, it is hardly surprising that newspapers for so long remained financially and organizationally fused with particular ideological,

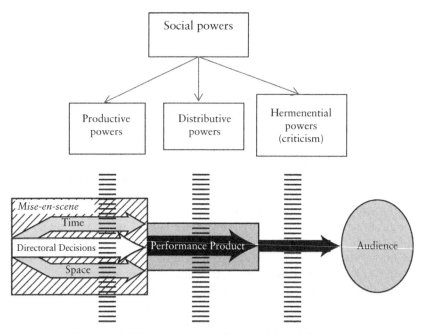

Figure 2.6. *Mise-en-scène* interfacing with social powers.

economic, and political powers (Alexander 1981; Schudson 1981). Fusion allowed those who held hegemonic structural positions to decide which of their performances should be distributed and how they would be framed.

As social power becomes more pluralized, the means of recording and distributing social dramas have been distributed more widely, media interpretation has become more subject to disputation, and performative success more contingent. Even in the "iron cage" of nineteenth-century capitalism, British parliamentary investigations into factory conditions were able to project their often highly critical performances on the public stage. Their hearings were reported widely in the press (Osborne 1970: 88–90), and their findings were distributed in highly influential "white papers" throughout the class system (Smelser 1959: 291–2). Even after Bismark outlawed the socialist party in late nineteenth-century Germany, powerful performances by militant labor leaders and working-class movements challenged him in "rhetorical duels" that were recorded and were distributed by radical and conservative newspapers alike (Roth 1963: 119–35). In mid-twentieth-century America, the civil rights movement would have failed if Southern white media had monopolized coverage of African-American protest activities. It was critical that reporters from independent Northern-owned media were empowered to record and to distribute sympathetic interpretations, which allowed psychological identification and cultural extension with the black movement's cause (Halberstam 1999).

Differentiating the elements of performance, then, is not just a social and cultural process but a political one as well. It has significant repercussions for the pluralization of power and the democratization of society. As the elements of performance become separated and relatively autonomous, there emerge new sources of professional authority. Each of the de-fused elements of performance eventually becomes subject to institutions of independent criticism, which judge it in relation to criteria that establish not only aesthetic form but also the legitimacy of the exercise of this particular kind of performative power. Such judgments issue from "critics," whether they are specialized journalists employed by the media of popular or high culture or intellectuals who work in academic milieux.

Such critical judgments, moreover, do not enter performance only from the outside. They also are generated from within. Around each of the de-fused elements of drama there have developed specialized performative communities, which maintain and deploy their own critical, sometimes quite unforgiving standards of judgment. The distance from the first drama prizes awarded by the City Dionysius festival in ancient Greece to the Academy Awards in postmodern Hollywood may be great in geographic, historical, and aesthetic terms, but the institutional logic (Friedland and Alford 1991) has remained the same. The aim is to employ, and deploy, autonomous criteria in the evaluation of social performance. As the elements of performance have been differentiated, the reach of hegemonizing, hierarchical power has necessarily declined. Collegial associations, whether conceived as institutional elites, guilds, or professional associations, increasingly regulate and evaluate the performance of specialized cultural goods (Parsons 1967). In complex societies, continuous critical evaluations are generated from within every performative medium and emergent genre – whether theater or feature film, blog or website design, documentary or cartoon, country-and-western song or rap, classical recording, sitcom, soap opera, news story, news photo, editorial, feature, or nightly newscast. Such self-policing devices aim to "improve" the possibilities for projecting performance in effective ways. These judgments and awards are determined by peer evaluations. Despite the power of the studios and mega-media corporations,

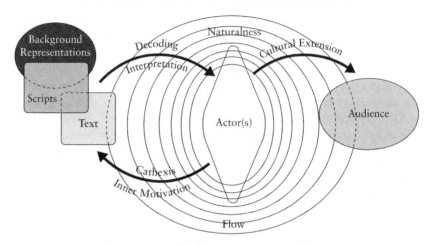

Figure 2.7. Double fusion: text-actor-audience.

it is the actors, cinematographers, editors, directors, script and speechwriters, reporters, ad writers, graphic designers, and costume designers themselves who create the aesthetic standards and prestige hierarchies in their respective performative communities.

In less formal ways, critical interpretive judgments circulate freely and endlessly throughout dramatic life, in both its theatrical and social forms. The public relations industry, new in the twentieth century, aims to condition and structure the interpretations such critics apply. Such judgments are also the concern of agents and handlers, of experts in focus groups, of privately hired pollsters, and spin doctors of every ideological stripe. The more complex and pluralized the society, the tighter this circle of criticism and self-evaluation is wound. Normative and empirical theories of power and legitimacy in the contemporary world must come to terms with how the conditions of performativity have changed everywhere. See Figure 2.7.

The challenge of being natural: Re-fusing actor and role

Even if the means of symbolic production are sufficient, the script powerfully written, and the *mise-en-scène* skillfully set in place, there is no guarantee that a performance will succeed. There remains the extraordinary challenge of acting it out. Actors must perform their roles effectively, and they often are not up to the task. Thus, while Veltrusky (1964: 84) acknowledges that signifying power resides in "various objects, from parts of the costume to the set," he insists, nevertheless, that "the important thing is . . . that the actor centers their meanings upon himself."

In smaller-scale societies, ritual performers act out roles they have played in actual social life or from sacred myths with which they are intimately familiar. In post-ritual societies, the situation is much more complex. In theatrical performances, actors are professionals who have no off-screen relation to their scripted role. In a neglected essay, Simmel (1968: 92) put the problem very clearly: "The role of the actor, as it is expressed in written drama, is not a total person . . . not a man, but a complex of things which can be said about a person through literary devices." In social dramas, actors perform a role they often do occupy, but their ability to maintain their role incumbency is always in doubt; their legitimacy is subject to continuous scrutiny; and their feeling for the role is often marked by unfamiliarity.[3]

As the actor in theatrical drama increasingly became separated from the role, the challenge of double fusion – actor and text on the one side and actor with audience on the other – became a topic of increasing intellectual attention. When social texts were more authoritative, less contested, and less separated from familiar social roles, professional actors could achieve re-fusion in a more indexical than iconographic way. In what later came to be seen as histrionic "picture acting," performers merely would gesture to a text rather than seeking actually to embody it. This overt exhibition of the separation of actor and role could have theatrical purchase (Aston and Savona 1991: 118) only because dramatic texts had a more deeply mythical status than they typically have today. By the late eighteenth century, when sacred and traditional social structures were being reconstructed by secular revolutions (Brooks 1976), this "anti-emotionalist" thespian style came under criticism. In *The Paradox of Acting*, Diderot (1957 [1830]) attacked acting that communicated feelings by gesture rather than embodiment. But it was not until the so-called new drama of the late nineteenth century – when social and culture de-fusion were considerably more elaborate – that the intensely psychological and introspective theater initiated by Strindberg and Ibsen demanded an acting method that placed a premium on subjective embodiment, or facsimile.

Just as Aristotle wrote the *Poetics* as a cookbook for script-writing once myth had lost its sway, so did the Russian inventor of modern dramatic technique Constantin Stanislavski (1989 [1934]) invent "the system" after the iconic potency of scripts could no longer be safely assumed. The challenge was to teach professional actors how to make their artificial performances seem natural and unassuming. Stanislavski began by emphasizing the isolation of the actor from scripted text. "What do you think?" he admonished the novice actor. "Does the dramatist supply everything that the actors need to know about the play? Can you, [even] in a hundred pages, give a full account of the life of the dramatis personae? For example, does the author give sufficient details of what has happened before the play begins? Does he let you know what will happen when it is ended, or what goes on behind the scenes?" (1989 [1934]: 55).

That the answer to each of these rhetorical questions is "no" demonstrates the challenge of re-fusion that contemporary actors face. "We bring to life what is hidden under the words; we put our thoughts into the author's lines, and we establish our own relationships to other characters in the play, and the conditions of their lives; we filter through ourselves all the materials that we receive from the author and the director; we work over them, supplementing them out of our own imagination" (Stanislavski 1989 [1934]: 52).

The art of acting aims at eliminating the appearance of autonomy. The ambition is to make it seem that the actor has not exercised her imagination – that she has no self except the one that is scripted on stage. "Let me see what you would do," Stanislavski advised the neophyte, "if my supposed facts were true" (1989 [1934]: 46). He suggests that the actor adopt an "as if" attitude, pretending that the scripted situation is the actor's in real life. In this way, "the feelings aroused" in the actor "will express themselves in the acts of this imaginary person"– as if she had actually "been placed in the circumstances made by the play" (1989 [1934]: 49; see also Goffman 1956: 48). If the actor believes herself "actually" to be in the circumstances that the script describes, she will act in a natural way. She will assume the inner motivation of the scripted character, in this way re-fusing the separation of actor and script. Only by possessing this subjectivity can an artfully contrived performance seem honest and real (Auslander 1997: 29). "Such an artist is not speaking in the person of an imaginary Hamlet," Stanislavski concludes, "but he speaks in his own right as one placed in the circumstances created by the play" (1989 [1934]: 248).

> All action in the theater must have an inner justification, be logical, coherent and real . . . With this special quality of *if* . . . everything is clear, honest and above board . . . The secret of the effect of *if* lies in the fact that it does not . . . make the artist do anything. On the contrary, it reassures him through its honesty and encourages him to have confidence in a supposed situation . . . It arouses an inner and real activity, and does this by natural means. (Stanislavski 1989 [1934]: 46–7, italics altered)

If social and cultural de-fusion has shifted the focus of theatrical acting, we should not be surprised that the acting requirements for effective social drama have changed in a parallel way. When social and political roles were ascribed, whether through inheritance or through social sponsorship, individuals could be clumsy in their portrayal of their public roles, for they would continue to possess them even if their performances failed. With increasing social differentiation, those who assume social roles, whether ascriptive or achieved, can continue to inhabit them only if they learn to enact them in an apparently natural manner (e.g., Bumiller 2003; Von Hoffman 1978). This is all the more true in social dramas that instantiate meanings without the benefit of a script, and sometimes without any prior clarification of an actor's role.

It is not at all uncommon, for example, for the putative actors in an emergent political drama to refuse to play their parts. During the televised Watergate hearings in the summer of 1973, even Republican senators who privately supported President Richard Nixon felt compelled to join their fellow Democrats in public expressions of outrage and indignation at the Republican president's behavior (Alexander 2003c; McCarthy 1974). By contrast, during the televised Clinton impeachment hearings in 1998, the Democrats on the House panel distanced themselves from the script, refusing to participate seriously in what Republicans leaders tried to perform as a tragic public event (Mast 2003, 2006, forthcoming). Their refusal destroyed the verisimilitude of the social drama. Actors on both sides of the aisle seemed "political," offering what appeared to be contrived and artificial performances. Despite the tried-and-true authenticity of the political script, the political drama failed because the actors could not, or would not, fuse with their parts.

The causal impact of acting on performance is so large that even bad scripts can be a great theatrical success. "We know where a bad play has achieved world fame," Stanislavski (1989 [1934]: 52) observes, "because of having been re-created by a great actor." Simmel (1968: 93) writes that the "impression of falsehood is generated only by a poor actor." If an actor experiences flow, then he or she has succeeded in fusing with the scripted role. The idea, according to Stanislavski, is "to have the actor completely carried away by the play" so that "it all moves of its own accord, subconsciously and intuitively" (1989 [1934]: 13). Only when flow is achieved can the actor fuse with audience as well. To seem real to an audience, "it is necessary that the spectators *feel* his inner relationship to what he is saying" (1989 [1934]: 249, original italics; see also Roach 1993: 16–17, 218).

Even the best acting, however, cannot ensure that the audience gets it right.

The challenge of reception: Re-fusing audience with performative text

One-sidedly cultural and pragmatic theories share one thing in common: each eliminates the contingent relationship between performative projection and audience reception. Viewing performance purely in textual terms, semioticians implicitly tie audience interpretation directly to the dramatic intentions of the actors and the culture structure that performance implies. The role of the spectator, according to Pavis (1988: 87), is simply to decipher the *mise-en-scène*, to "receive and interpret . . . the system elaborated by those responsible for the production." If such a theoretical position makes psychological identification and cultural extension seem easy to achieve, then the purely pragmatic position makes it seem virtually impossible. The founder of audience response theory, Iser (1980: 109–10), spoke about "the fundamental asymmetry between text and reader," asserting that the "lack of common situation and a common frame of reference" is so large as to create an "indeterminate, constitutive blank." Speaking in a more historical vein, his French counterpart, Leenhardt (1980), observed that "with the formation of a new reading public," the "organic relationship to the producer has nearly disappeared." The "codes of production of literary works" have now become utterly "alien" to the "spontaneous codes of readers" (1980: 207–8).

It is a mark of social and cultural complexity that the audience has become differentiated from the act of performance. Reception is dictated neither by background nor foreground representations, nor by social power, effective direction, or thespian skill. Yet neither is reception *necessarily* in conflict with them. Every dramatic effort faces uncertainty, but re-fusion is still possible.

Boulton (1960) articulates this contingent possibility when she describes the audience as the third side of "the great triangle of responses which is drama." Will the audience remain apart from the performative experience, or will it be "cooperative," proving itself capable of "submitting itself to a new experience" (1960: 196–7)? Boulton points here to the psychological identification of audience with enacted text. By "accepting a sample of life and tasting it," she writes, an audience is "sharing in the lives of imaginary people not altogether unlike known live persons." It is revealing that the

74

psychoanalyst who created psychodrama, J. L. Moreno, focuses also on the contingent relation between audience and stage and on the manner in which this gap is bridged by identification. "The more the spectator is able to accept the emotions, the role, and the developments on the stage as corresponding to his own private feelings, private roles, and private developments, the more thoroughly will his attentions and his fantasy be carried away by the performance" (Moreno 1975: 48). The paradox that defines the patient-performance is "that he is identifying himself with something with which he is not identical." Overcoming this paradox is the key to therapeutic success: "The degree to which the spectator can enter into the life upon the stage, adjusting his own feelings to what is portrayed there, is the measure of the catharsis he is able to obtain on this occasion."

The audience–performance split also has preoccupied the theatrical avant-garde. Some radical dramatists, such as Brecht (1964) or the Birmingham School of Cultural Studies (Hall and Jefferson 1976), have sought to accentuate defusion, in theory or in practice, so as to block the cultural extension of dominant ideology. By far the greater tendency among radical dramatists, however, has been the effort to overcome the de-fusion that makes theatrical performance artificial and audience participation vicarious and attenuated. Avant-garde performances have tried to create flow experiences, to transform mere theater into rituals where script, actors, and audience become one. In his 1923 Geneva address, Copeau (1955 [1923], in Auslander 1997: 16) observed that "there are nights when the house is full, yet there is no audience before us." The true audience is marked by fusion, when its members "gather [and] wait together in a common urgency, and their tears or laughter incorporate them almost physically into the drama or comedy that we perform." Exactly the same language of re-fusion is deployed 50 years later by Brook (1969) when he describes the aim of his "Holy Theatre." Only when the process of "representation no longer separates actor and audience, show and public" can it "envelop them" them in such a manner that "what is present for one is present for the other." On a "good night," he comments, the audience "assists" in the performance rather than maintaining "its watching role" (1969: 127).

Postmodern theatrical analysts are acutely aware of the fact that "theatre is attended by the 'non-innocent' spectator whose world view, cultural understanding or placement, class and gender condition and shape her/his response" (Aston and Savona 1991: 120). Film and television producers and distributors try to protect their investments by targeting specific audience demographics and by staging test runs that can trigger textual readjustments in response. Politicians may be committed vocationally rather than aesthetically and financially to generating an audience, but they display an equally fervent interest in re-fusing the audience–performance gap. They "keep their ear to the ground" and try to gauge "feedback" from the grassroots in front of whom their social performances are staged. That this testing of the demographics and responses of potential audiences is now conducted by candidate-sponsored scientific polling (Mayhew 1997) does not change the performative principle involved. The goal remains to achieve performative success by overcoming social-dramatic de-fusion.

If large-scale societies were homogeneous, this segmentation of performance from an audience would be only a matter of layering (Rauer 2006). Performances are projected first to an immediate audience of lay and professional interpreters and only subsequently to the impersonal audience that constitutes the vast beyond (see also Lang and Lang 1968: 36–77). In real life, however, the problem is much more difficult than this. Audiences are not only separated from immediate contact with performers but also are internally divided among themselves. Even after the intensely observed ritual ceremonies that displayed, and intensified, the growing political consensus about Nixon's impeachment, poll data revealed that some 20 percent of Americans did not agree that the president was guilty even of a legal violation, much less of moral turpitude (Lang and Lang 1983). In opposition to the vast majority of Americans, this highly conservative group interpreted the impeachment as political vengeance by Nixon's enemies (O'Keefe and Mendelsohn 1974).

Copeau (1955 [1923]) rightly linked the fusion of audience and performance to the internal unity of the audience itself. "What I describe as an audience is a gathering in the same place of those brought together by the same need, the same desire, the same aspirations . . . for experiencing together human emotions – the ravishment of laughter and that of poetry – by means of a spectacle more fully realized than that of life itself" (in Auslander 1997: 16). In complex societies, the main structural barrier to re-fusing social drama and audience is the fragmentation of the citizenry. Social segmentation creates not only different interests but also orthogonal subcultures – "multiple public spheres" (Eley 1992; Fraser 1992) – that produce distinctive pathways for cultural extension and distinctive objects of psychological identification. More and less divided by ideology, race, ethnicity, class, religion, and region, citizen-audiences can respond to social performances in diametrically opposed ways (Liebes and Katz 1990). For this reason, group-affirming social dramas are much easier to carry off than universalizing ones. This particularistic strategy informs recent identity politics, but it has always been the default position of social drama in complex societies. When these structured divisions are exacerbated by political and cultural polarization, the seamless re-fusion of audience and performance becomes more difficult still (Hunt 1997).

Whether or not some shared culture framework "really exists" is not, however, simply a reflection of social structure and demographics. It is also a matter of interpretation. Audience interpretation is a process, not an automatic result. For example, Bauman (1989) suggests that a consciousness of doubleness is inherent in the interpretation of performance – that every performance is compared to an idealized or "remembered" model available from earlier experience. In other words, audience interpretation does not respond to the quality of the performative elements per se. Audiences of social and theatrical dramas judge quality comparatively. Scripts, whether written or attributed, are compared to the great and convincing plots of earlier times. Did the fervor over President Reagan's trading of arms for hostages constitute "another Watergate," or did it pale by comparison (Alexander 1987b; Schudson 1992b)? In his role as chair of the House Impeachment Committee, how did Representative Henry Hyde's efforts stack up against Sam Ervin's bravura performance as chair of the Senate Select Committee during the Watergate hearings? How do the participants in today's presidential debates compare to the towering model of the Lincoln–Douglas debates that, according to American mythology (Schudson 1992a), made civil-dramatic history more than a century ago? Did President Obama's seemingly hands-off response to the Gulf oil spill represent "another Katrina," such that he was performing as badly as his predecessor, George W. Bush?

When audiences interpret the meaning and importance of social dramas, it is such comparative questions that they keep firmly in mind. If their answers are negative, even those who are within easy demographic reach will be less likely to invest their affect in the performance, and neither psychological identification nor cultural extension will likely occur. Fragmented performance interpretations feed back into the construction of subcultures, providing memories that in turn segment perceptions of later performances (Jacobs 2000). If there are some shared memories, by contrast, audiences will experience social drama in a deeper and broadened way. As audiences become more involved, performance can draw them out of demographic and subcultural niches into a more widely shared and possibly more universalistic liminal space. See Figure 2.8.

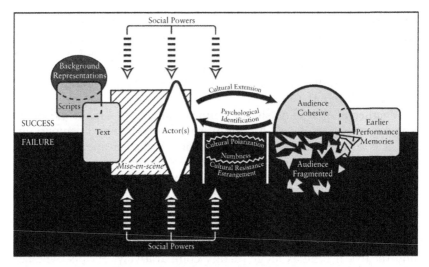

Figure 2.8. Audiences and performance.

Conclusion: Cultural pragmatics as model and morality

Why are even the most rationalized societies still enchanted and mystified in significant ways? The old-fashioned rituals that marked simpler organizational forms have largely disappeared, but ritual-like processes most decidedly remain. Individuals and collectivities strategically direct their actions and mobilize all their available resources, but their instrumental power usually depends on success of a cultural kind. This does not mean that the explanation of their success should be purely symbolic. It means that pragmatic and symbolic dimensions are intertwined.[4]

It is such a cultural-pragmatic perspective that has informed this chapter. I have developed a macro model of social action as cultural performance. In the first section, I proposed that performances are composed of a small number of analytically distinguishable elements, which have remained constant throughout the history of social life even as their relationship to one another has markedly changed. In the second section, I demonstrated that as social structure and culture have become more complex and segmented, so the elements that compose performance have become not only analytically separable but also concretely differentiated – separated, and de-fused in an empirical way. In the third section, I showed that whether social and theatrical performances succeed or fail depends on whether actors

78

can re-fuse the elements of which they are made. In the fourth section, I explored the challenge of modern performance by investigating the complex nature of the demands that each of its different elements implies.

In simpler societies, Durkheim (1996 [1912]) and Mauss (1979) believed, rituals are made at one time and place, after which the participants scatter to engage in activities of a more instrumental and individualistic kind. In complex societies, things are rarely so cut and dried. All actions are symbolic to some degree. In social science, it is best to convert such dichotomous either/or questions into matters of variation. The aim is to discover invariant structures, how they vary, and to suggest the forces that propel this change over time.

In complex societies, the relative autonomy and concrete interdependence (Kane 1991) of performative elements ensures variation both within and between groups. Even for members of relatively homogeneous communities, performances will range from those that seem utterly authentic to those that seem utterly false, with "somewhat convincing," "plausible," and "unlikely but not impossible" coming somewhere in between. For performances that project across groups, the range is the same, but attributions of authenticity are made less frequently. Such attributions also can be seen to vary broadly across historical time.

It might be worthwhile to offer a figurative rendering of the discussion I have presented here. Figure 2.9 presents a graphical, highly simplified schematization. The x-axis plots the variation in social and cultural structures, from simpler to more complex; the y-axis plots the elements that compose/organize a performance, from fused to de-fused. Three empirical lines are plotted in a hypothetical way. The higher horizontal plot line (a) traces performances that achieve fusion – ritual or ritual-like status – no matter what the degree of social complexity. The lower horizontal plot line (b) graphs failed performances, or those that fail to re-fuse the elements of performance, once again without regard for the state of social complexity. The diagonal plot line (c) graphs the average expectations for successful performance, which decline in stepwise and symmetrical fashion with each increment of social complexity. It has a downward, 45-degree slope, for each increase in social and cultural complexity stretches farther apart – further de-fuses – the elements of performances, which makes success that much more difficult to achieve. Performances above the diagonal (c) are more successful than expected, given the historical conditions of performance; those below are less.

79

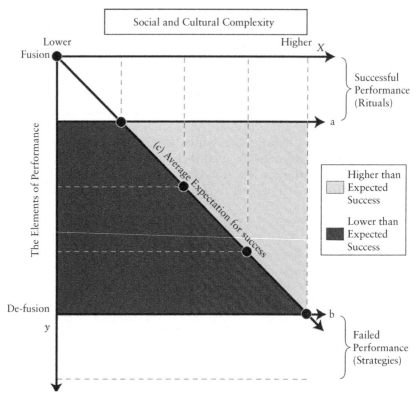

Figure 2.9. The historical conditions of social performance: structured variation.

Wariness about authenticity is intrinsic to the pluralism and openness of complex societies, whether ancient, modern, or postmodern social life. Nietzsche (1956 [1872]: 136) bemoaned that "every culture that has lost myth has lost, by the same token, its natural and healthy creativity." But from a moral point of view, it is often healthy to be skeptical of myths, to see through the efforts of actors to seamlessly re-fuse the elements of performance. When political democracy made its first historical appearance, in ancient Greece, Plato (1980) feared that demagogy might easily sway the polis to undertake immoral acts. In terms of the perspective set out here, Plato was an implacable opponent of performance, deeply suspicious of its cultural-pragmatic effects. In one of his dialogs, he portrayed a master of oratory, Gorgias, as bragging about its extraordinary persuasive powers. "You might well be amazed, Socrates, if you knew

. . . that oratory embraces and controls almost all other spheres of human activity . . . The orator can speak on any subject against any opposition in such a way as to prevail on any topic he chooses."

Socrates answered caustically, relativizing performative skill by connecting success to mere audience acceptance. "The orator need have no knowledge of the truth about things," Socrates exclaims; "it is enough for him to have discovered a knack of convincing the ignorant that he knows more than the experts." Socrates continues in an equally sarcastic vein: "What happens is that an ignorant person is more convincing than the expert before an equally ignorant audience. Am I right?" Gorgias responds cynically, asking: "Isn't it a great comfort, Socrates, to be able to meet specialists in all the other arts on equal terms without going to the trouble of acquiring more than this single one?" Socrates is furious. He acknowledges that orators need "a shrewd and bold spirit together with an aptitude for dealing with men," but he denies that it can be called an art. "Oratory certainly isn't a fine or honorable pursuit," he avows; indeed, "the generic name which I should give it is pandering." As a moral philosopher, Plato sees sincerity as the victim of performance. He insists that "the supreme object of a man's efforts, in public and in private life, must be the reality rather than the appearance of goodness."

From the normative point of view, performative fusion does need to be unmasked, and rational deliberation provides the means. From a cultural-sociological perspective, however, embracing rationality as a norm does not mean seeing social action itself as rational. Culture is less toolkit than storybook. Why else are critical efforts to question a performance almost always accompanied by creative efforts to mount counter-performances in turn (Alexander 2004)? Re-fusion remains critically important to complex societies. One must insist that social power be justified and that authority be accountable, but one also must acknowledge that even the most democratic and individuated societies depend on performative abilities to sustain collective belief. Myths are generated by ritual-like social performance (Giesen 2006). Only if performances achieve fusion can they reinvigorate collective codes, allowing them to be "ubiquitous and unnoticed, presiding over the growth of the child's mind and interpreting to the mature man his life and struggles," as Nietzsche (1956 [1872]: 136–7) astutely observed.

—— 3 ——

PERFORMANCE AND THE CHALLENGE OF POWER

In this chapter, I approach the phenomenon of power from the perspective of "cultural pragmatics," which is, at once, a micro theory of action theory and a macro theory of institutions and culture. Each of these three levels is imbedded, moreover, inside a theory of historical change, which describes deep transformations in the conditions for social performance. It is these historical shifts in the interrelation of action, institutions, and culture that form the backdrop for new thinking about power.

Cultural pragmatics intertwines the traditions of culturalism and pragmatics that were pitted against each in seemingly endless conflict throughout the last century. There were, of course, significant efforts to transcend this throughout that time. If the current effort is different, one reason is that it seeks resolution neither through a one-sided and polemical *coup de main*, which purports to demonstrate that the other side is hopelessly wrong, nor through a kind of arithmetic process that sets empirical conditions for when one side or the other "really" matters, an additive and subtractive effort at resolution that might be called the variable approach. With the idea of cultural pragmatics, I propose to resolve this long-brewing conflict in a more synthetic manner, which means, in effect, starting over. We need to begin from the beginning, with a basic philosophical or theoretical rethink. We need to do away with the traditional concepts of action and structure, and to dissolve, not reify, such dichotomies as culture versus institution and instrumental versus normative.

Actions are performative insofar as they can be understood as communicating meaning to an audience. For the purposes of understanding such performance, it does not matter what meaning "really"

is, either for actors themselves or in some ontological or normative sense. What matters is how others interpret actors' meaning.
This does not mean, however, that the meaning of an action can be
understood as simply emergent from interaction. Much more that is
"structural" is involved.

How can we understand the "success" of a performative action?
The notion of success, of course, comes from pragmatics, but success
actually also has a lot to do with meaning, and hence with communication. For an action to be successful, an individual or collective actor
must be able to communicate the meanings of their actions that they
consciously or unconsciously want others to believe.

Communication of belief is accomplished, metaphorically speaking, by becoming an actor in a script. Then, you need to get the others
who constitute the putative audience for your action to take this
script as real, to experience it, not as a "script" – not as symbolic or
contrived – but as completely real, as having an ontological status.
Such successful conveyance means that you, as an actor, seem authentic to your audience. If they are to identify with you and to connect
emotionally with your script, then they must believe you. They must
accept your symbolic projection. They must speak your language, so
that you are both reading from the same page.

From the manner in which I have put this, it should be clear just
why we need to connect sociology with performance studies. It is in
discussions about theatricality that we can find the tools we need to
understand social action as performance. Performance studies is a
broad field inside and outside the United States. Emerging from the
collaboration between the avant-gard dramatist Richard Schechner
and the anthropologist Victor Turner, it draws also from Erving
Goffman and Clifford Geertz and from John Austin's language philosophy, which was taken up by Jacques Derrida and elaborated by
Judith Butler. To this theoretical brew there is added more than a
dash of traditional theater and media studies and, more recently, a
pinch of postcoloniality. *Voila!* You have the heady mix that makes
up performance studies today.

For a specifically *sociological* approach to performance, it seems
essential to begin with the notion that every social performance is
composed of certain elements. It is with the description of these elements, their interrelation and their historical variability, that the
sociology of performance begins.

1 Actor. This could be an individual, a group, an organization, and
  may reference any level from casual and unstructured flow to class,

gender, and national conflicts, such regional identities as Europe, or processes in the global civil sphere. Actors can be skillful or not, lifelike or wooden, imaginative or dull.

2 Collective representations. The languages actors speak are multiple, and the words and phrases that come out of their mouths are singular, but they are speech acts, not languages in the semiotic sense. Every speech is a play upon the variations of a background structure, the collective representations that define the symbolic references for every speech act. For most of human history these background representations had nothing written about them, though they were highly organized. When these representations are first objects of writing, it marks a major watershed in social performance, for it crystallized the distinction between more latent background representations and scripts, the action-related subset of symbols that constitutes the immediate background for speech.

3 Means of symbolic production. In order to communicate such foregrounded representations, actors need real material things, which are themselves, of course, meaningfully defined. For the messages of an actor to be projected, they need a stage, whether this is a place in the sand, a tree or a high spot of ground, a newspaper, television transmission, video cam, or website. Performers also need props, which can be a parrot beak, full costume regalia, background music, spotlight, or the semi-automatic rifle cradled casually in one's arms.

4 *Mise-en-scène.* Literally "putting into the scene," this French phrase has come to represent what directors do. It is the arranging, and the doing, of actors' movements in time and space. It is the tone of voice, the direction of the glance, the gestures of the body, the direction and intensity of the spot lighting.

5 Social power. This dimension of social performance, often invisible, is critical in making the elements of performance available, or not. It can be defined as resources, capacities, and hierarchies, but it involves also the power to project hermeneutical interpretations of performance from outside political and economic power narrowly defined.

6 Audience. All of the above become significant only insofar as they allow or prevent meanings from being successfully projected to an audience. Audiences are placed at different removes from actors, and they can be more homogeneous or divided.

Each of these elements can be examined in terms of its respective performative structure, which has critical implications for patterning performance. For example, the better the script, the more it is agonistic. From tension between pure protagonists and impure antagonists there can emerge the twisting and turning that grabs and intensifies reader identification. But scripts cannot be too complicated, for simplicity and clarity are also critical to performative force. Drawing on theatrical and literary theory, we can explore such critical technical considerations for each of the elements we have considered.

The challenge for social performance is to make its component parts invisible. If they are not invisible, action will *seem* to be performed. Not seeming to be contrived, making a performance seem real, is the *sine qua non* for successful performance. To create verisimilitude is to seamlessly string together performative parts. Everything must appear to be created for the here and now. Meaning must seem to come from the actor if it is to seem authentic, not from scripts, props, power, or audience. Performative success depends on connecting the audience to the actor, without mediation. Audiences see themselves in the action. They are pulled in; they identify. Artificiality disappears. There is fusion between actor and audience and, indeed, among all the elements of performance. To make artifice seem natural: this is what it takes to be believed, to get others to accept your meaning.

In the course of historical time, the relationship among performative elements has been transformed. The simpler the society – the smaller, the less differentiated, stratified, and complex – the easier it is to achieve fusion, and, indeed, the more often it occurs. This is why, from the beginning of social science, analysts have associated "rituals" with simpler societies, a designation that can refer to family, peer group, and ethnic enclave and not only to simple collectivities in the historical sense. Rituals are the quintessence of fused performance. It is easier to weave the elements of performance seamlessly together if they are not too separated to begin with. If a society is simpler, then it is more likely that actors will be understood, that scripts will be believed, that audience and actors will be familiar with one another, that dramatizations will seem natural rather than forced, and that power will be invisible or, at least, accepted as a natural thing.

Achieving verisimilitude is never automatic. It is always a performative accomplishment. But as societies become larger, more stratified, and more complex, it becomes more and more challenging. The reason is that the very elements from which performances must be put together have become increasingly de-fused.

1 When writing emerges, structures of background representations become transformed into objectified texts. Authenticity is,

in this way, much more subject to scrutiny, with texts themselves becoming subject to continual revision and reconstruction.

2 Actors are more likely to perform before audiences they do not know, with whom they do not share prior background understandings.

3 Those who possess social power lead vastly different lives from audiences. In fact, they often are involved in deeply exploitative relationships with the very people whom they must performatively convince. Think here of the Egyptian Pharaohs, who sat at the top of a stratified social pyramid, but who needed to engage in continuous public ceremonies to maintain collective belief. It is no wonder that Weber called such leaders mystagogues.

4 The means of symbolic production become more difficult to employ and to obtain, even as their roles become more crucial. For, with the growing separation of audience from actors, elaborate forms of projection must be brought into play.

As the elements of performance become so de-fused, critics and intellectuals emerge. Conflict over interpretation becomes an always present dimension of social life. Even as state, class, and religious power become centralized and distant, so do audiences. As they become more distant, they are more doubting, more alienated, more fragmented by class and such other qualities as ethnicity, region, gender, race, and religion. No wonder that counter-publics develop and oppose the performances of centers. Or that as popular cultures enter into the public sphere, they are simultaneously a roadblock to the successful projection of high and official meanings and a source for enlarging the reservoir of authentic performance available to marginalized subaltern groups.

Even as the elements of performance become separated from one another, the challenge for performance remains determinedly to re-fuse them. Yet with this de-fusion, it becomes increasingly difficult to create the seamless sense of the real upon which success depends. Whether re-fusion can be achieved becomes, for every performance, increasingly an open question. No longer ascribed or automatic, re-fusion must now be achieved, and the process of legitimation becomes of great interest to social science. It becomes a moral and aesthetic question, too. Since romanticism, philosophers and artists have worried about the problem of authenticity, railing against artificiality, bad art, and bad faith. These vocabularies of criticism enter every human society as the elements of performance become de-fused.

The paradigmatic representation of this de-fusion process is theater. Theatrical drama grows out of religious ritual, emerging in periods of sharply increasing social complexity. Greek drama grew out of Dionysian rituals, which explains why the fusion-haunted Nietzsche hated it so, and European drama emerged, during the early modern period, from the medieval mystery plays performed at Easter time.

In the world of theater, the de-fusion of performative elements becomes recognized, the challenge of overcoming artificiality institutionalized. In ancient Greece, competitions were staged and prizes awarded for play writing and for acting. Today, Oscars and Emmys are given to masters at producing and staging the now much more variegated elements of mass performance. One should note here how crucial is collegial control. The ability to effectively produce the elements of performance, and to bring them seamlessly together, cannot be ordered from outside. These are matters of craft, and their evaluation is subject to the horizontal authority of practitioners, not the vertical dictate of bureaucrats or bosses. The surprises endemic to award ceremonies remind us that the effectiveness of performance is always open for grabs, no matter how great power or reputation, or how much money is spent.

It is not accidental that theater develops alongside the emergence of publics of potentially empowered citizens. From the perspective I am developing here, citizenship can be conceived as the separation and autonomy of a critical element of social performance. Citizenship is the legal capacity for skeptical viewership, the right to criticize and choose among performances, and the right to form one's own performances in response.

The implications of performance theory for understanding power are clear. According to conventional conceptions, whether Weberian or Marxist, power is institutional-structural. It is the ability to make somebody do something whether they like it or not. Coercion, or the ability to threaten it, is critical from such a perspective, which leads to the centrality of such ideas as control over means of production or monopolization of the means of violence. From this point of view, you don't need ideas to exercise power; you just need resources and capacities.

Such thinking about power is as simplistic as it is omnipresent, but it also has element of truth. By identifying something as power, as compared, for example, to love, religion, or prestige, we dictate a dimension of social life in which coercion *can* be evoked. Resources and capacities matter.

What's wrong with emphasizing them alone? It is because, while supplying some of the most distinctive bases for exercising power, by no means do they supply all. Indeed, they leave the "action" of power

87

– the *performing* of power – untouched. Power theories concentrating on resources or capacities leave out the independent shaping power of background symbols and forms, the figures and forms of script, the contingency of *mise-en-scène* and actor interpretation, and the extraordinary significance of audience separation. Perhaps most importantly of all, this approach neglects how performing power is always mediated by accounts of its meaning and effectiveness, via the intervention of reports by journalists and critics, and by the inchoate but deeply resonant currents of the public's opinion.

The institutional-structural approach seems to assume, in other words, that the performance of power is easily fused. It is as if theater had never developed, as if there were no such thing as the public stage and no capacity for counter-power at all. Yet the public is a stage. It is not easy for power to bring the de-fused elements of performance into alignment. The capacity for counter-performance is omnipresent.

Before elaborating on the new panorama of power opened up by this performative understanding, I wish to acknowledge there is a different alternative to institutional-structural theory, one which brings in "ideology" and "knowledge." In the power theorizing first of Gramsci, then Althusser, and more recently of Foucault, there developed within the institutional-structural position a new emphasis on representations and scripts. In the hands of these thinkers, however, such emphases, otherwise welcome, actually become part of the problem, not the solution.

Such concepts as hegemony (Gramsci), interpellation (Althusser), and power-knowledge (Foucault) obscure the contingency of performance and the complexity and independence of its elements. They replicate, in fact, the problems of linguistic structuralism. Concentrating on language at the expense of speech, they ignore the very contingency of performance that cultural pragmatics aims to embrace. The problem is not that these approaches are materialistic. They do not ignore representations. What they do, instead, is to assume powerful scripts, great actors, compliant audiences, corrupted or brainwashed journalists, and bought-off critics. With a wave of the hand, texts become automatically transformed into successful action. Whether it is law, school books, movies, political campaigns, or wars, background representations are assumed to speak, and to speak persuasively. But we know from living our own lives and from the experience of history that this cannot be so. No text automatically achieves performative success. Neither does any actor, social power, or *mise-en-scène*. To look at language as power is no different than

88

looking at power as if it were simply a language; it is to make Claude Levi-Strauss into Pierre Bourdieu.

If power cannot simply be coercive, it needs to be performative. If power is to be effective, performing power must be a success. To be really powerful means that social actors, no matter what resources and capacities they possess, must find a way to make their audiences believe them. To think about power more clearly, then, we need to consider the elements of performance, their internal complexity, and their independence. Judith Butler (1993a) writes that "there is no power construed as a subject that acts, but only a reiterated acting that is power in its persistence and instability," and she refers here to the relatively straightforward task of convincing an audience about one's gender. Shorn of the post-structural language, Butler is saying that power is not *only* a subject acting. An actor, the purveyor of power, cannot make power, or more accurately sustain it, through his or her action alone. Power is subject to the rigors of perform-ance. The rigor of greatest interest to Butler is the need for power to constantly "iterate" background narratives and codes. Performing power depends, however, on much more than that. It not only needs to iterate earlier beliefs but to sustain a productive relation to all the other elements of performance as well. Faced with such rigors, power can indeed exist only in its instability.

In *Disappearing Acts: Spectacles of Gender and Nationalism in Argentina's "Dirty War,"* Diana Taylor (1997) studies the Argentine Junta in terms of the performance of masculinity and aggression. With its uniforms, parades, and militant moralism, the dictator-ship sought to transform tradition and Catholicism into militant and intimidating force. With its often very public abductions, which allowed thousands of invisible executions, it put coercion on display. Yet, despite the Junta's extraordinary control over state resources and capacity, its performances of dictatorship eventually came to naught. The "mothers of the disappeared" formed in the public square of Buenos Aires. The durability and visibility of the *madres* constituted a counter-performance, quietly but insistently recalling the regime's murdered enemies and silenced opponents. The *madres'* spectacle unfolded in the great public square of Buenos Aires everyday, and their symbolic authority, which drew upon some of the same tradi-tional values as the Junta, was too great for them to be physically dispersed. Eventually, this performative power had tremendous effect. Certainly other factors were involved, but Taylor demonstrates that the performance of counter-power by the *madres* was one important reason why the Junta eventually disappeared.

Dictatorship is the ability for central power to re-fuse every element of its own performance, while preventing other potential powers from ever doing the same. In this manner, there is a primitivization of power: social performance is pulled back under the center's control. Such central control over the elements of performance can be sustained, however, only with tremendous ideological work and the relentless exercise of force. Certainly it is possible, even in modern and complex societies, for dictatorships to be successful. The repression and mass murders of Stalin, Hitler, Mao, and Pol Pot are proof. But even inside these brutal historic regimes there were latent counter-publics and audience alienation, and at some times and places counter-performances broke through. Fusion is much more difficult to sustain when dictators are less totalitarian in their ambitions and can draw on less complex and abundant ideological and material resources.

Let us turn from outright dictatorship to the concerted exercise of power inside of more democratic regimes, where the consequential de-fusion of the elements of performance is given much freer rein. Despite neo-conservative aims, energy, and interests, and their control of the reigns of national political power, the Bush administration's run-up to the Iraq war depended on the success of a complex production process (see chapters 8 and 9 below). Such a war could have been launched, for example, only after September 11, 2001, an explosive trauma that which strongly energized elements of a Manichean plot. It also depended upon a successful out-of-town run, or rehearsal, in Afghanistan. Even with this, the Iraqi hawks still had to engage in endless performative evocations of the necessity for war, which they acted out in public speeches, interviews, talk shows, and op-ed pages. But these performances met with only partial success. The ability to launch a legitimate war eventually came to depend on Secretary of State Colin Powell's giving the "performance of his life" before the Security Council at the United Nations.

Even after the ineptitude and tragedy of the Bush administration's war-making became evident, the American citizen-audience remained more receptive than it might because of the performative weakness of the other side. Instead of a compelling counter-narrative, the military enemies of the American and British occupation engaged primarily in murderous terror and projected a fundamentalist script repulsive to most democratic sensibilities. Nonetheless, despite the president's control over the levers of structural power, the performative success of his war-making has steadily declined. His performance of war was mediated, and undercut, by critical accounts of journalists and pundits, by foreign leaders and intellectuals, and by angry parents of those who have died. The applause meter of public opinion polls registered a slow but steady decline.

Skeptical audiences are the key to causing the performances of institutional power to fail. But the instability of power involves something more, the possibility of converting turned-off audiences into turned-on counter-powers through the staging of successful alternative plays. Democracy, in fact, might be conceived as a system that allows counter-performances always to be made. It does so by ensuring the independence of the elements of performance, making it illegal for any social actor to monopolize them. Of course, efforts at monopolization are always made. Power corrupts, but in differentiated and fragmented social orders it is very difficult for power to corrupt absolutely. Scandals and social movements confront such monopolizing efforts with cries of corruption, and they are performances too.

— 4 —

SOCIAL, POLITICAL, CULTURAL, AND PERFORMATIVE

Power seems like a pretty simple idea, but for millennia it has been an essentially contested concept.

One party to this dispute sees power primarily on a vertical axis. Power is not about developing links to others but about orders from above, about command and force. It is a matter of hierarchy not solidarity, of subordination not respect. This view of the order of things rests on an instrumental idea of action. Twenty-five hundred years ago, Thracymachus summed it up pretty well: "'Just' or 'right' means nothing but what is in the interest of the strongest party . . . In all states alike, 'right' has the same meaning, namely what is for the interest of the party established in power, and that is the strongest" (Plato). This approach to power became associated in early modern philosophy with the so-called "realism" of Hobbes and Machiavelli, and in modern social science with Marx.

Against such realism stands the "normative" view, connecting the exercise of power with morality. The key term here is legitimacy. To be legitimate, power must be deployed in a manner that can be justified according to an ethical ideal. Legitimate power solicits not only conflict but cooperation. When it succeeds, power becomes authority. Authoritative power is more stable and easier to deploy than naked compulsion or force. In early modern philosophy, Locke's more consensual and democratic contract theory provides an answer to the *Leviathan* of Hobbes. Weber introduces the idea of legitimacy to modern social scientific discussions of power, though he himself remains deeply ambivalent, developing an upgraded realist approach at the same time. Authoritative power is systematically conceptualized by Parsons, and Gramsci argues that, under the condition of ideological hegemony, those with less material power acquiesce voluntarily, allowing dominant classes to rule more easily. Foucault insists that power and knowledge are always intertwined, but follows Nietzsche in conceptualizing legitimacy more as camouflage than ethical claim (Foucault 1970; Gerth and Mills 1964; Gramsci 1971; Hobbes 1651; Locke 1694; Parsons 1967).

These general and abstract disputations inform empirical argument about democratic politics. According to the tradition of Thracymachus, the idea of speaking, acting, and moralizing citizens ruling themselves is naïve, a dangerous illusion. Marx economizes Thracymachus when he argues that capitalist democracy can be only formal, never substantive, that the ruling class dominates every political struggle. Michels bureaucratizes Thracymachus when he asserts oligarchy is inevitable because elites monopolize organizational resources. Weber sociologizes Thracymachus when he argues that democracy can be sustained – against impersonal bureaucracy – only by the force of amoral demagogues and ruthless party organizations. Drawing on Marx, Michels, and Weber, Mills describes America as ruled by a power elite. Combining military, economic, and political power, this callous clique wields its power against a pulverized mass, citizens pacified by a culture industry that has transformed the once democratic public into mere publicity (Marx and Engels 1962 [1848]; Michels 1962 [1911]; Weber 1978, Mills 1956).

Against this pessimism camouflaged as realism, there stands a line of social science thinkers who believe that democracy is possible and not only desirable – because horizontal ties of solidarity can be built upon values, specified in law, and represented through elections. Tocqueville elaborates the intertwining of religion, law, and democratic association in his studies of early nineteenth-century America. Durkheim shows how solidarity can be woven into institutions via energetic symbolic actions that sustain collective symbolic representations. Dewey observes that "Democracy is more than a form of government," that "it is primarily a mode of associated living, of conjoint communicated experience," and Mead explains how individuation emerges from common feeling and association. Arendt develops the most culturally sensitive democratic philosophy of recent times. Against visions of purely material and vertical power, she writes that "the reality of the world is guaranteed by the presence of others, by its appearing to all," that political action is "transacted in words," and that "to be political, to live in a polis" means everything is "decided through words and persuasion and not through force and violence" (Arendt 1958; see also Dewey 1966 [1916]; Durkheim 1996 [1912], 1957; Mead 1964; Tocqueville 2004 [1835, 1840]).

Certainly, democratic theory should be hard-headed, not naïve or fanciful. But it should not conceive politics mechanistically, presuppose cynical and instrumental reason, or imagine democratic order as merely external or institutional. If we confine ourselves to the tradition of Thracymachus, we have no access to the interior domain of politics, to the structures of feeling, the habits of the heart, the worlds of moral sense and perception that make living together in a democratic manner possible. We cannot illuminate the mysterious process by which citizens so often agree, willingly and without coercion, to uphold rules whose utility they scarcely understand and whose effect may be detrimental to their self-interest narrowly conceived. Democracies are not only about differences, interest, and antagonism; also they are sustained by shared morality and nurtured by community. This is exactly what Tocqueville meant by insisting that in democracies self-interest can be "rightly understood," not in a narrowly calculating way (2004 [1835, 1840]).[1]

The continuing vitality of democratic discourse and the robustness of solidarity help sustain a civil sphere that is relatively independent from money and brute force. In earlier work on civil culture and institutions, I develop a model of democratic societies that pays attention to shared emotions and symbolic commitments, to what and how people speak, think, and feel about politics (Alexander 2006a). I stress the critical role of social solidarity, the we-ness of a community, whether regional, national, or international, that defines feelings of connectedness in a manner that can transcend particularistic commitments, narrow loyalties, and segmented interests. The civil sphere is a form of social and cultural organization rooted simultaneously in a radical individualism and a thoroughgoing collectivism, a combination well captured in Habermas' notion of the "sphere of private people come together as a public"(1989 [1962]). The phrase "We, the people," which begins the US Constitution, references the civil in struggles to broaden social participation and extend equality. Yet, if solidarity gestures only to collective obligation, it will support repression at the expense of liberty. In the wake of their successful revolution against kingship, Americans insisted that the Constitution proposing a new state be amended by a Bill of Rights enshrining individual liberties.

The social and the civil

How does all this relate to the empirical study of elections? While not denying the existence of electoral campaigns and voting, those examining them through the lenses of Thracymachus tend to brush their significance aside. They view campaigning and voting as a merely political means to the end of social power, with "social" defined in a broadly economic-material way. Focusing on social power denies an independent significance to politics, to the meaning-in-the-moment that constitutes political action itself. In Harold Laswell's classic formulation, politics becomes simply who gets what and why (1936). It is not about cultural justification, about aligning political struggle with moral right, about civil and anti-civil meaning-making, about symbolizing candidates so they represent the collectivity in a discursive way. Modern political sociology elaborates this social reduction, focusing its empirical studies on social cleavages that determine electoral outcomes. As Lipset formulates it, elections represent simply the "democratic translation of the class struggle." Bell once explained McCarthyism by "deep changes taking place in the social structure that are reworking the social map of the country." Such contemporary political sociologists as Brooks and Manza explain today's voting patterns by the "post-industrial trends [that] have enhanced the electoral significance of the professional and managerial segments of the electorate." Emphasizing the external, material environment of political action makes political actors self-interested and calculating. Political campaigns become a market, the candidates sellers, the voters buyers. For Downs, "Each citizen casts his vote for the party he believes will provide him with more benefits than any other"; for Crick, politics is "the marketplace and the price mechanism of all social demands." Political scientists frequently employ the model of neoclassical economics, speaking of elections as "the marketplace of democracy," conceptualizing "the median voter's policy preference" as driving "electoral competition between two viable candidates" in which "everyone is fully informed" and which produces "benefits to the general community"(Crick 1962; see also Bell 1963; Brooks and Manza 1997; Dahl 1961; Downs 1957; Lipset 1981 [1960]).

Accounts of the 2008 presidential election typically engage the same reductive language of social cause and political effect. In *How Barack Obama Won*, NBC News Political Director Chuck Todd and Elections Director Sheldon Gawiser write, "The actual results of the presidential race were as expected," that they were "quite unremarkable if one understood how the fundamentals of the political landscape so favored the Democrats . . . in a year in which the economy was extremely weak and the Republican party brand was as poor as it had been since the Great Depression" (Todd and Gawiser 2009). Looking "inside the American election of 2008," their account headlines, "Demographically Speaking: Times Are Tough for GOP." Another post-election analysis, this one by a raft of academic political scientists, explains, "Larger political and societal forces were at work and drove the election" (Crotty 2009). In a section entitled "Social Groups and the 2008 Presidential election," the volume's editor elaborates:

> As the campaign progressed, the group divisions among voters became clearer. There were few surprises. The electoral coalitions broke along traditional party lines – income, class, race, ideology, and gender – and in the expected directions. Obama attracted the working class, the better educated, liberals, Democrats moderates, independents, and women, especially single and professional women [and] the exact opposite of Obama's pattern of support characterized McCain's. (Crotty 2009)

In the volume's conclusion, another political scientist explains that 2008 was a "transforming election" because it "represented a moment when a new demography caught up to a new politics"(White 2009).

Against this view of the social determinism of politics in 2008, I would insist, not that social conditions do not matter, but that the political has an independent force. Even Todd and Gawiser acknowledge that, among those Americans who saw the economy as tanking, 44 percent still voted for Republican John McCain, whose conservative, stand-pat policies did not promise economic change (Todd and Gawiser 2009). If elections really were socially determined, then how could that be? Similarly, while noting that the percentage of Democratic voters declined for three decades to rough parity with Republicans in 2004, these NBC journalists report an abrupt reversal between 2006 and 2008, with Republican identification dwindling and Independent affiliation rising (Todd and Gawiser 2009). How could there have been such a history-shifting departure from a long-term pattern of secular social change? "The conditions of life can never 'explain' what we are or answer the question of who we are," Arendt contends, "for the simple reason they never condition us absolutely." If social conditions could actually determine the political, she continues, "action would be an unnecessary luxury," merely "a capricious interference with general laws of behavior." Political action and speech are necessary precisely because they are not luxuries. They are the core of democracy, and they have significant and independent effect. "With word and deed we insert ourselves into the human world," Arendt explains, and "this insertion is not forced upon us by necessity." With political action, "something new is started which

96

cannot be expected from whatever may have happened before," and "the new always happens against the overwhelming odds of statistical laws and their probability" (Arendt 1958).

Because politics matter, elections matter, and demographic groups are neither unitary nor determining. In February 2007, almost two years before the presidential election, *Rolling Stone* magazine described Obama's entry into the campaign as "one of the more startling and sudden acts in recent political history." Providing a rationale for his unexpected decision, Obama tells the magazine he felt "a call from the crowds" as "a summons to a new role." Arendt is right to suggest that in politics, "the new always appears in the guise of a miracle" (Arendt 1958):

> What is at stake is the revelatory character without which action and speech would lose all human relevance . . . The connotation of courage, which we now feel to be an indispensable quality of the hero, is in fact already present in a willingness to act and speak at all, to insert one's self into the world and begin a story of one's own . . . Courage and even boldness are already present in leaving one's private hiding place and showing who one is, in disclosing and exposing one's self. (Arendt 1958)

"For many years," write the media scholars and election analysts Kathleen Hall Jamieson and Paul Waldman, "political scientists have endeavored to create models that would predict the outcome of presidential elections using only information available before the campaign begins in earnest"(2001). If such predictive models really do hold sway, then the political disappears and the significance of electoral democracy is whisked away. If elections simply transform social into political hierarchies, then focusing on democratic elections seems beside the point. Electoral campaigns block such automatic translation. In order for the ruled to become the rulers – Aristotle's straightforward definition of democracy – voters must be protected by the relative autonomy of a civil sphere. Democracy allows the production of a new kind of power. In a democracy, it is civil power, not social power, that decides who will control the state. Civil power is solidarity translated into government. To the degree that the civil sphere is independent, "We the people" can speak, via communicative institutions that provide cultural authority and via regulative institutions that carry legal force. The civil sphere regulates access to state power by constituting a new and different power of its own. To the degree that society is democratic, voting is the gatekeeper of state power. It is the civil power produced by electoral campaigns that opens and closes the gate.

The cultural and the performative

Philosophy may assert the independence of the political and justify it normatively. But the political actually achieves autonomy from the social only if nested inside the cultural, and this, political theorists typically do not explain. Social meanings have their own internal logic. Patterned by binary codes and temporal narratives, culture structures are as forceful, organized, and independent as social structures of a more material kind. When political actors act and speak, they evoke meanings and symbolic weight. They see themselves in terms of exemplary models of speaking and acting that culture provides, and they wish to persuade audiences to view them in the same way. To enter into the state, to be in a position to pull the levers of organizational and material power, those who struggle for democratic power must first become authoritative. They gain authority by speaking on behalf of sacred values and against profane ones. By evoking such cultural valences, claims for power gain legitimacy from citizen-audiences before electoral decisions are made.

To understand modern politics, the structured meanings upon which political speech and action draw must be interpreted and explained. The need to do so brings us right up to the edge of a truly cultural sociology. Before actually stepping into it, however, we must maneuver through another thicket of long-standing intellectual debate. Since the middle of the nineteenth century, sociologists of modernity have been announcing that tradition has vanished, that once-enchanted earlier societies have lost their magic, that iconic aura has been displaced by mechanical reproduction, that alienation makes it impossible to experience meaning. As Marx and Engels put it in 1848, "All that is holy is profane." If the modern world is actually so deracinated, then contemporary efforts at symbolic action must be explained away. Symbols become superfluous superstructures. The motivation for ethical discourse is seen as instrumental pursuit of material interest. Ideas are reduced to ideology. Traditional approaches to meaning in sociology treat culture as a dependent variable, while social power, social structures, and material interests are treated as independent variables that have a causal status. In this manner, sociology turns from culture to its unmoved mover, "society" as a noncultural force. Thus is the social reduction of politics camouflaged in cultural form.[2]

Instead of such a reductionist sociology *of* culture, I have argued for a *cultural* sociology. Just as we need to respect the independence of the political vis-à-vis the social, we must also give the independent

98

structuring power of culture its due. Modernity has eliminated neither deep meaning nor encrusted tradition; it has, rather, changed the content of meaning and multiplied its forms. Modern culture still provides anchoring codes and narratives, even if they often evoke rationality, individuality, skepticism, and social transformation more often than mystery, hierarchy, stasis, and metaphysical belief. As far as the role of meaning goes, according to Durkheim, no great divide exists between the aboriginals who believed in totemic gods and "the religious man of today." Modern people still engage in emotional and ritual action, energizing symbols that can become powerful collective representations, dividing the sacred from profane.[3]

Not long after Durkheim's declaration, and quite likely in response to it, there emerged a dramatic transformation in linguistic understanding that continues to ramify in the humanities and the social sciences. Ferdinand de Saussure and Roman Jakobson propose that words gain meaning not by referring to things "out there" in the real world, but from their structured relation to other words inside of language. Meaning is relative and relational, organized by binaries. A color is called black not because it is a dark hue, but because the English language pairs the idea of blackness with the color it designates as white. The physical hues we associate with the words white and black are defined relationally as opposites; only then do they become so in terms of empirical and social fact. In his later philosophical investigations, Ludwig Wittgenstein reaches the same conclusion by a different route. Before we can understand a word as denoting a specific worldly thing, we must see it as part of a "language game" identifying the relevant general category of things. So the meaning of a thing cannot exceed the conventions of linguistic culture at a given historical time (Jakobson 1990a; Saussure 1966 [1916]; Wittgenstein 1953).

As these revolutions in philosophy and linguistics took hold, they turned intellectual attention away from the vexed problem of consciousness, accessible only via the mystery of empathy, to the actual words that sentient actors employ. Seen, heard, and written down, symbolic languages externalize subjective meaning. These cultural forms can be interpreted and analyzed in a more rational and disciplined manner, though the experiences and sensibilities of social analysts necessarily continue to come into play. This so-called linguistic turn facilitated a broader "cultural turn" in the human sciences. Not only speech but also culture itself comes to be modeled as language: binary symbols pre-structure social action, as language does with speech. Levi-Strauss was the first social scientist to move semiotics from language to the study of human societies, though he still held fast to the modernist faith that semiotic tools are confined to the "savage mind." Barthes drew exactly the opposite conclusion, demonstrating the myriad manners in which binary symbolic relations structure modern meanings. As symbolic anthropology flourished, the concepts and methods of Douglas, Turner, and above all, Geertz spread widely throughout the humanities and social sciences (Barthes 1972b [1957]; Douglas 1967; Friedland and Mohr 2004; Geertz 1973d; Levi-Strauss 1967, 1973 [1955]; Rorty 1967; Turner 1969).

Until well into the 1980s, cultural sociology remained an oxymoron, sociologists insisting on the great divide between meaning and modernity and the sociology of culture winning the day. Meaning was studied as the wagging tail of social power, as resistance to hegemony, disguised governmentality, organizational isomorphism, cultural capital, or symbolic politics.[4] As the cultural turn has broadened, more strongly cultural sociologies finally emerged. Solidarity is modeled less as interest than discourse; stratification interpreted more in terms of symbolic rather than material boundaries; social movements less as conflicts for power than as struggles over representations and framing; material life more as material culture; and markets as economies of signs (Eyerman and Jamison 1991; Lamont 1992; Lash and Urry 1994; Miller 1987; Sewell 1980; Zelizer 1985). In my own studies of political and social conflict, I locate a binary discourse revolving around democratic purity and anti-democratic pollution. This discourse of civil society (Table 4.1) propels meaning-making in the mass media and allows voters to make critical judgments about who's who in the struggle for electoral power. It is not issues per se that determine voters' political judgments, and even less the social interests at stake. It is the manner in which these issues and interests are related to the underlying social language of civil purity and impurity (Alexander 1992, 1996; Alexander and Smith 1993).

According to this cultural perspective, the factual status of "issues" – what is rationally ascertainable about social problems and the policies proposed to solve them – is relatively insignificant in the struggle for power. Problems and policies are ostensible referents. What students of social power miss is the symbolic language within which issues are framed and claims for legitimacy made. Journalists, bloggers, and voters themselves see campaigns as about personalities, issues, and ideologies, about being liberal or conservative, pro- or anti-abortion, military intervention, affirmative action, surveillance, gay marriage, immigration, free trade, financial regulation, health

Table 4.1   The discourse of civil society

Civil		Anti-civil
	Motives	
Active		Passive
Autonomous		Dependent
Rational		Irrational
Reasonable		Hysterical
Calm		Excitable
Self-controlled		Wild-passionate
Realistic		Distorted
Sane		Mad
	Relations	
Open		Secretive
Trusting		Suspicious
Critical		Deferential
Honorable		Self-interested
Altruistic		Greedy
Truthful		Deceitful
Straightforward		Calculating
Deliberative		Conspiratorial
Friendly		Antagonistic
	Institutions	
Rule regulated		Arbitrary
Law		Power
Equality		Hierarchy
Inclusive		Exclusive
Impersonal		Personal
Contracts		Bonds of loyalty
Groups		Factions
Office		Personality

care, unions, the minimum wage. But it is symbolic identifications that are the *ends* of the struggle for power, whatever the *means*. Everything is done as if words and images matter, and they do. Campaigns refer to things that exist in the world, but they are not exclusively about these "real" things. In themselves, things are signifieds, social references redolent of symbolic signifiers. Every issue must be associated with the sacred or profane side of the civil binary, and this applies not only to conflicts inside the civil sphere but also to those concerning its boundaries. As former political press secretary and publisher of the *Columbia Journalism Review*, Evan Cornog writes, "For all the campaign talk about resumes and experience, issues and qualifications, it is the battle of stories, not the debate on issues, that determines how Americans respond to a presidential contender" (Cornog 2004). Difference gathers temporal power in heroic narratives that promise the transformation of social life. Democratic stories are fueled by dramas in which protagonists cast themselves as civil heroes fighting against ruthless and scheming protagonists whose election would endanger the very fundaments of civil life.[5]

Yet, while a fundamental referent of political action, the codes and narratives that structure discourse in civil society are not determinate. There is agency. Political actors and campaigns *struggle* for power. They are compelled to create performances, and their success is uncertain, contingent. It depends on skill and fortune, on commanding an effective stage, on media interpretations, on shifting historical constellations, on audiences being prepared and responding in felicitous ways. The discourse of civil society creates the vocabulary for political speech, but it is flesh-and-blood actors who make this script walk and talk, who speak the words, form intonations, create tropes, and time rhetorical flow. These are not matters of culture's structure but its pragmatics (Alexander 2006b).

To challenge more static understandings of language, John Austin introduced the idea of performativity (Austin 1957). When a politician emphatically states that the world is like this, declares in no uncertain terms that his opponent is doing that, he seems to be making constative statements, statements that present themselves as descriptions, as denoting something out there in the real world. Performative statements, by contrast, rather than referring to a putatively existing fact, work to bring some condition into being through the very act of talking. When political candidates make emphatic declarations about the state of the world, and ringing declarations about their opponents, they would like us to believe their words are constative. Mostly, however, they are performative. Politicians do things with words. Candidates are less describing the world than wanting to bring that world into being in the imaginations of their listeners. They want to convince us of how things are. If their performances are successful, we are persuaded. Whether we become convinced is less a matter of rightness in a moral or cognitive sense than of aesthetic power, of whether a political performance has "felicity." Is it structured in manner that evokes our concerns, builds pictures in our minds, allows us to share their worldly visions? About the time that Austin philosophizes performance, Goffman draws on theatrical metaphors to develop a sociology of the performative in social interaction. Turner later describes the movement from ritual to theater as a pivotal transition marking modernity, and Geertz employs theatricality to understand cockfighting rituals in Bali. Crossing anthropology and theater studies, Schechner creates the new discipline of performance studies (Geertz 1973b; Goffman 1956; Schechner 1988; Turner 1982).

In my theory of cultural pragmatics, I deconstruct social performance in terms of background representations, scripts, actors, means of symbolic production, *mise-en-scène*, social and interpretive power, and audiences. When felicitous performances fuse speaker and audience, these complex mediations become invisible, and audiences do not, in fact, see actions as if they are performed. We endow them with verisimilitude, so that scripted actions seem spontaneous and real. We believe that the words of politicians are true and their selves authentic. As societies become modern and more complex, however, the elements of performance become more separated one from another, and fusion becomes a much more difficult thing. Authenticity becomes problematic, and communication much more to achieve. Figure 4.1 presents the historical separation of key performative elements schematically, and fusion and re-fusion as well (See chapter 2 above).

Cultural pragmatics allows us to capture the self-interest and contingency of the struggle for power without jettisoning meaning and returning to Thracymachus. In contemporary societies, audiences for political performances are often physically distant and emotionally disconnected, without affection or understanding for the mediated figures they see struggling for power. Citizen-audiences do not feel compelled to believe the truth of what they hear or see, much less to attribute to political performances moral and emotional force. While political performances must achieve success, contemporary audiences are increasingly de-fused from the powers that be. The struggle to re-fuse speaker and audience, to connect with the members of civil society through felicitous performance of the codes and narratives that define it – this is what the democratic struggle for democratic power is all about.

— 5 —

DEMOCRATIC POWER AND POLITICAL PERFORMANCE: OBAMA V. MCCAIN

What happens when a politician struggling for power addresses a crowd, speaks to interviewers, debates an opponent, makes a comment on TV? The politician emphatically states that the world is like this, declares in no uncertain terms that his opponent is doing that. Austin called these constative statements; they present themselves as descriptions, denoting something that is out there in the real world. The contrast with such constative statements are performative ones. Rather than referring to the existence of some fact or quality as if it exists already, performative statements actually bring the situation into being by the very act of talking. Insofar as they are doing so, they are, to evoke his most famous phrase, "doing things with words." When making emphatic declarations about the state of the world, and ringing declarations about their opponents, politicians struggling for power would like us to believe their words are constative. Mostly, however, they are performative. They are less describing the world than wanting to bring that world into being in the imaginations of their listeners. They want to convince us that this is the way things are. If their performances are successful, we will be persuaded. This persuasion depends, Austin tells us, on whether political performances have "felicity," whether they are structured in an evocative manner that relates to our concerns, builds pictures in our mind, makes us identify with them and share their worldly visions. Felicitous performances create fusion between speaker and audience. When performances fuse, we endow them with verisimilitude. They seem real. We think the words of politicians are true and their selves are authentic.

To achieve performative power, politicians project their performances on elaborate stages, against evocative backdrops of flags, columns, and war-torn buildings; in front of bleachers and stadiums filled with cheering people; drive motorcades down streets lined – thanks to "advance men" – with attentive and adoring fans. Yet, despite these and other efforts, political performances face a major problem: large segments of their audiences are far away and feel disconnected. Modern societies are fragmented, segmented, and differentiated. Large swathes of the audiences for political performers do not have any particular affection for those who are struggling for power. Many of those who listen to their words and look at their images have no particular reason to believe what they hear or see, much less to attribute to these performances moral and emotional force. The goal of successful performance is fusion, but the audiences of modern societies are increasingly de-fused from the powers that be.[1]

The struggle to re-fuse speaker and audience, to connect with the members of civil society through felicitous performance – this is what the democratic struggle for power is all about. Those who want power must be elected, and they will not get votes unless their performances are successful, at least to some degree. This is why politicians and their advisors must put their heads together, run focus groups and conduct polls, and do daily interpretive battles with journalists as well as those on the other political side. They must project their ideological messages to audiences whom they do not know.

And to make this even more difficult, between politicians and their audiences there stands an entire profession and institutional framework. Journalists and media institutions interpret political performances before they reach even the most positively inclined voter-audience. To these audiences, news media present political performances denotatively, as fact; but they are already connotative: they are interpretations. Not only do journalists filter political performances, but also they inform audiences how they themselves have reacted to these interpretations.

Cultural sociology of political power

It should be clear why struggles for political power need to be rethought in more meaning-centered terms. In political sociology, power is typically conceived as control over instruments of domination, as maximizing resources, as asymmetrical exchange, as contingent struggle for strategic advantage or as reproducing elite power, whether that of state, class, gender, race, civilization, or religion. These instrumental approaches to power presuppose theories drawn from Marxian and Weberian traditions – from ideas about hegemony and interpolation, from ideas about political parties as "houses of power" and about rational-legal legitimacy as providing merely a democratic framework for class struggle, and from economistic theories about rational choice. Such reductionism in political sociology is echoed by the subservient manner in which "weak programs" in the sociology of culture (Alexander and Smith 2003) have treated meaning as the wagging tail of power – a subordination formulated in slightly different ways by the Birmingham school of Stuart Hall, by Foucaultian students of governmentality, and by neo-institutionalist studies of strategic isomorphism, as well as by earlier American work on "symbolic politics" by such figures as Murray Edelman.

Neither political sociology nor weak cultural programs have been able to conceptualize key empirical processes that are central to understanding power in formally democratic societies. Inside the civil sphere, struggles for power take place as struggles for persuasion, as performances that unfold before an idealized audience of rational, responsive, and putatively solidary citizens. Gaining power depends on the outcome of struggles for symbolic domination in the civil sphere. It is cultural victory that determines control of the state, and, potentially, over every other non-civil sphere as well, such as the economy, religion, ethnic association, and family.

To understand and explain the symbolic communications that structure civil society, a strong theory of meaning-making is required. What is needed is a cultural sociology, not a sociology of culture, a strong, not a weak approach to social meaning. It only seems paradoxical that, in order to understand power, we must give relative autonomy to culture. But it is coding and narrating that channel the construction of political motives inside the civil sphere, smooth the pathways for political relations, and set up the framework for consequential institutional changes in society and state. Taking state power in a democratic society is a struggle for position vis-à-vis is the binary discourse of civil society. The goal of those who struggle for political power is to identify themselves, their campaign "issues," and their broader ideology with the sacred side of this binary and to project convincing accounts of their opponents as embodying anti-civil evil. Those who struggle for power seek to expand these cultural constructions beyond their immediate ideological and organizational groupings, to become iconic objects of emotive identification for populations far and wide.

Collective representations and ritual

To struggle for power in a democratic society one must become a collective representation (Durkheim 1996 [1912]); one must become a symbol of the civil sphere, but also of at least some of these other, extra-civil spheres that generate nondemocratic, often primordial values that real existing civil spheres are compelled also to represent. To become a symbolic representation in the struggle for power is not only to achieve this status with one's immediate supporters and party group, but also to project this symbolic stature throughout the civil sphere and also outside of it, over a much wider domain. Struggles for power project meanings and styles to citizen audiences that are layered from close by to far away, and which are fragmented in all the familiar demographic ways. Winning power depends on creating performances that successfully breach some of these great divides.

What is a politician? He or she is a collective representation, one that can be energized through a process of symbolic communication and, by this process, become a carrier of intense social energy. A former comrade from Barack Obama's early Chicago days, interviewed by the *New York Times*, remembers the young community organizer as somebody who displayed a remarkable "energizing capacity to connect with the people in these neighborhoods" (Kovaleski 2008). Political life is a back-and-forth process of "behavioral" interaction and symbolic communication, one in which psychic energy flows between symbolic public texts and actual living and breathing persons. This explains why, even in the virtual age, politicians must mingle, and be seen to mingle, with real voters, why they shake so many real hands and speak not only digitally but in all their throaty sweatiness to throbbing and heaving rallies.

Candidates experience and channel the energy of human contact. These ritual interactions are textually mediated, and they are televised and circulated as symbolic images in turn. The sounds and images of audiences whistling and applauding, and of beaming, back-slapping and fist-pumping candidates, reflect this energy back to the candidate and upward, via communicative institutions, into the broader civil sphere. This circulating energy cannot be supplied simply from studio performance. While digitally produced or even created political performances are, of course, technically feasible, in a civil society it would be considered immoral to employ them. Nor would they trigger the recursive processes of symbolic representation central to the political sociology of democracy.

Political rallies can become pure, old-fashioned, fused performances – true rituals with the touching of hands to charismatic leaders, the tremendous effervescence of crowds flowing into a single symbol, the political collective representation. In the presidential campaign season, this ritual begins with small groups in living rooms in Iowa and New Hampshire, morphs into larger settings after primary victories and defeats, and culminates in the carefully choreographed scenes of mass hysteria, laced with ritualized gravitas, that characterize party conventions. In the personalized contact process that defines the ground game of political campaigns, "advance men" are crucial. It is their aim to create fused performances. Campaign image-makers organize the candidate's website, write blogs, send reporters spinning messages throughout the 24-hour news cycle and millions of digital messages daily to contributors and fans, and meet face to face with journalists and influence peddlers in private and in public. They aim to extend this ritual experience, via the mass media, to larger audiences of voters.

Reporting on Hillary Clinton's June 7, 2008, concession speech in the historic National Building Museum in Washington, DC, CNN's Wolf Blitzer remarks, "We're listening to this crowd getting *excited*," publicly interpreting the convention center's immense interior space, with its vaulting modernist arches, as "dramatic and imposing," and "most appropriate" for the sad and sweet denouement of a powerful and controversial campaign. Blitzer also observes, as Senator Clinton addresses her cheering fans, how she is elevated on a platform high above them. It is, indeed, as one of Blitzer's colleagues observes, as if the politician were in a great church, offering a sermon to devoted worshipers. "Hillary" – the chants are ubiquitous – offers thanks to her staff and all the volunteer workers, the priests and the laity of her political religion. We witness the production of myth, of fallen heroes and martyrs in the struggle for civil power. The next day, the *New York Times* described the event as "a dramatic – and at times theatrical – end to a candidacy that transfixed the country," observing how "many of her supporters watched, some weeping, turning out to witness and appreciate the history of this latest turn in the Clintons' story" (Nagourney and Lebiovich 2008).

The ritual nature of fused political performances, the manner in which deeply affected, breathless journalists break down the barrier between actor and audience, and the extraordinary collective energy and symbolic power produced – these were quintessentially expressed much later that summer in Mile High Stadium in Denver, Colorado, when Barack Obama formally accepted the Democratic nomination for the presidency. Above are notes from a "media ethnography" about MSNCB television coverage in the afternoon and evening of that day, August 28, 2008. They might be entitled "Building Fusion." We begin with the run-up that mixes religion with entertainment.

Looking forward to the big moment, the Reverend Al Sharpton evaluates its potential significance – and simultaneously tries to ensure its performative success – by quoting from Martin Luther King's "I Have a Dream" speech, delivered 45 years before on this very day to the March on Washington. Presenting that earlier, historic speech as an eerie adumbration of Obama's candidacy, Sharpton recalls how Reverend King had proclaimed his faith that "someday people will be judged not by the color of their skin but by the content of their character." Sharpton tells NBC correspondent David Gregory that Obama's victory in the primary is perfect proof that King's prophecy has come true.

Then, Congressman John Lewis is interviewed. The former civil rights activist had been a key organizer of the March on Washington in 1963 where King had delivered his famous speech. Lewis proclaims, "We are dedicated this evening to Reverend King and his Dream speech." There follows an evocative video about King and his tragic-heroic quest. We are presented with his iconic face, and reminded that he believed in the glory of God and egalitarian promises of the American civil sphere. Bernice King, daughter of Martin and the recently deceased Coretta Scott King, offers the benediction.

Afterward, Keith Olbermann, MSNBC co-anchor, narrates a video about racial discrimination that focuses on the great Yankee baseball player Elston Howard. Chris Matthews, Olbermann co-anchor, frames the world-historical importance of what is to follow, declaring that the United States will become "the first Western Hemisphere country" nominating a person of African origin for president. Olbermann equates the nomination with such other "completely unforeseen" and dramatic historical events as the fall of Germany's Berlin Wall and the end of South Africa's Apartheid. The two anchors exchange remarks about historical significance. Matthews calls this "an amazingly democratic moment." The essence of democracy, he avers, is that everything is open. In the struggle for power, nobody knows what will happen in advance. "Elections matter," he observes. "If you

110

sit at home" and don't participate, you are "an idiot in the Greek sense," somebody with no connection to the polity. Olbermann characterizes Obama's nomination as an undeniable demonstration of the possibility for "concrete change," something that is "real for many, many people." For David Gregory, it "represents the future, not the past" – it's "change, that's the key."

This inflationary framing is momentarily brought back to earth by NBC correspondent Andrea Mitchell, who reveals what she clearly believes to be the wires behind the evening's event. "The whole point of coming," Mitchell says, is "organizing," getting attendees to sign up to do grunt campaigning work. The events at Mile High Stadium, in other words, amount to simply "a massive recruitment effort." You get a free ticket if you agree to do six hours of volunteering. This is good reporting in a professional, journalistic sense. Reducing the event from rhetoric and dreams to planning and base, it implies fakery, not idealism, and exchange, not altruism. In the present context of ritual fusion, however, Mitchell's observations appear discordant, symbolically out of place even if empirically true. Anchor Chris Matthews is affronted, warning, "Andrea, this seems to me immensely Machiavellian!"

What follows on-screen is a performance by African-American recording artists Will.i.am and John Legend performing Obama's campaign slogan "Yes We Can." For the commentators, and perhaps many white viewers, these back-to-back screen events are beginning to appear too black, enmeshing the Obama symbol in a minority, still partially stigmatized subculture. Such a segmented performance would prevent the wider connection with whites that political performances in the contemporary American civil sphere need to succeed. Implicitly addressing this performative anxiety, Olbermann observes, "that's one of the dangers here"– the "need to keep these people entertained for two hours" before the evening's main speakers arrive.

Then something rather surprising happens. The televising of Obama's acceptance speech is wrenched out of its black-versus-white frame, out of the world of entertainment, and pulled from the past and anniversary to the future and celebration. Joe Scarborough, a conservative ex-congressman who is now an influential MSNBC morning talk show host, proclaims, "I can't think of any event that approaches this. They are hitting a home run here, I'll tell you that. After this speech, none of us will have any questions at all about what 'change' means." This skeptical observer has judged the ongoing event at Mile High stadium to be authentic, and he has declared admiration. Asked by Matthews about Senator McCain's sarcastic references to the link between large stadiums and arrogant celebrities, Scarborough reminds viewers that "JFK took over the L.A. Coliseum" for his acceptance speech in 1960, repeating information published earlier that day in the *Times*. "I need to tell you again," Scarborough insists, "that this is the most extraordinary event I've ever seen. Watch for Colorado to swing Obama's way." This outspokenly conservative commentator has been engaged by the dramaturgy and meaning of the ritual process. His testimony suggests the performative power of the occasion, its capacity to create a cathartic moral experience after the up and down narrations of the Convention's previous days.

The MSNBC coverage now turns to "youth reporter" Luke Russert interviewing John Legend, the recording artist who wrote and performed "Yes We Can." Legend is articulate and forceful. Asked about the celebrity attacks on Obama by McCain and others, he issues a warning to conservatives and predicts their performative failure: "Don't be jealous because you haven't aroused emotion." Russert describes Legend's song as a media sensation, with 15 million hits on YouTube alone. Russert paraphrases Legend's remarks in a generational way: "You [aging] boomers think seeing a woman or black in power is a big deal, but to us it isn't. For us, it's not, 'cause we've grown up with this."

Coverage moves to the stadium's stage, where Sheryl Crow is rocking out. After projecting this bite of popular culture, televised attention shifts to Olbermann interviewing Chicago Mayor Richard Daley. "What a throwback to yesterday," the co-anchor remarks, referring to the tumultuous 1968 Democratic convention over which Daley's father had presided in Chicago, contrasting today's civil ceremony with the provocative displays of youth culture, violent political protest, and controversial police repression of that earlier time. On split-screen the television displays Sheryl Crow in skin tight white jeans and cowboy hat, still singing her heart out. Daley responds to Olbermann's remark by mentioning that earlier in the week Michelle Obama, asserting that in her speech "she connected." The Chicago Mayor insists that today, as compared with 40 years ago, "it's the economy" that matters, identifying Obama not with sixties radicals but with the most popular liberal president of the twentieth century, Franklin Roosevelt. Matthews asks, "How did you in Illinois manage to elect two black Americans senators?" Daley continues to emphasize the contrast, answering that today, "We have an open society."

This insistence on the contemporary reality of civil solidarity is underscored as the camera shifts to Stevie Wonder singing about "the united people of these United States." He calls out, "now everybody repeat after me: Barack Obama, yes we can, yes we can." Enthusiastically joining in, the crowd applauds loudly, offering shouts of "We love you Stevie." The singer replies by underscoring this moment of civil fashion: "I gotta do this, I gotta do this, I gotta do this one: 'Signed, Sealed, Delivered (I'm Yours).'" Here, at the center of contemporary popular culture, African-Americans are being fully incorporated, at least performatively. Stevie Wonder has been Barackobamized. As Wonder sings, the camera scans the booth to find Rachel Maddow, Maureen O'Connell, and Eugene Robinson – two white MSNBC correspondents and an African-American reporter from the *Washington Post* – swinging and dancing to Wonder's "Signed, Sealed, Delivered."

The camera scans to the mixed-race stadium audience, much of which is also standing and swaying back and forth to the music. Amidst this aura of fusion, there is a complaint. The right-wing political commentator Pat Buchanan, sporting dark wraparound sunglasses that give him a rather sinister Darth Vader look, seems bemused. "God bless our country, the United States of America," he intones sarcastically. Pat, don't you want to join "the MSNBC dance back up band?" Olbermann asks. Even if Buchanan refuses to dance, Olbermann quips, he has contributed to the scene by looking like one of the "Blues Brothers."

Connecting this ritual build-up more directly with the struggle for power, focused attention shifts in the next scene to the speech by former Vice President Al Gore, the hard luck Democratic presidential candidate who lost the disputed vote to George W. Bush in 2000. Since that loss, Gore has become famous as an environmental campaigner, winning a Nobel Peace Prize and an Academy Award for his documentary about global warming.

Democracy gives us an opportunity to change, Gore exclaims. Elections do matter. Remember the 2000 election. Let's not allow that to happen again. This election matters so much. Throughout Gore's remarks – as it had with the remarks of those who had preceded him – the camera shifts revealingly back and forth between the speaker and individual faces in the audience.

This shifting measures whether speaker and audience are connecting or de-fusing, whether the performance hits home or not. As Gore speaks, we see the audience laughing and joking with each other, not particularly engaged. America cannot continue, Gore thunders, with an "indifference to facts," subordinating the general good to the benefit of the few. Global warming is a "planetary emergency." McCain has allowed his party to browbeat him into abandoning measures that could prevent this imminent environmental apocalypse. Gore attacks "the special interests who control" the Republican party "lock, stock, and barrel." He declares that we can restore solidarity and rationality at the same time: "You understand that this election marks a clean change from the politics of partisanship and division." Drawing a parallel between President Abraham Lincoln and Obama, Gore asserts that our present crisis is as great as the Civil War. Obama represents "the best of America." He "will restore *e pluribus Unum*," and "allow us Americans speak with moral authority to other nations."

The MSNBC commentators now discuss the content of Obama's upcoming speech, selections from which have just been supplied. Noting its confident, sometimes even aggressive tone, Olbermann says this is "an alpha male moment," recalling Bill Clinton's acceptance speech in 1992, where he proclaimed, if "Bush doesn't want to use the powers of the presidency, I'll do it." Matthews proactively deepens the civil moment. "This is not something cute and personal," he instructs viewers, but "something serious and powerful." The speech shows "here is my order of battle, here's what I bring to the table." It "will be a dramatic and compelling speech by Barack Obama, by all accounts – at the top of the hour." Olbermann increases the anticipation: "You can't just read from this and get what it's going to be like. You need to think stylistically because of the optics." Buchanan himself concedes, "it may be the most decisive moment of the entire election, it's that important a speech." Allowing it a sacred place, Buchanan describes the upcoming speech as possessing "gravitas." Rachel Maddow immediately agrees, but she points to the performative challenge of the speech: "It is long! How will he be able to manage that?" Buchanan, a former speechwriter to Richard Nixon, explains that "You've got to 'talk through' the applause." Olbermann adds, "this is *his* voice." Buchanan responds, "this is written for the ear, not for the eye," it's not Al Gore. "It should be a tough man's speech," he says.

Once again, the camera scans the crowd. The sun has set and the stadium is now filled to overflowing, like a festival or a football game. Thousands of tiny American flags waving, old folks with grandchildren, blond haired All-American girls and Ivy-Leagued jacketed preppies, men and women of every color and shape, banners waving "Latinos for Barack."

Illinois Senator Durbin steps to the podium, offering the formal introduction. He declares there is "hunger for more authenticity," a need "to renew the faith of the American people in a leader." Because "Americans want to believe," Durbin explains, suggesting why Barack Obama has become a collective representation. "I've been close to Barack Obama for many years, but now, many Americans feel close to this man." Averring fusion, the Senator prophesies that Obama embodies the sacred discourse of liberty in a transcendental way. Obama has "judgment" and "wisdom," and with him "the future of our nation is in the hands of hard working Americans, who want to believe that America's best days are still to come. Tonight, as the stadium's lights are going dark, we will come to the dawning of the new day!" If we accept his "message . . . that the greatness of America will return," we "can turn the page, and welcome a new generation. Yes, America can, yes we can." Barack Obama and Joe Biden "will lead us to a better place." Fused with them, "we will be by their side every step of the way." We are in the realm of the civil sacred, passing from the evil past and the mundane present into the idealized space of the future. Taken by the hand by caring and prophetic leaders, we can make the American dream of a perfect civil society come true.

Barack Obama has been well and truly introduced, his imminent speech lauded for its power and meaning, liminally set off from mundane reality, and his person adulated in a salvationary way. The flesh-and-blood nominee now emerges. His face set

115

in serious demeanor, Barack Obama strides forcefully up to the podium.

As the Democratic nominee delivers his speech, the camera scans to show whites, blacks, old folks and youngsters nodding in affirmation. Obama directly challenges the recent withering criticism of his Republican opponent. "I don't know what kind of lives John McCain thinks celebrities lead, but this is mine." Offering ambitious proposals to repair the nation's torn social fabric, Obama's speech fluidly moves from the practical and mundane to the utopian premises of the civil sphere – "that's the idea of America, the promise that we rise and fall together, than I am my brother's keeper, my sister's keeper."

The commentarial responses are filled to overflowing with praise. When Andrea Mitchell likens Obama's words to those of President Andrew Shepherd in Aaron Sorkin's movie *The American President* – which morphed into the long-running, legendary television show, *The West Wing* – the factual and the fictional media of communication meet halfway, merging poetry and prose. Declaring "the Hell with my critics," Chris Matthews speaks in the first-person plural to underscore the intensity of the personal-cum-civil connection Obama has achieved: "I think what he said was about us, and that's why we care. Our strength is not in our money or military, but in the American promise." Adding "let me tell you how" Obama did this, Matthews explains Obama asked, "Was my upbringing a celebrity's upbringing?! How dare you say this election is a test of [my] patriotism!" Obama was declaring "Enough!" He supplied not only his usual inspiration, but all the specifics that his critics said he had until now neglected in the campaign – "twenty-nine specific policy pledges and at least nineteen failures of the McCain campaign." He supplied "four direct punches to George Bush and four more to the Republican party. No shots were left unthrown. There has been an extraordinary laying down of the glove."

As if to prevent critics from intervening between Obama's speech and his audience, the MSNBC commentators provide responses before potential critics of Obama's speech have a chance to reply. They attribute their positive reactions not to their interpretive powers but to the actual speech, its performative effect. Olbermann asks, "As political theatre, where *doesn't* this rank in our recent history?" Brian Williams, anchor of

NBC Nightly News, answers by making an analogy between Obama's rhetoric and the fictional prose of *West Wing* writer Aaron Sorkin. Chuck Todd, NBC pollster and political analyst, observes, "I was struck by the little nods here to political responsibility." Obama is "trying to appeal to Missourra [*sic*], not Missouri. He is saying I'm going to fight. The toughness of the speech is what's still going to stand out." McCain won't "know how to react to this speech. I'll tell you, I don't know how the Republican Party is going to be able to go against this show." Tom Brokaw, the iconic former NBC news anchor and best-selling popular historian, adds: "Barack felt a certain license to throw a punch back. There was something personal and combative here that I haven't got so far . . . This guy is just a step above no matter what you think of him or his politics." After "three days of *mishigas*," Williams observes, "we can now look at this as a narrative, a four day narrative." Matthews turns to his normally cool, rather politically conservative colleague, Michelle Bernard. The African-American commentator offers that, immediately after the speech, she fled to a room backstage "so I could weep alone." Matthews asks, "Is this nomination of Obama a 'willingness of the heart'? Are we beyond an ethnic nation? There was a sea of black, white, and Asian faces. Is the era of ethnic politics over?" Iowa did it first, he recounts, on the day of Obama's early primary victory. Responding that "Iowa was the greatest day in our nation's history," Bernard affirms that, after today, "America will never be the same again." Mitchell recalls how, during Obama's speech, "people jumped to their feet and started shouting when he attacked McCain." She testifies, "I've never witnessed anything quite like this. The stagecraft was so phenomenal. I don't know how they could have made it any better."

These remarks are repeated in the *New York Times* coverage the next day (Stelter and Rutenberg 2008). According to media constructions, the fusion inside the stadium generated not only local ritual but amplified outside, gaining the largest audience in the history of televised conventions, larger by one-third than the opening night of the Beijing Olympics. This suggests that the television commentators gasping, ah-ing, and oh-ing over the previous evening's scene must have appeared as felicitous to many.

Becoming a hero: The mythical narrative

In a major profile about Obama's political qualities, *Times* reporter Michael Powell explains the Democrat's performative effectiveness in terms of identification, a quality demanded for successful performance: Obama "has the gift of making people see themselves in him." Powell supplies an empirical description of how this trick is turned. Obama produces psychological identification by virtue of his narrative's textual qualities. Obama is a "protean political figure, inspiring devotion in supporters who see him as a *transformative* leader." It is "as if there were a Barack-the-immaculate-pol quality to his rise." Powell employs allusive terms that evoke the emergence of a biblical prophet. Obama, he writes, "has taken just 11 years to run the course from state senator to the first black presumptive nominee who holds thousands spellbound" (Powell 2008a).

Why is a prophetic narrative necessary? Every struggle for big-time political power is narrated in terms of crisis and salvation. Characters can become heroes, after all, only by overcoming great odds, by resolving overwhelming challenges. According to our would-be presidents, Americans face a unique moment in history. There are unprecedented dangers and opportunities, a world-historical crisis domestically and internationally that threatens to derail America's mythical history. National collapse looms. Only during such a "crisis of our times" (Alexander 2003d) can heroes be made. Electoral defeat will bring apocalypse. Not just survival, but transcendence and refounding are at stake.

Obama declares in his post-primary acceptance speech on June 4, 2008, "this is our time, this is our moment." He draws a sharp and redolent red line between the dark past and the bright golden future. He presents himself as a force that mediates darkness and light. He will purify the American project and pull it from the past to the future, into the bright sunshine of a new day. Drawing from the same culture structure, John Kennedy, too, had once memorably promised symbolic transformation. "A new day is dawning," he declared in his 1960 inaugural address; "the torch has been passed to a new generation." As for Obama, a few days after his June 4 speech, he wove this salvationary theme into a major economic address (Broder 2008).

"Mr Obama said again that a McCain presidency would be a continuation of President Bush," the *Times* reports, pointing to how Obama narrates his opponent inside a framing of past, present, and future. To be in the present, a position that allows you to reach to the future, a political actor needs to break sharply with the past.

118

Obama insists that McCain is only nominally in the present: his real attachment is to the past. "We've been there once," Obama warns the Bush presidency, and "we're not going back." The *Times* observes that "Obama posed the choice between him and McCain as a fundamental one between the future and the past, the ground on which he hopes to fight his campaign." Obama declares, "This is the choice we face right now, a choice between more of the same . . . or change . . . Not an argument between left or right . . . It is time to try something new." McCain thinks we are already in the future, according to Obama; "He says we've made great progress in our economy these past eight years."

In this economic address, Obama inserts economic "facts" into the binary of then and now, past and future. This rhetorical gesture reveals the role of binary historical divisions. Heroes are constructed by inserting a political actor into world-historical time. It's not only about saying somebody is a hero – this rarely happens as such. It's about narrating time, about constructing a fundamental and significant temporality, and weighting it with immense importance, significance, if possible. This radically discontinuous temporal narrative is deepened by a coding that pollutes the opponent as anti-civil. Time becomes vital, and the salvationary narrative possible, to the degree that the other candidate is truly and deeply dangerous, such that electing him would plunge us into an apocalyptic situation. If the other candidate is elected, the progress of the nation will be halted, and we will not be able to move into future time. During the 1996 presidential contest, Bill Clinton promised to build a bridge to the twenty-first century, something that Bob Dole could not.

To become a hero, one must establish a sense of great and urgent necessity. The moment is precarious and burdened with terrible significance. America has fallen on tough times; the Dream lies in tatters. The nation has fallen off the hill. We have been desecrated and polluted by the second Bush presidency. We must be purified, and for this we need a new hero. Obama presents himself as having overcome great personal adversity on the road to auditioning for this position of national hero. Born into a deeply polluted racial group, he was inspired by an earlier African-American prophet-hero whose rhetoric about the dream of justice had become deeply etched in the collective consciousness of American civil society. After Obama secured the nomination, on June 4, joyous proclamations of imminent salvation were offered by African-Americans and circulated by the communicative institutions of American civil society. His victory seemed to

119

presage an end to race hatred and the realization of the true solidarity promised by American civil society. In Africa, Obama's Kenyan relatives and their countrymen described his ascension as signaling redemption, the possibility of global solidarity.

When Obama spoke after clinching the nomination, the present became a rhetorical pivot between the enslaving past and redemptive future. "Generations from now, we will be able to look back and tell our children that this was the moment when we began to provide care for the sick and good jobs for the jobless; this was the moment when the rise of the oceans began to slow and our planet began to heal" (in Kristol 2008). An op-ed columnist heard "echoes of the gospels and Genesis," recalling the candidate's Wesleyan speech a week earlier, in which he had openly declared that "our individual salvation depends on collective salvation" (Kristol 2008). The next day, the *Times* ran a large photo depicting Obama as a Jesus-like figure offering salvation. He is elevated above a teeming crowd, with hundreds of hands stretching out to touch him. He has become a charismatic vessel, filled with the sacred promise of civil repair.

To become a hero is to enter into myth. It is to cease being merely a mortal man (or woman) and to develop a second immortal body in Kantorowicz's sense (Kantorowicz 1957), an iconic surface that allows audiences an overpowering feeling of connection with the transcendental realm of a nation's idealistic political life that lies just underneath. Obama has begun to grow this second body. He is no longer just a human being – a skinny guy with big ears, a writer, an ordinary man – but a hero. As an iconic hero, this symbolic body will not die. It will be remembered no matter what happens to the living man. Most political figures cannot grow such second skin. They are respected or liked, or even deferred to, but their second body, the mythical public body, is weak and puny, so they remain politician rather than myth. Overshadowed and wimpified by their opponent, they are "wounded" in political battles, revealing their mortal natures. Jimmy Carter was wounded by Ted Kennedy's late primary run, and injured further by Teddy's overwhelming and vainglorious speech at the Democratic convention. Carter faltered in the general election campaign, watching helplessly as the once mundane Ronald Reagan grew a sacralizing and mythical second body. Bill Clinton versus George H. W. Bush ran this play in reverse. Decades before, Richard Nixon's five o'clock shadow, not properly covered by make-up, darkened and polluted him, allowing John Kennedy to shine like a bright young god during their decisive presidential debate (Greenberg 2004).

120

As the actual events of the primary were winding down – it "concludes Tuesday" – the *Times* alludes to a routine narration. There has "developed such a reliable story line that pundits can recite in their sleep." This narrative is about the two "firsts" almost tearing the party apart, the first woman and the first black. But, while this "story" has a "numbing familiarity," this shouldn't obscure "what makes this nomination singular." In explaining this singularity, the narrative first thickens in such a manner that the primary narrative can become world-historical and thus mythic once again. The primary campaign surely "stands alone in the history of American presidential politics," so much so that "there's nothing that's remotely close" to it. The depth of democratic participation has achieved a transcendental level. The *Times* explains that the primary process started in efforts of Progressive era reformers "to give voters, rather than party bosses, a greater voice." But this reform didn't really matter that much until now. Only today has the democratic promise of the primary idea paid off. The voters have triumphed (liberty) finally over the bosses (repression). The primary process is "shattering records . . . The scale of this thing is just extraordinary . . . Their performance is all the more striking because it defies the normal laws of political gravity . . . Remarkable" (Harwood 2008a).

The primaries have defied the natural laws of the world, not only the corruption of society's social laws. The media weaves this mythical tale about Barack and Hillary, whose supporters together have made democracy real, and for the first time.

Cultural agency and scripting

From the perspective of the audience, the hero politician is anything but self-made. Neither coded nor narrated, her heroic stature is natural, essentialized. For the citizen-audience, it is simply a matter of learning who the candidate for power really is, and has always been. From the perspective of the politician struggling to take power, however, becoming a collective representation is a project, an action requiring extraordinary agency. He becomes a character in his own script, writing a story in the unfolding of his personal lifetime. Such self-fashioning must be responsive to unending contingency, even as it strives to maintain the arc of its coded narrative themes.

Obama entered the campaign for the presidency with a script that was public in an unusually formal way – his autobiographical book, *Dreams from my Father*. Since then, not only he but the reporters covering him have folded every political contingency into these already existing narrative strands, evaluating the meaning of new events against these background representations.

Obama's community-organizing was a vital part of his self-fashioning. He began this soon-to-be public phase of his *Bildung* two years after his Columbia college graduation and concluded it, three years later, on his way to Harvard Law School. At the farewell reception for Obama at the Altgeld Gardens project in south Chicago, he told the small, 60-person gathering that he would eventually return to Chicago "to pursue a career in public life" (Kovaleski 2008). The story is reconstructed by the *New York Times* from interviews with those who were there, as part of the paper's ongoing effort to create some narrative framing for Barack-the-immaculate's mysterious early life. But it was Obama himself who first scripted these events inside the frame of his autobiography, *Dreams from my Father*. His stint as an organizer was not important because of the successes he achieved on the ground. "We made very little progress," Obama recalled (Kovaleski 2008). Its importance derived from its being part of a *telos*, not a means–end relation – as culture, not as practical reason. The years represented a stage in the Obama story, a step in his *Bildung*, his moral development. As the *Times* reporter does not fail to note, this relatively brief stint of Chicago community-organizing occupies fully one-third of the 442-page public narrative that was devised to script it. A political campaign builds upon already existing informal and formal scripting. Its aim is to instantiate these background representations in political time and space, to create an iconic power that condenses memories, dreams, and interpretations into the surface image and depth meaning of a powerful hero.

The image as object and strategy

Staffers and reporters are deeply concerned with the "image" of the candidate, speaking about it as if it were an objective, rather than a subjective thing. Certainly, it is a social fact in Durkheim's sense, a collectively constituted representation whose contours, once established, are independent of the power of any single individual, no matter how powerful. It is because of this only seemingly paradoxical combination of massive objectivity and insistent subjectivity – of social determinism and individual agency – that "controlling the image" becomes a matter of overwhelming concern to every political campaign. To encounter the image is to recall a collective representation that transcends the candidate as an individual. It is to engage his second, immortal body, the one that can make an ordinary and mortal politician into a king. The image must be kept pure and unsullied. It must be handled and framed. Campaigns project a protected space around their candidate, a sacred aura that must not be profaned. They fight to keep it inviolate; they struggle to keep every possible polluting contact at bay.

In June, Politico.com revealed that campaign staffers had removed two headscarf-wearing Muslim women from the background of an Obama photo op. (Rutenberg and Zeleny 2008). Faced with this exposure of apparent deceit and possible intolerance, the campaign apologized, even while it defended its right to be "tight" and "vigilant." Control is necessary, they explained, in order to fight against "erroneous information that has spread on the internet" identifying the Senator as Muslim himself. While it is good strategy to defend the pure image from pollution, it is bad strategy when such efforts to preserve the sacred end up polluting it, allowing the candidate to be constructed in anti-democratic terms. To neutralize such mistakes, political staffs open up space between the candidate and the campaign. Acknowledging their "mistake," Obama staffers maintain it was their own, not the candidate's, asserting it "doesn't reflect the orientation of the campaign." The *Times* reporter explained that the incident "pointed to pitfalls the campaign faces as it moves into the general election and seeks to maintain control of Obama's image by tightly managing his public appearances." Despite this temporary setback, such control must still be maintained. While Obama staffers acknowledge the battle had been lost, they assert that the war against "misinformation" will not be. A senior aide remarks, "We're going to deal with that very aggressively through a number of mediums."

Obama's apparent decision to allow his children to be interviewed on TV reveals a similar dynamic. On the one hand, the interviews are effective, projecting the sacred and innocent space of the family circle around sometimes wavering public images of the candidate himself. However, a backlash ensues that threatens pollution. Why did Obama bring his family into the public sphere, his small children into harm's way? Obama blames his staff, even as he acknowledges it was his own decision. He employs the ambiguous royal we. Even as they exposed this slip, journalists recorded their own and others' admiration for how successfully Obama's campaign had, in fact, been able to assert control over the candidate's image.

Yet another illustration surfaces when Obama's staff welcomes reporters and photographers to meet with the campaign's new national security team, composed primarily of retired military officers. It is revealed that staffers actually had barred cameras, though not reporters, when Obama had mixed with a large gathering of black civic leaders only days before. They had also recently refused to provide names of African-American religious figures with whom Obama had privately met during a visit to Chicago. Still, efforts to control the image are widely accepted, and often admired. In response to the spike of harsh questioning about Michele Obama's patriotism and temperament, the campaign had orchestrated a series of "friendly" television appearances and a "flattering spread in the pages of *US Weekly*." It was reported that such efforts had "won compliments from political professionals of both parties." The Obama campaign exhibited a "high level of discipline." It had matched "the stagecraft that was once so successfully practiced by the campaigns of Bush to the envy . . . of Democrats" (Rutenberg and Zeleny 2008).

Politics as war by symbolic means

Struggles for the presidency are not games. There is too much ultimate power at stake. Struggles for civil power to control the state are as vicious and aggressive as they are culturally and legally allowed to be. Organizers and observers alike compare political campaigns with war. They are plotted and remembered in terms of battles won and lost. "Now that the primary season is over," Senator Charles Schumer announces, "there is going to be a clear voice" for the Democrats: the party can finally begin "setting up the stark contrast with Mr. McCain." The *Times* reports that "with the Democratic stage to himself for the first time, Senator Barack Obama opened a two-week tour of battleground states on Monday, attacking Senator John McCain" (Broder 2008).

For these reasons, "partisanship" is the most fraught and ambiguous word in democratic politics. Solidarity is the *sine qua non* of the civil sphere, yet it is threatened by the agonism of the struggle for the political power to represent it. Intense and often sharply hostile conflict is unleashed in the name of a broad, inclusive, and pacific civil solidarity. Yet, sponsoring and promoting periodic bouts of political agonism allows the civil sphere to maneuver through complexity and to finesse fragmentation, to reconcile if never to eliminate opposing ideological and social interests. After these fierce battles are over, the winner becomes the representative of the civil sphere inside the state.

This paradox is not only conceptual. It is experienced as deeply dangerous. Electoral battles challenge the fellow feeling of solidarity and mutual identification upon which civil society depends. Yet, if being elected means convincing voters that your candidate truly represents the values of the civil sphere, then partisan attacks on the other candidate as much less civil, and indeed as anti-civil, must be the unwritten rule in every significant political campaign. As the *Times* reminds its reader, today's partisan hostility "may be no different than what prompted allies of Quincy Adams to run searing attack pamphlets . . . nearly 200 years ago: It works" (Rutenberg 2008). Nonetheless, there is continuous monitoring of the invisible line separating "healthy" and "normal" party conflict from pathologically anti-civil faction. Crossing this line is what "dirty tricks" are all about, when "off-line" and "under the table" expenditures pay for plumbers' operations and swift boat ads. There are continuous demands to maintain decorum and civility, which often are not met. In the American political system, these issues were crystallized in Watergate, the legendary occasion that remains etched in the collective memory of the civil sphere. It remains a memory of how partisanship can turn into anti-civil hostility, and of how even the best of democracies are sometimes done in. As the *Times* observes, candidates might promise nice "only to behave otherwise when the battle finally joins." Despite their promises, Obama and McCain are "locked in a minute by minute fight . . . with rhetoric that can be as harsh and misleading as that of any previous campaign." The *Times* observes, "Behind the scenes are amped-up campaign war rooms that between them send dozens of attack email messages to reporters on a given day." Obama reassures his supporters at a rally: "If they bring a knife to the fight, we bring a gun" – a line from the *Untouchables*, which demonstrates how party conflict challenges the plasticity of the discourse of civil society.

Agonism is exacerbated because the discourse of civil society is binary. If meaning is difference, then political legitimacy is even more so. Making oneself civilly pure, and one's opponents as anti-civil and impure, is the stuff of which victory is made. It is the irony at the heart of democratic politics.

The cultural construction of voters

The voting public, as such, is not physically active in this power struggle, which is directed by tightly organized campaign staffs, mediated by more and less civil associations, and fueled by enormous flows of money. Yet voters, if not physically co-present, are *imaginatively* central. As coded, narrated, and rhetorically projected, voters constitute the central audiences of political campaigns. They are held to be rational and independent and capable of immensely wise decisions.

They are the sacred of the sacred. According to the democratic myth, such enlightened citizens simply do not make mistakes. In any particular campaign season, voters may be constructed as angry, depressed, happy with the status quo, or anxious about the future. But such passions are taken to be expressions of their enlightened autonomy, of their rock-solid sense of the public interest upon which American democracy rests. Sometimes, of course, voters do support demagogues and liars, but it is universally held that they have done so not because they themselves are weak or dishonest. Rather, they have been knowingly and irresponsibly misled, typically by "the other side." Provided with false or inadequate information, voters have been unable to act on their best instincts and rational interests.

Those who struggle for power in the civil sphere must always show themselves as studiously respectful of voters. A candidate can never be seen as insulting or talking down to them. To engage in the former is to be elitist; to engage in the latter is to be pandering. Elitism and pandering are qualities that disqualify a candidate from representing the civil sphere. Voters have the last word in the struggle for political power. On voting day, by a magical process that is usually hidden from view, the secret votes of interested citizens are transformed into the publicly proclaimed general will. The beneficent force of civil solidarity reemerges to calm the passions and interests of potentially divisive partisan struggle (Schmidt in progress).

Those who fail to win the vote are constructed in a post hoc manner as having deserved their fates. Their character, campaign, and stance on issues were rejected by John Q public. No matter their earlier, pre-election days of respect and glory; they are now polluted, having fallen on the wrong side of the civil/anti-civil divide. Listen to Governor Bill Richardson's post-primary indictment of the Clinton campaign. Once a fervent supporter of Hillary Clinton, Richardson now opines that "what hurt them was their sense of entitlement that the presidency was theirs and all the acolytes fall in line." Because Hillary Clinton was rejected by the voters, she must now be situated as outside the civil sphere, or at least as peripheral to its central core. Richardson suggests that the Clintons were not democratic but arrogant, demanding subservience rather than facilitating autonomy. They put themselves above the voters, taking them for granted until it was too late. Even when the putatively arrogant Hillary finally did energetically court Democratic voters, late in her primary campaign, she was accused of pandering, of deceptively becoming a "working-class hero" rather than speaking truth to working-class stereotypes. She was also accused of being overly dependent on her husband,

126

subordinating herself to his pettiness and temper and his seemingly insidious racial slurs.

The cultural construction of candidates

In civil society, in order to become a hero, a protagonist must be placed at the center of America's *democratic* myth. What the political protagonist stories depends upon the binary discourse of civil society. Hillary comes to symbolize equality and mobility, a working-class hero – Rosie the riveter – and a superwoman breaking the glass ceiling. Barack becomes the great emancipator. Calm and reasonable, he is a black Abraham Lincoln promising a more profound and expansive solidarity. McCain is the wounded prisoner of war who breaks the bonds of enslavement and roars back to a corruption-fighting, maverick, and newly altruistic life. He bucks social pressures and material inducements to do what he thinks is moral and right.

A major scripting challenge emerges when Obama announces that he will withdraw from public financing, the major effort at post-Watergate civil repair, a strenuous if not terribly effective effort to control monetary influence upon the struggle for civil power. Symbolizing a democratic approach to the struggle for power, it was a funding system that Obama had always publicly embraced, to which McCain himself had also contributed. Obama's aides acknowledge that this abandonment "might tarnish" him (Luo and Zeleny 2008). Obama has adumbrated his doubts about public financing ever since his online fund raising capacity became evident, but he has promised not to abandon it. So, his honesty and ethics now seem threatened, and they are primary qualities of the discourse of civil society. Abandoning public financing seems to threaten democratic control over the struggle for power. It will, according to the *Times*, "likely transform the landscape of presidential elections, injecting hundreds of millions" of private money into what should be a civil process.

Obama moves immediately to defend his decision, which he claims, counter-intuitively, actually brings him more closely into alignment with the discourse of civil society. He has abandoned his promise in order better to *defend* civil society against secretive and manipulative agonism and aggression! He also maintains that online fund raising is the most civil form of financing ever developed, that it is far fairer than the kinds that the public financing system had been erected against. Obama asserts, in fact, that he needs to maximize private gift giving so that he can properly defend himself against the anti-civil tactics of Republicans. His Republican opponents are "masters at gaming the system and will spend millions smearing" him. The Republican National Committee has already acquired $50 million against the DMC's $10 million.

McCain accuses Obama of lying and flip-flopping: he has completely reversed himself, going back on his commitment to the American people. Again, Obama insists that online fund raising represents "a new kind of politics." The *New York Times* worries that Obama's turn to private money will intensify the agonism of the struggle for power, raising the dangerous possibility that partisanship will become anti-civil antagonism. Obama will now be able to place ads outside the "the traditional battle ground states." A Republican strategist, observing that Obama had purchased ads in Georgia, remarks, "I think the last guy to buy Georgia was General Sherman," concluding, "it's a very aggressive election strategy." Sherman was a nasty piece of work, a warrior who burned down Georgia in the finale of the (anti) civil war. The *Times* also warns of another possible anti-civil complication: abandoning public money will force Obama to spend more time raising private money and less time "meeting voters."

The agonism of partisan party struggle is emolliated by efforts to connect it to the democratic side of civil discourse. Each party calls out the other's antagonism as an example of incivility, while describing its own aggressive response as legitimate self-defense. McCain says Obama is "the type of politician who will advance himself before he advances the debate or the issues," an old, not a self-styled new politician (Rutenberg 2008). In a story headlining that Obama "Carefully Hones his Partisan Image," Michael Powell (2008b) documents Obama becoming more partisan, despite his earlier claims for unity. He reports but does not credit the campaign's claim that spins this new stance, not as partisan, but as simply exposing actual "difference," that is, that it's a reflection of the reality of John McCain, not a new and more aggressive strategic framing.

Difference is a semiotic truism, but it is also one of the major strategies of politics. As campaigns work the binaries, they try to simplify the meaning of every issue that comes up, bringing it into semiotic alignment, on one side or the other of the great divide. Everything must be made clear or dirty, and, whenever possible, the newly pure and polluted folded into the narrative arc of historical transformation. This spinning machine comes to an end on the first Tuesday of November, when the act of voting allows a purging catharsis, a spitting out of the negative, and a transformation of the individual into the collective will.

Until that day, politics is about creating difference, not overcoming

128

it. The principal strategy for protecting the purity of your candidate's image is to categorize the other candidate in polluted ways. If we are to be coded as clean and democratic, they must be made dirty in the litany of tried-and-true, anti-democratic themes. If our candidate is to be narrated as heroic, theirs must become a villain.

After securing the nomination, Obama announces notable policy shifts. He not only jettisoned public financing but publicly accepted the Supreme Court's decision that the Constitution gave citizens the right to carry guns. The *Times*'s Michael Powell offers the factual observation that Obama has "executed several policy pirouettes in recent weeks, each time landing more toward the center" (Powell 2008c). This has triggered challenges to Obama's scripted character, raising the question of whether these changes should be coded as responsible modulation or manipulative flip-flopping. Powell describes Obama as "this most observant of politicians," who has shown throughout his career "an appreciation for the virtues of political ambiguity." He notes, "Obama has taken calibrated positions" on a number of issues in the last week. He characterizes his recent response to the Supreme Court as "delphic," giving a classically democratic Greek spin but also suggesting that Obama's justifications cannot be proved either right or wrong. In America, if action is deemed pragmatic, virtue can be upheld (Table 5.1). Powell quotes historian Robert Dallek. Because every presidential candidate wants to "be seen as pragmatic," Dallek observes, so "shifting doesn't mean they are utterly insincere." He recalls that even the revered FDR "slipped and slid his way through the 1932 election," and that "Herbert Hoover called him a 'chameleon on plaid'."

Table 5.1 Shared civil coding

Pragmatic shifts	Flip-flops
Strong	Weak
Trustworthy	Untrustworthy
Flexible	Ideologically rigid
Sincere	Calculative
Authoritative	Indecisive

Obama carefully emphasizes the civil qualities of his motives and actions (Harwood 2008b). He explains, for example, that the Supreme Court's decision "reinforces that if we act responsibly" we can both protect individual rights and "the community" alike. We can still make laws against "unscrupulous gun deals" and keep

129

"illegal hand guns off the streets." His aides rush to supply extenuating context, which while reaching for reality, implicitly reveals a larger symbolic truth. "Flippers are important," they claim, only "when they reinforce a larger narrative about a candidate's negative attributes." Still, the coding of contingent policy is open; it can slide easily to the anti-democratic side.

"Operatives in both parties" agree that candidate John Kerry's "apparent equivocation on the Iraq war damaged his 2004 campaign." McCain staffers claim that Obama "is not a change agent but just a typical politician," in the *Times* words, a "stereotypically two-faced politician." For now, however, despite the candidates' evident shifting of positions, voters in both parties give both high civil scores "for being honest and straightforward."

Soon after, Obama suggests he will "refine" his Iraq policies after meeting with military commanders later in the summer. One explanation is that the surge has been seeming to work. In "Obama Fuels Pullout Debate with Remarks," the *Times* carefully observes simply that "violence declines" (Powell and Zeleny 2008). Obama maintains that, in essence, his policy on Iraq has not changed. He insists that if Iraq were actually to be democratic – the goal that President Bush set for the surge – then not only must violence be ended but there must be political "reconciliation" as well. It is on the failure to achieve the latter element of civil society that Obama rests the case for withdrawal now. Though violence has declined, Iraq is still not a democratic place. Withdrawing would also allow the American government to redistribute military spending to create more equality at home. Obama insists that he has always said that the pace of withdrawal will be responsive to commanders. He reaffirms his intention to "consult" with commanders, but also his refusal to subordinate himself to them. It's a matter of being rational and filtering all available "information." On his first day of office, he will give the Joint Chiefs a new mission, namely to end this war "responsibly, deliberately, but decisively." In other words, ending the war can be and will be civil.

In the early phases of the post-primary campaign, Obama faced the hermeneutical danger of flip-flopping. During this same period, McCain confronts the danger of not being able to do difference at all. Until late July, his campaign had not been able to get a handle on the negatives. If you can't do difference, you can't generate meaning, and without meaning the struggle for power will fail. Repeated stories assert that Obama is ahead because McCain has failed on this score. Reasons are offered as to why McCain has found this difficult to do:

Obama has not been in office long; McCain is wary of unleashing charges that "conservatives have overstepped and been criticized for racially tinged remarks"; it is said to be difficult to pollute "a movement candidate" (Healy 2008). Finally, McCain has promised to be civil, which inhibits an overly negative campaign. In fact, at this stage McCain is described as trying to be "respectful," and he's been forced to distance himself from some of the more intemperate ads that have been created and financed in his name. These stories also give Obama credit for preventing his own pollution. He "has proved defter and more fleet-footed at counter-punching" than either Kerry or Gore. He has not been "cowed" into apologizing.

By mid-July, these difficulties for McCain are well and truly overcome. He abandoned his scruples and began doing the binaries with a vengeance. It commenced with the advertising and internet campaign declaring, "Obama is the world's biggest celebrity," the desperate Hail Mary pass the Republicans threw just after Obama's foreign tour reached its zenith, the candidate hailed by a fused and adoring crowd of 200,000 in front of Berlin's Victory Arch, just steps away from the iconically democratic Brandenburg Gate. The performative injury to Obama's image was significant, sending the candidate's poll numbers into a tailspin from which they would not fully recover until the end of August. The celebrity became a mystery man who had appeared out of nowhere and would not tell the truth. When Obama responded that he would not answer the Republicans' "negative campaigning" with his own, he sustained his image as a hero who held to the sacred ground of civil purity, but he had difficulty recovering his ground.

While McCain had once been a hero, that was in the military and not in the civil sphere, and it seemed long ago and faraway. The rise of Sarah Palin seemed for a time significantly to rectify this disbalance. Her iconic image of moose-hunting frontiers woman emerged from the virgin land itself, from the primordial ooze of the old wild west. McCain may have first named "Joe the plumber," but it was Palin who married herself to this folk figure in mythical time. But only weeks after its emergence, Palin hero was done in by the binaries, battered by the mainstream media as corrupt, arrogant, deceitful, irrational, and stupid. The financial meltdown in mid-September was not determinate, but provided a setting for the binary dice to be rolled a final time. McCain's response to the crisis seemed motivated by cynical and strategic motives; he was depicted as impulsive, grandstanding, confused, and irrational. In this context of his negatively depicted antagonist, Obama emerged as a democratic protagonist, a hero who seemed effortlessly to embody civil discourse once again. He was depicted as calm and confident, as intelligent and lucid. So inserted into the heart of the civil sphere, this unlikely and once marginal candidate was voted into office by an overwhelming majority, and allowed to take power inside the state.

The new reflexivity

There is a reflexivity in the democratic struggle for power. The old reflexivity points to the self-awareness that has, for at least two centuries, been a structural dimension of power struggles in democratic societies. There has always been some differentiation between the communicative and regulative institutions of civil society – and even inside the communicative and regulative institutions themselves. This level of differentiation, internal and external, guarantees that, from the beginning of modern democratic civil spheres, there has been a high degree of self-reflexiveness, and institutional and value conflict. For example, the media watches out for its own interests against the interests of the law, against the campaigns of ambitious and crafty candidates, and against political parties. The candidates and their parties, in turn, are always cautious and often antagonistic to the media.

The Times reports that "strategists for Obama . . . have made it clear they have to control his image and protect against attack" (Rutenberg and Zeleny 2008). This both annoys and worries the media, for they are aware that they are routinely being lied to, by both parties and candidates. In the face of such prevarication, they feel the need to point it out and also to produce "the truth" as they see it from their professional-norm position. Otherwise, in their view, the people are being manipulated, and the process becomes anti-democratic. On the one hand, journalists wish to emphasize that Obama has a "stated desire to be unusually transparent and open," to be civil towards the media rather than being manipulative and controlling. At the same time, the *Times* reports that Obama is "at loggerheads with media organizations" who want greater access to the candidate and his staff. None of this is new. The media has long been reflexive about its relationships with political power.

By speaking about the "new" reflexivity, I wish to refer to a growing self-consciousness, not about institutional differentiation, but about the culturally constructed nature of the struggle for political power itself. The older, standard reflexivity was about the "natural" grounds of conflict and interest between institutions whose "real-ness" was taken for granted. For example, in democratic countries there has been an enduring conflict between free press and fair trial. This has produced reams of reflexive discussion about the respective roles of law and media and how to mediate their boundaries. Nonetheless, in the public journalism reporting on these conflicts, both sides are naturalized, referred to as essentialized entities with real interests rather than being deconstructed. Things are different today, when sophisticated print, television, and web commentators speak about the need for new narratives and control of the image. News and events are no longer presented as if they happen naturally. The media cover the spinning of the thing as much as the thing in itself, though they are careful in the process not to deconstruct themselves: they admit neither to spinning nor to narrating the news. Their professional ethics are too deeply held for that.

For at least two centuries, democratic and nondemocratic nations have sustained public spheres whose structuring has depended upon mass media, but it has only been in postmodern societies that self-consciousness about the mass-mediated production of the political image has assumed central stage. Politics has always been symbolic and cultural, but only in postmodern societies has public political action become reconceptualized as political "performance." Those who struggle for power in democratic societies have always worked to project powerful symbolic images of themselves on the public stage, and to control their interpretation. Today, however, political journalism has become increasingly focused on evaluating this performative task. Political journalism is concerned as much with the intricacies of political performance as with political events, as much with the staging of political discourse as with political discourse itself. Intellectual critics and critical sociologists often decry the emphasis on "symbolic politics" as manipulative and propagandistic, as a turning away from reality to pretense, simulation, and spectacle. Political practitioners speak simply about getting out truthful information about their message or their candidate. Political journalists tell us how the sausage is made.

Why is there this new reflexivity? It is not because politics has become deceptive and obsessed with spin where once it was guided by sincerity and concerned with truth. Neither is it because of the emergence of the "new journalism" after Watergate or the rise of Reaganism. These may have been efficient causes, but they were not the fundamental ones. Politics has always been performative, but the elements of this performance have become more and more de-fused – there are new roles, new paid specialties, and a new self-consciousness about these contributions, a new awareness. For example, the earlier you go back in democratic mass politics, the less likely it is that you will find speech writers. Even as speech writing became more common, moreover, it did not emerge as a specialized role, a "profession." And, when speech writing finally did become a firmly institutionalized role, it was not displayed on the public stage. Only in the last 30 years has "the speech writer" become a common trope and familiar presence in democratic politics, a figure who steps out of his role to take credit for the candidate's words (Lim 2008: 78–86). Journalists rarely fail to address themselves to the question of whether the words coming out of the candidate's mouth are actually his or her own words, and successful speech writers rarely fail to write books bragging about their own power – at the expense of the candidate's – at some later time. Because of this de-fusion, it is ever so much harder for fusion, the appearance of naturalness, to be gained. What the media are covering is the *effort* at achieving fusion as much as the candidates' conflict itself. Yet the possibility of achieving authenticity nonetheless remains. As in the theatre so in politics, what's regained is Coleridge's "willing suspension of disbelief."

The same movement from nonexistence to informal existence to hidden existence to publicly-reflected-upon-existence applies to many other aspects of the struggle for power. Once, there were no press secretaries; today, there are many for each presidency and campaign. Once, speeches were made without armies of spinners descending on journalists to mediate their interpretation; today, spinning, and the discussion of spinning, has become a publicly discussed craft. Once, campaign speeches were given with little advance warning other than an announcement the previous day. Today, there is a profession of "advance men" who arrive days before and whose job is to create a crowd. Once, it was primarily his friends who advised a man of power. Today, he or she hires professional teams of veteran strategists, who themselves deploy other specialized teams, such as pollsters, advertisers, media buyers, and public relations groups, not to mention make-up artists, lighting specialists, and costumers. The mass-mediating dimensions of performance have also become de-fused. The blogger has emerged as a new social role. It performs both the factual and interpretive roles of journalism in a nonprofessional way. The blogger is not just a new kind of factual gatherer, but a new kind of interpreter, one that speaks openly and ideologically and personally even while supposedly on behalf of the people themselves.

Such performative defusion has made it much more difficult for those struggling for power to make their image seem natural and real. Journalists have become interested in explaining why. In the new reflexivity, media have become very explicit about the elements of political performance. Everywhere there is talk about narrative, performance, and spinning, about stagings and settings, about the variability of scripted speech writing, about *mise-en-scène*, and about the contingency of audience reception.

Conclusion

Contrary to democratic and sociological theory, the factual status of issues is, per se, relatively insignificant in the struggle for power. Issues are the present, the visible of power struggles. But what is really important is the absent. Academic campaign observers – along with political scientists and sociologists who study power – tend to miss the invisible, unspoken symbolic language and speech that constitutes the actual referents of power struggles in formally democratic societies. Journalists, bloggers, and voters themselves see campaigns as about personalities, issues, and ideologies, about being liberal or conservative, pro- or anti-abortion, military intervention, affirmative action, surveillance, gay marriage, immigration, free trade, unions, minimum wage. In other words, they see campaigns as about real things that exist out in the world, either as values or interests, or actual people.

My argument has been that these are all signifieds. They are concrete issues and ideological positions that can equally be constructed in either a positive or a negative way. Contests for power are not decided by "real" things in themselves, but rather by aligning real things and "urgent" things with what really makes meaning, the background systems of signifiers. It is the tensions between democratic and anti-democratic codes, and between the past and future of mythical narratives, that are the actual referents of political campaigns. They are the be-all and end-all of the struggle for power. Everything is done as if words and images matter. And they do. Difference reigns supreme.

Still, while a fundamental and necessary referent, the discourse of civil society is not determinate. There is the element of agency. Political actors and campaigns need to struggle for power. They are compelled to create performances, and their success is contingent. It depends on skill and fortune, on commanding an effective stage, on media interpretation, on audiences being prepared by shifting social conditions in certain felicitous ways.

To control the state in a democratic society means to become the chosen representative of the civil sphere. Normative theorists of democracy have understood this to mean that the choice is a deliberative one. Social scientists have understood this choosing to be a reflection of social and economic conditions. In this essay, I advance an alternative view. To become a representative of the civil sphere is less a matter of rational deliberation than of symbolic representation. Politicians must become collective representations, textured and tactile images that inspire devotion, stimulate communication, and trigger interaction. This is hardly a matter of ritual, though the experience of highly affecting scenes of fusion is ardently sought. It is a matter of controlling the image. It is to become a hero, to work the binaries while watching the boundaries. Pollution and purity are the aim, but partisanship must be avoided at all costs. Politics is performance, but political image cannot be seen as constructed. The media's new reflexivity is everywhere a danger. It threatens to undermine authenticity. Artificiality may be an attribution, but it often has the power to kill.

— 6 —

A PRESIDENTIAL PERFORMANCE, PANNED, OR OBAMA AS THE LAST ENLIGHTENMENT MAN*

This is a disheartening story about the evacuation of the public stage, the emptying-out of a hero, iconic dissolution. Maybe it can still (here's that word) *change?*

The midterm elections of 2010 were staggering for a president whose performance of politics had once looked virtuosic, a dramatic turn for a new American century. Two years earlier, upon Barack Obama's election, the left was delirious with triumph, the center embraced "hope," and conservatives, becalmed by impotence, were bewildered as they exited stage right.

But where candidate Obama's rhetoric thrummed with hope, progress, and civil salvation, in office, he seemed unable to inhabit and animate his presidential role. Starting with his inaugural address, Obama projected a newly sober style, designed not to excite but to mediate the great hopes he'd aroused.

The opening act of the passion play, "Obama in power," found our presidential protagonist speaking of doom and difficulty, only rarely reaching toward hope and glory. Time and time again, he spoke the long arc of history, emphasizing the slow pace of change and withdrawing to the Oval Office for technical deliberation. It wasn't a thrilling performance, and the media didn't fail to notice. Now, after only a short run, demoralized Democrats can only watch in shock as the public square fills with conservatives, cloaked in the costumes of founding fathers and crying "Tyranny!"

How could Obama have done such an extraordinary job of performing politics during the rehearsals of his long presidential campaign, but faltered so disastrously on the big stage? For Republicans,

* Composed in early December 2010.

the answer is simple: Americans can see right through Obama. They know he's been no more than an actor, an inexperienced politician and an incompetent administrator who looked the part, but could never really inhabit the role.

This partisan parsing is too easy, though. It takes reality for granted, as if facts and events can somehow be considered outside a cultural frame. My answer is different: we need to look at Obama's symbolic representation. Sometime after his inauguration, he lost his ability to symbolize for the left and the center of the citizen-audience. This dramaturgical disability created a symbolic vacuum and energized Americans on the right.

From mainstream cable to newspapers, partisan blogs and journalistic websites, report after report has diagrammed the president's failure to generate excitement. He's called distant, academic, disengaged, out of touch. This political actor's routine has fallen flat, and he's not connecting with his audience. Indeed, Democratic voter participation dropped drastically from 2008 to 2010. Conservatives were excited this time around, and their energy was contagious. Collective actors, like the Tea Party, emerged and captured the attention of conservatives and attentive independents. The audience for "Obama in power" seems to be dribbling away.

Worse, as Obama's poll numbers fall, he is still left with an array of problems, any one of which would be daunting enough. After promising to nurse markets back to health, and spending stupendous sums to do so, Obama still confronts high unemployment, economic stagnation, and a rapidly rising national deficit. After twelve months of toil on health reform, the results so far are nil, and conservative judges are beginning to intervene. Financial reform has gone virtually nowhere, negotiation with America's putative enemies appears to be at a standstill. Iran threatens, China rises, the earth warms, and oil still cripples America's Gulf Coast.

Oddly, none of this is to say that Obama has, in nuts and bolts terms, been an ineffective president; it's just that he's *seemed* to be. An effective and satisfying plotline would move us swiftly from initial antagonism to a tense standoff, then onward to climactic resolution, catharsis, and denouement (with a few thrilling twists and turns along the way). In the languid "Obama in power" play, we are, instead, mired in the muddled middle, without a clear end in sight. The president's supporters are anxious and unfulfilled, and the meaning they thought they had made by electing him is dissolving before their eyes. On the other side of the aisle, though, conservatives might give this performance rave reviews. Forget Broadway: the Tea Party is "symboling" on all four cultural cylinders, and the right is happily plotting its own Pennsylvania Avenue revival.

Three productions

In the days and weeks leading up to the November congressional election, three mass rallies unfolded on the sacred stretch of ground between the US Capitol building and the Lincoln Memorial. The first to take to the Mall was Glenn Beck, gathering the faithful with his "Restoring Honor" rally. On the 47th anniversary of the Reverend Dr Martin Luther King, Jr.'s iconic "I Have a Dream" speech, Beck, who's been described as America's most gifted conservative demagogue since New Deal opponent Father Coughlin, did what he does best. With 90,000 boisterous fans at his feet, Beck's inspirational public sermon, like his own character, was carved from antagonism. With us-versus-them (and them-versus-us) zeal, Beck rued the moral laxity of progressives, ranted about the sloth and indebtedness of this Democratic presidency, raved against foreignness, and denounced Obama as a socialist. He bellowed and prayed, lectured about God and family, and exhorted his audience to repent for its political sins. The greatest nation in the world, Beck believes, was founded by men who believed equally in God and the freedom of individuals to achieve, but it has been going downhill ever since. His takeaway message? Restore our honor. Take our country back (Lilla 2011).

In late October, Comedy Central's Jon Stewart, host of *The Daily Show*, and Stephen Colbert, host of the eponymous, tongue-in-cheek "conservative" spinoff *The Colbert Report*, inhabited the same sacred space. Their "Rally to Restore Sanity and/or Fear" brought together an estimated 200,000 quizzical, but intrigued, presumably liberal and politically frustrated fans. They weren't really sure why they had come, or even, by the end, what they had seen. For three hours, Stewart, Colbert, and an almost incomprehensible host of guest stars (from feminist professional wrestler Mick Foley, lauded for his reasonable nature, to Cat Stevens/Yusef Islam and Ozzy Osbourne singing a disjointed duet) reveled in an exercise in irony, not passion. Without mentioning the upcoming elections or denigrating conservatives, they pointed to "the country's twenty-four-hour political pundit perpetual panic conflictinator" and emphasized their distance from, not their connection to, politics. They implicitly left Obama and his party behind. Resignation and humor, not commitment or principle, created the unifying theme for this cosmopolitan gathering.

139

Sandwiched between these two revealing, massively publicized events was the "One Nation Working Together" rally. Left-leaning interest groups including the NAACP, the AFL-CIO, and the Sierra Club, with help from the National Teachers' Association, National Baptist Convention, Gay and Lesbian Task Force, and Communist Party USA amassed on the mall, but the rally was dispirited and badly attended. It had a sober tone, awkward and unpracticed performers, and a straggling audience. Whatever gusto speakers, sign-carriers, and listeners could muster went toward supporting progressive agenda items such as single payer and public health plans. Obama's name went conspicuously unmentioned; it was made clear that supporting liberal ideals was not to be conflated with support for the president himself.

In these vignettes, home viewers saw the character and performative strategies of the three principal "carrier groups" of American politics, c.2010. There was fervent outrage, transcendental passion, and energy on the right; ironic detachment and apolitical skepticism among moderate liberals; and righteous resentment and sagging spirits on the left.

And while it is true that the center of the political spectrum, an undecided or weakly affiliated group that amounts to no more than 20 percent of the electorate, decides American elections, the center is not active in the creation of political performance. Centrists are watchers, waiters, late deciders. What they saw in the 2008 election led them to, eventually, sign on with the Democrats, but over the subsequent two years, they either lost interest or moved to the right. An extraordinarily active government saw Obama push through major bills and initiate massive federal policy and agency restructuring, but the left reacted with resentment to the betrayal of its faith in the president's transformational promise. The right, on the other hand, reacted – overreacted – with fear and outrage. When Obama most needed his connection to the centrists who had effectively elected him, artful responses eluded him, his active base went AWOL, and the center deserted him for the right.

Becoming invisible

Although he is an activist president who has succeeded in the tasks of making novel law and policy, Obama is pushing himself and his party to the wings of the public stage – lead players, they're nearly invisible. Take the tale of the automotive bailout.

140

In the spring and summer of 2009, Obama fought Republican opposition and accusations of both socialism and profligacy to win Congressional action on the auto sector's financial crisis. Obama's aggressive moves included $50 billion in loans, the appointment of a Car Czar, and the retooling of General Motors' board, executive structure, and, indirectly, its marketing and production methods. After 18 months, the newly profitable GM staged a stock IPO that garnered $23 billion, at a stroke repaying a third of the government's investment and vastly raising the economic value of what remained. Hoopla and high-fives erupted in all corners, but applause for Obama's judgment, vision, and political courage seemed missing.

In the fervid run-up to the IPO, Warren Buffet, the revered financial guru, wrote a *New York Times* op-ed in which he extravagantly praised "Uncle Sam" for pulling the economy back from the brink of disaster. Buffet said it had been "pretty good government work," and intellectuals and pundits on the right attacked him for it. But while he mentioned a few officials still active in the Obama administration (Ben Bernanke and Tim Geitner among them), Buffet actually reserved his most fulsome praise for an unlikely hero: "Although I never voted for George W. Bush, I give him credit for leading."

Remarkably, the Democratic incumbent's name never came up. Obama had staked his reputation on a specific path of government intervention and the IPO seemed evidence that his plan had worked, but the world's most famous capitalist credited his reckless predecessor for the win. It was as if Obama, the character, had simply disappeared.

The last Enlightenment man

After his soaring victory, Obama had a magical aura. He had slain giants in the form of Hillary Clinton and John McCain, and he had broken the color barrier. But as revealed in his autobiographical and political writings, charisma was never the hallmark by which Obama presented himself. Instead, he viewed himself as a man of reason, both his own reason and others'. So leaving behind the dramaturgy of the extended campaign season, it was a reasonable man who took office.

Obama was a problem-solving policy wonk, not a conquering hero in a postmodern media age, but, perhaps, the last Enlightenment man. In an earnest tone, Obama eschewed metaphor and set to correcting the problems of a crumbling country. Building "a new foundation" was mentioned, but it seemed a speech writer's afterthought. Obama would get down and dirty, attacking real problems as discrete issues, solving puzzles one piece at a time. And that, as it turns out, may be practical, but it doesn't inspire public passion.

As the president deliberated, conservatives' allergic reaction to his election spawned the Tea Party, which only really entered the public imagination in the late summer Congressional break of 2009. "Bipartisan negotiations" had been stalled for months, and Tea Party activists suddenly seemed everywhere, launching vituperative, aggressive, sometimes even physical attacks in highly public and typically performative ways. Critics on the left, administration officials, and the mainstream media all failed to appreciate the dramatic effect of these polarizing Town Hall performances. Tea Party assaults were constructed as anti-democratic, angry, and irrational. But Obama's own reasonableness was already being questioned. The stunning upset victory of Scott Brown, chosen to fill "Uncle Teddy" Kennedy's seat on behalf of Massachusetts, demonstrated how the symbolic tide had turned. The Democrats' dream had become a nightmare.

The economy

An Enlightenment mind assesses the situation, gathers facts, and uses science to define strategy and solve the problem. It assumes that the democratic and universal access of reasonable minds to empirical fact will lead to consensus, harmony, and progress. Obama surveyed the economic crisis exploding in the first months of his presidency. He explained the extent of the problem, worse than he had imagined, to the public, but promised it would be solved with a comprehensive $750 billion stimulus package. Along the way, the economy would be saved, education would be reformed, science would be upgraded, state and local governments would be funded (and refunded), and the environment would be purified. There would be progress for everybody and everything. Best of all, the resulting economic prosperity would stanch the hemorrhaging national debt. Essentially, America would get a re-do.

These proposals were presented as rational and pragmatic, and Obama clearly expected the support of reasonable men and women on both sides of the political spectrum. Still, he worked to ensure moderate support; he offered almost 40 percent of the stimulus package in the form of tax cuts, just as conservatives had ardently hoped. But Republicans condemned the stimulus as liberal ideology and bad policy besides. Perhaps it was unreasonable, but the public swallowed hard and Democratic majorities approved the measures anyhow.

Reason be damned, they didn't seem to work. Obama had tied his fate to a progressive narrative promising economic amelioration. Yet, as the stimulus went into effect, hundreds of thousands of additional people lost their jobs, companies went bankrupt, and local governments failed. In early 2010, progress seemed possible, with month-by-month up-ticks in various indicators, but the economy cooled off quickly and fears of a double-dip recession looked all too real. As the narrative of change struggled to explain the reality of stagnation, conservatives stepped in with a narrative of moral laxity, indebtedness, and national decline. Obama now looked not only unreasonable, but profligate, a big spender casting caution (and cash) to the winds.

Health care

As a candidate, Obama denounced gaping inequities as threats to the American commonality and solidarity that underpin democratic citizenship. He singled out health care as a key differentiator: 50 million Americans were uninsured, he said. "We are not red states and blue states, but the United States," he said at whistle-stops; he would work with his reasonable colleagues across the aisle to fix the health system and restore solidarity.

Once he had passed the economic stimulus package, Obama devoted nearly the whole of his first year as president to shepherding health care reform through Congress. While they had succeeded, the left emerged from the long struggle disappointed, despondent, and facing a movement of outraged, defiant, and energized right-wing opponents. The last Enlightenment man had trusted in the reasonableness of the Senate's Republican negotiators, but he was played for a fool. Obama had unwittingly given the power to symbolize to Republican "colleagues" who were, instead, passionate antagonists. The rhetoric of bipartisanship, a myth of conciliation, trapped Obama and gave Republicans veto power over the president's narrative success. If he didn't offer enough concessions to win them over (and it was certain that nothing would ever constitute "enough"), Republicans could now frame Obama as "unreasonable." For its part, the left clung insistently to "the public option," attacking Obama for kowtowing to Republicans and accusing him of "selling out."

The final vote on health care was a scramble, but it passed. Moderate liberals called the achievement "historic," and *Time* magazine went so far as to suggest Obama was invincible: he had snatched victory from the jaws of defeat. It was a Pyrrhic victory. Left and right were further apart than ever, and the need for compromise in the bill had pushed the actuality of substantial financial benefits off for years. Health care would not be able to figure into a still hoped-for economic recovery; still a serious trophy, this particular victory would not come together with the stimulus bill to form any coherent legacy. An effective leader continued to look like he was treading water.

The great fear

In American democracy, the president is the well-spring of law-making and organized action. A latent, secondary function of the highest office is assuring Americans of social order. The president maintains poise and manages anxiety so that the center will hold. But as Obama's image deflated and he abandoned the public stage, as angry and aggressive new collective actors stepped into the spotlight, and the economy stubbornly resisted control, Americans became increasingly worried. Just three weeks after Obama muscled health care reform through Congress, a British Petroleum oil rig exploded in the Gulf of Mexico.

Millions of gushing gallons of oil – it was a performative test worthy of the great emperors, but in the face of the new crisis, Obama seemed inert. He issued terse statements, arriving on the scene a few days later, but put the Nobel laureate Secretary of the Interior in charge of communications with the oil company. The media narrative enumerated Americans' frustration. After nearly 90 days, the well was cauterized and the disastrous flow halted, but fishermen were out of work, tourism had disappeared, and the news was filled with pictures of pathetic, crude-covered animals. It seemed like "nobody was in charge." Once again, Obama had chosen the path of reason, technique, and conciliation, but it took the strength and money of a giant British oil conglomerate to tamp down both the problem and the public anger.

Charismatic calculus

When popular presidents face enduring opposition, they can draw on a store of charismatic power. And since charisma depends on aura, presidents evoke their symbolic powers in a "personal" way. John F. Kennedy seduced the public with witty press conferences, Reagan spoke over the heads of Congress to the common sense of the American public. Even bad boy Bill Clinton charmed the center as he suffered withering attacks from a morally outraged right. So it was

144

that Obama, in his first months in office, made rhetorical appeals, projecting charismatic charm and moving public opinion at critical points.

As his efforts stumbled, though, this last Enlightenment man lost his grip on charismatic power. Even when he did take to the bully pulpit, Obama seemed deflated. Words, so often cited as the key to his appeal, failed him.

It was not only performative contradictions that depleted Obama's charisma. Personal and idiosyncratic factors also figured into this charismatic calculus. Aside from a few conspicuous patricians, Obama was the first president not to be born and raised in small-town America. He was black. His charisma was more "urban cool" than "folksy Americana." He was great on a basketball court, but laughable at a bowling lane. He never fought in a war or looked comfortable wearing the American flag lapel-pin seemingly issued to all candidates. Clinton may have played a saxophone on a late night show, but he put it away in favor of country boy comments like "that dog won't hunt!" and trips to church with Hillary. Obama's "real American" Christianity was questioned when he and Michelle stayed in on Sundays. Even more telling, where Clinton had publicly committed himself and his party to law-and-order politics by funding 100,000 beat cops, Obama sided with Henry Louis Gates, a black, Ivy League professor against a white police officer, holding a painfully awkward "beer summit" at the White House to feign a reconciliation between the two. Every possible comparison fell to pieces; Obama was just wholly different from any president who had come before, and rumors of even more significant differences (secret Muslim! secret Kenyan! secret Socialist!) couldn't be put down.

Reason had gotten two years, and it looked like a failure as Americans headed to the polls in November 2010. "Wimpified" by the left as a gutless compromiser, Obama was vilified by the right as an out-of-touch radical liberal who would *not* compromise. In local and state elections, crucial centrist voters turned away from the party of the president and toward the energized, dramatically effective Republicans. Even more telling, key segments of Obama's 2008 electoral coalition stayed home, and the election was a symbolic slaughter, what Obama himself called, somehow perfectly, a "shellacking."

For Obama's faithful, hope remains. The show isn't over; there are still two years' worth of scenes to play out. Since political characters are made, not born, new personae can be made, unmade, and remade again. Further, in a highly connective and highly reactive culture, set pieces and plot devices shift quickly. With a skillful set of actors, and an increasingly attentive audience as the 2012 election looms, there is still the possibility for a happy ending. It's the long arc that will tell fairy tale from tragedy.

PERFORMING COUNTER-POWER: THE CIVIL RIGHTS MOVEMENT

Since their first institutionalizations in the seventeenth century, the universalistic promises made by the civil spheres of even formally democratic nation-states have been mocked by gross exclusions and inequalities. With the help of the bifurcating discourse of civil society, these "destructive intrusions" have entered into the very construction of the civil spheres, distorting its norms, institutions, and interactions. Yet, insofar as the universalizing ideals of the civil sphere have retained some independence and force, and they often have, there has always remained the possibility, in principle, for "civic repair."

In this chapter, I wish to suggest that the social movement against racial oppression that unfolded in America during the 1950s and 1960s should be regarded, among other things, as just such a movement of civil repair.[1] In social systems that include a partially independent civil sphere, every actor might be said to occupy a dual position. He or she is a subordinate or superordinate actor in a whole series of vertical hierarchies and, at the same time, a member of the putatively horizontal community of civil life. Even for a dominated and marginalized minority, duality allows the possibility, in principle, of struggles for empowerment and incorporation. One metaphorical way of putting this is to say the vertical relationships of the non-civil spheres – economic, political, religious, familial, ethnic, and scientific – are challenged by membership in a horizontal, civil "environment" that in principle surrounds them.

Duality is missed by social movement theories that focus exclusively on resistance to domination and the accumulation of scarce resources. It is not only the system of resource allocation that is crucial for stimulating social movements, but the system of normative integration, however that may be defined. If this integrative

147

environment is at least partly a civil one, conflicts against domination become more than simply "wars of position" whose outcomes depend on which side accumulates more power and more effectively threatens, and sometimes exercises, coercion and force.

Duality means that social movements also involve demands for recognition and for the expansion of civil solidarity that recognition implies. Achieving power remains vital, but it can only be gained by civil means. Organizations and resources remain crucial for social movements, but what they provide, in the first instance, is access to the "means of persuasion." In a social system that contains a substantial civil sphere, it is communicative institutions that provide leverage for affecting regulative institutions – the legal codes, the office obligations, and the electoral outcomes that effectively control the allocation of the state's money and force.

How do these theoretical considerations apply to the American civil rights movement? It goes without saying that there was little civil mediation in the vertical relationship between black subjects and white dominators in the American South. Because there was no civil mediation, blacks often felt compelled to try to seize power directly, through revolts and other kinds of violent confrontations. When they did so, their efforts were invariably put down with overwhelming force.

As the notion of duality suggests, however, even in the Southern states the vertical relationship of racial domination was surrounded by implicit, not yet articulated constraints that emanated from the horizontal civil sphere of the North. It was this duality – not the accumulation of instrumental power and the exercise of direct confrontation – that promised the possibility of justice for dominated Southern blacks. The challenge was how could this duality be activated? The challenge was to find a way to reach over the anti-civil domination of white southerners to the other, more civil side in the North.

Contemporary American historians and sociologists have tended to portray the civil rights movement as a power struggle between blacks and whites, emphasizing grassroots organizing and direct, face-to-face confrontations between organized masses of African-Americans and their immediate oppressors on the local scene (Morris 1984, 2007). As I see it, however, the civil rights movement must be understood in a different way. It aimed, first and foremost, at persuasion. Its goal was to achieve a more influential and hence more dominant position in the "national" civil sphere directed from the North. Only after achieving such civil influence could movement leaders, and the masses they were energized by, trigger regulatory intervention and accumulate power in the more traditional sense.

There were many so-called structural factors that made such communicative mobilization possible, and these have been the focus of various empirical studies. Theorists and empirical social scientists alike have identified such factors inside the black community as industrialization and urbanization; increasing secondary and higher education; the independence, wealth, and power of the black church; and the significance of black newspapers. What facilitated the emergence of the black counter-public in more contingent, historically specific terms was the massive African-American participation in World War II, which heightened expectations for full empowerment.

The force of structural factors outside the black community have also been frequently noted, most often the increasingly responsive legal order of the surrounding Northern civil sphere. This new legalism was itself stimulated, in no small part, by the growth of the National Association for the Advancement of Colored People (NAACP), which constituted a kind of "shadow" regulatory institution vis-à-vis white civil society. The NAACP initiated the US Supreme Court's *Brown v. Board of Education* decision, which made school desegregation illegal in 1954. I would add to these well-known structural factors the emergence of Northern news journalism as an independent profession with its own universalizing and increasingly idealistic ethics. Once Northern white news reporters entered the South to cover the nascent civil rights movement, they functioned as the eyes and ears of the Northern civil sphere. Without this organizational feature, there would have been no success for the black movement for civil rights.

Such structural-institutional factors – resources and capacities – did, indeed, make possible the emergence of the black movement for civil rights. But what was also crucially important – and what has remained virtually unstudied – was the process of communicative mobilization itself, the cultural-symbolic process that these structural factors facilitated but did not determine in a causal sense. By communicative mobilization, I refer to the ability of movement leaders to frame and reframe their complaints, their selves, and their groups in a manner that allowed their demands to leapfrog Southern officials and Southern media and to gain the serious, and eventually, the rapt attention of less racist whites in the Northern civil sphere.

From this perspective, the black leaders of the Southern movement, the "movement intellectuals" in Eyerman and Jamison's apt term, can be understood as enormously skillful mobilizers of communication.

In effect, they functioned as translators, reweaving the particular concerns of the black community by stitching them together with the tactics of Gandhian nonviolence, Christian narratives of sacrifice, and the democratic codes of the American civil sphere. What I am suggesting, in other words, is that in order to establish a relationship with the surrounding civil sphere, the black movement was compelled to engage not only in instrumental but in symbolic action. It aimed not only at accumulating and leveraging structural power but also at creating performative power, which depended on producing a compelling, arresting, and existentially and politically encompassing narrative. Its challenge was to create a "social drama" with which the Northern audience could identify and through which it could vicariously participate in the struggle against racial injustice in the South. In the late 1970s, James Bevel, one of the movement's most effective nonviolent leaders, retrospectively explained movement "action" in precisely these terms. "Every nonviolent movement is a dialogue between two forces," Bevel said, "and you have to develop a drama, [you have] to dramatize the dialogue to reveal the contradictions in the guys you're dialoguing with."

This dramaturgic element provides the elusive key to understanding how duality was triggered during those years of heightened mobilization and structural reform. How could white Northern civil society be there, in the South, yet not be there at the same time? When its physical presence was barely tangible, how could its moral presence eventually become so strongly felt? How could the North's representative officials be compelled to intervene in a society towards which they had earlier evinced so little interest and against which they had so often claimed to exercise so little control?

Duality was activated only because the Southern black movement created a successful social drama. Only such a symbolic vehicle could break through the structural constraints on the local scene. The symbolic power of the civil rights drama facilitated emotional and moral identification between Northern whites and Southern blacks. Eventually, these intertwined processes of emotional identification and symbolic extension created an historically unprecedented widening of civil solidarity, one that extended for the first time significantly beyond the color line. Insofar as solidarity expanded, Northern whites reacted with indignation and anger to the violation of black civil rights, especially to the anti-civil violence that white Southern officials often unleashed against the nonviolent protest activities of Southern blacks. This white outrage eventually affected Northern officials, who felt compelled finally to begin to repair the destructive intrusion of race into the Southern civil sphere, and eventually, and with much more ambivalence, in the Northern civil sphere as well.

Only through the concepts and methods of cultural sociology can we observe, and begin provisionally to explain, power processes of this kind. I am not suggesting that other approaches to power should be abandoned, but that conventional understandings of power – as consisting of resources and capacities – must be modified in a fundamental way. In the *Poetics*, Aristotle explained that drama compels identification and catharsis. Tragic drama, he wrote, excites in the audience pity and terror, and sympathy for the protagonists' plight. The progression of protagonist and antagonist eventually allows catharsis, the emotional working through that affirms not only the existence but the force of higher moral law. Of course, the civil rights movement was not scripted; it was a social movement, not a text. Nonetheless, the contingent, open-ended nature of its conflicts were symbolically mediated and textually informed. Life imitates art. In the dramas created by the civil rights movement, the black civil innocents, who were weak, were pitted against the white anti-civil antagonists, who were strong. The forces of civil good unexpectedly but persistently emerged triumphant. If such an outcome made the process ultimately more melodramatic than tragic, melodrama shares with tragedy an emphasis on suffering and the excitation of pity and terror.

Civil rights leaders became heroes only because they first were victims; they gained repeated triumphs only after repeated experiences of tragedy. As the movement gained experience, its organizers learned how to dramatically display their victim position more effectively. What they knew from the very beginning, however, was that Southern black protestors could redeem their suffering only if they maintained their civil dignity in the midst of defeat, if they refrained from anti-civil violence aggression, dishonesty, and deception. The protestors had to be viewed by the Northern audience as keeping faith with civil good in the face of anti-civil abuse and the temptations of despair.

The modern civil rights movement began with the Montgomery bus boycott in 1955–6, a drama that brought Martin Luther King into the spotlight and captured the attention of Northern communicative media and citizens. After Montgomery, King and his colleagues formed the Southern Christian Leadership Conference (SCLC). For the next four years, this strongly networked organization devoted itself to winning voting rights by launching campaigns to register and educate potential black voters. These campaigns were bound to fail.

They aimed at achieving regulatory intervention and political power directly in the South without first addressing communicative institutions and achieving influence in the North. Movement leaders learned the hard way that they would have to put first things first. They would have to mount a full dress, years-long social drama for the benefit of the civil audience in the North. Only if they succeeded in this communicative effort could they produce the regulatory intervention – first via voting, then via positive law and office regulation – that eventually would give them political power on the local scene.

The critical learning experience that changed leaders' minds was the sit-in campaign that black college students launched in 1960. As a result of this spectacularly successful movement, lunch counters were desegregated in Greensborough and Nashville and hundreds of other Southern cities. The most important effect of the sit-ins, however, was to introduce what came to be called "direct nonviolent action." With this new tactic, the civil rights movement's understanding of itself was permanently changed. Without ever explicitly acknowledging it, leaders discarded the Gandhian approach to nonviolence. For Gandhi and early movement leaders, nonviolence had been an end in itself; they believed that love and tolerance could alter the consciousness of the oppressor. After 1960, nonviolence became a tactic, a means to a dramaturgical end. Its function became not to efface the anti-civil violence of racist officials but rather to provoke it, allowing movement activists to draw attention to their own civil composure in turn.

The drama-producing status of direct nonviolent action became evident in the next year, in the "Freedom Rides" of 1961. For several weeks, the leaders of CORE (Congress for Racial Equality) and SNCC (Student Non-Violent Coordinating Committee) organized a "protest bus" to test laws outlawing discrimination in public transportation throughout the South. Every few days, the riders on this Freedom bus would be brutally beaten, sometimes nearly to the point of death, by the white vigilante posses that gathered to receive them in the bus stations of the deep South. This campaign did not succeed in making the South enforce its antidiscrimination laws. It did succeed, however, in providing for Northern whites an extraordinarily compelling melodrama about racial power, suffering, and heroic justice. This dramaturgical power was suggested by the fact the Freedom bus eventually came to be filled with more journalists and national guardsmen than movement activists, and in the end was trailed by many more carloads of the same.

The endgame of these serial civil dramas was to so deepen emotional identification and symbolic extension between Southern blacks and Northern whites that powerful Northern officials were compelled to undertake the very serious political costs of what came to be known as "the second Reconstruction." The 1963 Birmingham campaign marked the tipping point, after which the Northern civil sphere became so communicatively engorged that it did indeed transmogrify public feeling into regulative intervention.

The year before Birmingham, in 1962, the movement had suffered a disastrous political and symbolic defeat in Albany, Georgia. The black protest leaders learned from this experience. In their effort to penetrate the symbolic space of the Northern civil sphere, they vowed, in the future, to leave much less to chance. Until Birmingham, King and his organization had entered local civil rights contests rather haphazardly, leveraging the black hero's national prestige and the civil deference he commanded into dramatic power over an ongoing flow of events. After the Albany fiasco, protest leaders realized that, in order to frame white violence effectively, they would have to exert significantly more control over their own performance and, if possible, over their antagonists' as well.

The very choice of Birmingham as the target for this exercise in systematic provocation reveals the movement's heightened self-consciousness. Birmingham was picked, not because of its potential for progressive reform, but for the opposite reason. As a deeply reactionary city, its chief law enforcement officer, "Bull" Connor, had a serious problem containing his temper and maintaining self-control. Only if there were a clear and decisive space between civil good and anti-civil evil could the conflict in the street be translated into a symbolic contest, and only if it became such a symbolic context could the protest gain its intended effect. Agonism is essential to the plot of every successful performance.

In the days leading up to the campaign, the dramatic tension between protagonists and antagonists reached a fever pitch. Ralph Abernathy, King's principal assistant, promised "we're going to rock this town like it has never been rocked before." Bull Connor retorted that "blood would run in the streets" of Birmingham before he would allow such protests to proceed.

Providing an over-arching narrative for this imminent clash, King drew upon the book of Exodus, the iconic parable of the Jews' divinely inspired protest against oppression. The SCLC leader publicly vowed to lead demonstrations until "Pharaoh lets God's people go."

Despite elaborate preparation, however, the social drama initially failed to ignite, and the performance did not develop as planned. The demonstrations began on cue, and King went to jail. Yet Birmingham's black civil society did not rise up in solidarity and opposition, and the surrounding white civil sphere in the North became neither indignant nor immediately involved. Even King's "Letter from the Birmingham Jail," later accorded canonical status in American protest literature, failed to generate any significant response from the Northern media, much less from their audience.

The routine of daily marches, arrests, and nightly mass meetings continued, but the national reporters begin to drift away from Birmingham for lack of "news." It became increasingly difficult to mobilize support beyond the small core group of dedicated activists. The problem was that the sequence of demonstration, arrest, and mass meeting was, indeed, becoming routine. It would have to be disrupted by something "abnormal." An event would have to be staged that would have the performative power to create a breach in the ongoing social order.

After intensive discussion and self-doubt, movement leaders made the decision to allow Birmingham's school children to enter the fray. In the historical literature, the motivations and the repercussions of this decision are typically represented in quantitative and material terms, as making up for the falling numbers of adult participants. Much more significant, however, was the potential for altering the moral balance of the confrontation. Children would appear even more well-meaning, sincere, and innocent than the movement's nonviolent but powerful and determined adults, and this greater vulnerability would provide an even sharper contrast with the irrational, violent repression that the movement intended to provoke from Southern officials.

When the "children's crusade" began, and hundreds of young people were herded off everyday to jail, the drama did, in fact, sharply intensify. Attendance skyrocketed at the nightly mass meetings, and a sense of crisis was in the air. Birmingham was back on the front pages, and the local confrontation had succeeded in projecting itself into the symbolic space of the wider civil sphere. As the long-time local leader of Birmingham's freedom movement, Fred Shuttlesworth, proclaimed to the overflow crowd who showed up in his church the evening after the children were first jailed, "the whole world is watching Birmingham tonight."

It was the pressure created by this intensifying external scrutiny, not simply the material constraint of the city's jails being filled to overflowing, that managed to incite Birmingham's bad-tempered sheriff. Bull Connor finally unleashed the repressive violence that underlay white domination. Stepping outside the constraints of civil society, he resorted to physical force, turning fire hoses on the protestors, setting police dogs loose on them, and allowing his officers to use electric cattle prods. Because of his local power, the sheriff thought he could act with impunity. Yet, while he did succeed in gaining control of the immediate situation, he could not control the effect that this exercise of unbridled power would have on the civil audience at one remove. The sheriff ignored duality at his peril. Bull Connor won the physical battle but lost the symbolic war.

By engaging in public violence, these Southern white officials allowed themselves to become antagonists in a civil drama written and directed by the black protest movement. The melodrama presented Southern evil in an almost gothic way. Graphic reports of horrendous, lopsided physical confrontations between civil good and anti-civil evil were broadcast over television screens and splashed across front pages throughout the Northern civil sphere. Fiercely rushing water from high-pressure fire hoses swept little girls and boys dressed in their Sunday best hundreds of feet across Birmingham's downtown square. As they were pinned against a brick wall, the civil interpreters from the North transmitted the children's screams of terror and their pathetic efforts to shield themselves from the violent force. Growling German shepherds and their police handlers in dark sunglasses lunged forward into the youthful crowd. Northern journalists, both reporters and photographers, recorded the viciousness of the animals and the arrogant indolence of the men, and they captured the fright, helplessness, and righteous rage of their nonviolent victims. The emotional resonance these photos generated in the Northern civil sphere was palpable, and became only more profound with the passing of time. From being symbols that directed the viewer to an actual event, the photographs of the confrontation became icons, evocative embodiments of the fearful consequences of anti-civil force in and of themselves.

It is important not to forget that these media messages were representations, not literal transcriptions, of what transpired in Birmingham during these critical days. Even if the events seemed to "imprint" themselves on the minds of observers, they needed to be interpreted first. The struggle for interpretive control was waged just as fiercely as the struggle in the streets, and its outcome divided just as cleanly along local versus national lines. In their own representations, Birmingham's local media completely inverted the indignant interpretive frame provided by media in the North. For example, when the *Birmingham News* reported on the fire hosing of demonstrators, it presented a photograph of an elderly black woman strolling alongside a park, holding an umbrella to protect herself from the mist produced by the gushing fire hoses nearby. "Just another showery day for a Negro stroller," read the caption below the photo, offering the further observation that the woman "appears undisturbed by disturbances" from the riot nearby. Headlining statements by city officials, the local media broadcast the Birmingham mayor's condemnation of the "irresponsible and unthinking agitators" who had made "tools" of children and turned Birmingham's whites into "innocent victims."

For Northern communicative institutions and their audiences, however, the linkage of anti-civil violence to white, not black power proved much more persuasive. Portraying the black demonstrators as helpless victims at the mercy of vicious, inhuman force, these reports evoked feelings of pity and terror. For the audience in the surrounding Northern civil sphere, in other words, the narrative of tragic melodrama was firmly in place. Northern whites' identification with the victims triggered feelings of civic outrage and moved them to symbolic protest. Angry phone calls were made to Congressional representatives, indignant letters fired off to the editorial pages of newspapers and magazines. In the *Washington Post*, an angry citizen from Forest Heights, Maryland, poured out her personal feelings of outrage and shame. Her simple and heartfelt letter provides an eloquent expression of the indignation she evidently shared with many other white Americans in the North. From the perspective presented here, it is of particular interest that she explains her outrage as motivated by her identification with the black protestors, to whom she effortlessly extends her own ethical and civic principles.

> Now I've seen everything. The news photographer who took the picture of a police dog lunging at a human being has shown us in unmistakable terms how low we have sunk and will surely have awakened a feeling of shame in all who have seen that picture, who have any notion of human dignity. This man being lunged at was not a criminal being tracked down to prevent his murdering other men; he was, and is, a man. If he can have a beast deliberately urged to lunge at him, then so can any man, woman or child in the United States. I don't wish to have a beast deliberately urged to lunge at me or my children and therefore I don't wish to have beasts lunging at the citizens of Birmingham or any other place. If the United States doesn't stand for some average decent level of human dignity, what does it stand for?

The experience of moral outrage was so widely shared in the days after Birmingham that it set the stage for regulatory intervention and fundamental civil repair. Martin Luther King declared that "the hour has come for the Federal Government to take a forthright stand on segregation in the United States," and President Kennedy responded by assuring the public that he was "closely monitoring events." The President sent Burke Marshall, the head of the Justice Department's Civil Rights Division, down to Birmingham. With Marshall's prodding, settlement negotiations were begun. In the eye of the hurricane of communicative mobilization, white and black leaders for the first time spoke cooperatively face to face. As the local negotiations continued, high officers from the surrounding civil sphere – President Kennedy and his cabinet secretaries – placed calls to strategically placed local businessmen and to corporate executives outside the South who could exercise leverage on the local elite. These interventions eventually produced a pact detailing goals and timetables for ending Birmingham's economic segregation.

While these progressive local reforms certainly deserve praise, it was to the community beyond the city, indeed beyond the region, that the Birmingham demonstrations were aimed. It was their success in mobilizing the North's more democratic and, potentially at least, much more powerful civil sphere that made Birmingham into "Birmingham," a watershed in the history of the racial movement for civil justice in the United States. "Birmingham" would enter into the collective conscience of American society more powerfully and more indelibly than any other single event in the history of the movement for civil rights. In the days immediately following the Birmingham settlement, a weary President Kennedy summed up this new world of public opinion in a complaint to his Majority Leader in the Senate: "I mean, it's just in everything. I mean, this has become everything." Three months later, a White House official remarked to the Associated Press, "This hasn't been the same kind of world since May." In 1966, Bobby Kennedy recalled the period during an interview. "Everybody looks back on it and thinks that everybody was aroused about this for the last three years," Bobby remarked. "But what aroused people generally in the country and aroused the press," he insisted, "was the Birmingham riots in May of 1963."

This dramatic deepening of Northern white identification with protesting Southern blacks had political effect. The profound arousal of civil consciousness, which "Birmingham" simultaneously triggered and reflected, pushed the civil sphere's elected representatives in the direction of regulatory reform. That summer, the Kennedy administration drew up far-reaching legislation, submitted to Congress as "The Civil Rights Act of 1963." With this action, the symbolic space of communicative mobilization became transformed into the details of law and sanction that would eventually allow massive regulatory intervention in the Southern states.

It is a matter of historical debate whether this civil rights legislation could have been passed without Kennedy's martyrdom in November, 1963, and the accession to the presidency of Lyndon Johnson, the former Senate Majority Leader who was a master of the legislative craft. That the very introduction of this far-reaching legislation represented a fundamental fork in the road, however, is beyond dispute. Johnson organized passage of the first major civil rights legislation in 1964. In March of 1965 Martin Luther King led the extraordinary "March on Selma," whose dialectic of tragedy and triumph triggered passage of the second civil rights bill, the "Voting Rights Act of 1965." Yet, despite the momentous events that followed in the two years after Birmingham, they can be properly understood only if they are seen as iteration, as amplifying and filling in the symbolic and institutional framework that had become crystallized by the early summer of 1963. What began as counter-performance became a powerful core narrative for a new post-racist American way of life.

— 8 —

PERFORMING TERROR ON
SEPTEMBER 11

To understand the sociological processes that created "September 11" (hereafter also referred to as "9/11") and what transpired politically, morally, and humanly during that tragic time and its aftermath, and also to understand how to prevent a tragic eternal return, we must reflect on the theoretical presuppositions that underlie our empirical perceptions. We need to theorize terrorism differently, thinking of its violence not only in physical and instrumental terms but also as a particularly gruesome kind of symbolic action in a complex performative field. If we do, we will understand, as well, how the American response, while initially thwarting its nihilistic intention, established a cycle of performance and counter-performance that continues to structure the cultural pragmatics of national and international politics today.

Terrorism as (post)political

Terrorism can be understood as a form of political action, one of a very specific type. It is distinguished first by the sustained violence of its principal methods, in contrast to a politics that relies primarily on organization and communication or one that rests, like those of most nation-states in their foreign relations, on the periodic but discrete application of coercion and force. Terrorism is distinguished, second, by the isolation of its practitioners, in contrast not only to the communal character of mass organizations but also even to the vanguard politics of Bolshevism and Fascism, which seek to establish thick network relations with groups whose ideology they can mold and whose solidarity they can claim.

Finally, terrorism is distinguished by the relative diffuseness of its ideology. Drunk on grandiose delusions of the millennium and on visions that make worldly success impossible in realistic terms, terrorist ideology does not spell out political steps to achieve its ideological aims. Because of this yawning gap between ideals and realities, the working ideology of terrorism focuses almost exclusively on tactics and rather little on broader strategy. Another way of putting this is to say that terrorism focuses on deeds more than words.

These disjunctions reflect the institutional failures that breed a politics of terror, which flourishes only in social situations where *politics*, in the classical sense of the term (Crick 1962), has not been allowed free play. In much of the contemporary Arab-Islamic world, national and regional institutions have flattened drastically and have narrowed the dynamics of political will-formation. Discursive, democratic, and humane forms of political expression have frequently become impossible.

Hobsbawm (1959) once called banditry and peasant riots *prepolitical* – to differentiate them from the militant and sometimes violent revolutionary politics that characterized what he took to be the normal, class-war politics of his day. Contemporary terrorism might be called *postpolitical*. It reflects the end of political possibility. In this sense, 9/11 expresses, and displaces, the bitterness of an Arab nationalism whose promises of state-building, economic development, and full citizenship lay in tatters throughout the North African and Middle Eastern world. Terrorism is post – rather than pre – political in another sense as well. Its profound experience of political impotence is expressed not merely in cultural or metaphysical terms but in a hungry will to power and a manifest ambition to rebuild the umma, a great Arab-Muslim state.

Rather than defeating its opponents through political struggle, terrorism seeks to draw blood. Its tactics deliver maiming and death; they serve a strategy of inflicting humiliation, chaos, and reciprocal despair. Beyond these primordial ambitions lie three destabilizing aims. These flow in increasingly powerful ripples from the initial drawing of blood:

1 To create *political* instability by murdering key leaders and overwhelming the immediate political process;
2 To achieve *social* instability by disrupting networks of exchange and by sowing such fear that distrust becomes normal and chaos ensues; and
3 To create *moral* instability by inducing authorities to respond to these political and social threats with repressive actions that will

160

delegitimate key institutions in their own society. Such repression may be domestic or foreign, and it is less a matter of actual engagement in violent and suppressive actions than of how these actions are framed.

The postpolitical and the civil

Does terrorist action typically succeed in these aims? This depends on context. Success is a direct function of the authoritarian nature of the regime against which terrorism takes aim. Postpolitical tactics are much less likely to succeed in societies that allow politics to mediate power, and this is particularly the case in legitimate, deeply rooted democratic regimes. Postpolitical action certainly does produce significant, sometimes world-historical, and almost always existentially horrendous effects. In societies that have more developed civil spheres, however, such effects are not nearly as transformative as their initiators had hoped.

The seemingly demonic ferocity of terrorists, their ruthless willingness to sacrifice the lives of others and their own, draws blood and often creates social and political chaos and instability. The slaughterhouse of World War I began with terrorist assassination. Anarchist and syndicalist violence in late nineteenth-century America marked new phases of anti-capitalist agitation. The activities of the Red Brigades, Baader-Meinhof gang, and Weathermen in the late 1960s and early 1970s sent shock waves of terror throughout significant parts of the Italian, German, and American populations, respectively. White militia groups wreaked terrible havoc in Oklahoma City and elsewhere in the 1990s.

Still, none of these terrorist waves, so effective in narrowly postpolitical terms, succeeded in translating their immediate tactical "achievements" into the broader strategic aims of moral delegitimation and regime change. The reason is clear: in civil societies, to eschew the tactic of politics is to be blinded in broader strategic terms. In democratic societies, in order to achieve broad effects political actors must orient their tactics to address the moral frameworks that compel the larger population. Yet, this is precisely what terrorism cannot do. It is hardly surprising then that, on 9/11, the terrorists who attacked the Twin Towers produced the opposite effect than the one they had in mind.

This broad sociological claim about the ineffectiveness of terrorism in a civil society might be countered by pointing to earlier terrorist movements, from the Irish and South African to the Zionist and

Palestinian, which seemly did achieve institutional success. It would take a different and more comparative essay to respond fully to such counter-claims. Here I focus only on one terrorist act. Still, we might consider the Palestinian Liberation Organization (PLO) as one brief case in point. While it first came to world attention through acts of terror, the PLO began to achieve its aims of territory and quasi-statehood only later, during the years of the first *Intifadeh* (uprising).

This youth-centered, stone-throwing protest movement against Israeli occupation engaged not in murderous, postpolitical terrorism but in highly effective political dramaturgy (Liebes 1992a, 1992b). The young Palestinian "Davids" created sympathy, not only outside Israel but also within it, for their struggle against the Israeli military "Goliaths." What eventually followed was an occasionally enthusiastic but more often resigned acceptance of the Palestinians' national ambition among influential segments of the Israeli public that had been steadfast in their opposition to the PLO during its terrorist days. By contrast, the second *Intifadeh*, which began after the breakdown of peace talks in 2000, made terrorism more central and had much less successful political effects (Alexander and Dromi 2011; Shoshan 2010).

A dramaturgical framework of politics

Despite the critical importance of politics, the difficulty that terrorism has in gaining success cannot be explained in purely instrumental terms. Success and failure in politics is not a game. It neither responds simply to available resources nor is guided exclusively by rational choice. Terrorism has a moral reference, and its understanding demands a cultural-sociological frame.

We must consider terrorism as a form not only of political but also of symbolic action. Terrorism is a particular kind of political performance. It draws blood – literally and figuratively – making use of its victims' vital fluids to throw a striking and awful painting upon the canvas of social life. It aims not only to kill but, in and through killing, also to gesture in a dramatic way. In Austinian (1957) terms, terrorism is an illocutionary force that aims for perlocutionary effect.

Performative actions have both a manifest and a latent symbolic reference. Their explicit messages take shape against background structures of immanent meaning. Social performances, like theatrical ones, symbolize particular meanings only because they can assume more general, taken-for-granted meaning structures within which their performances are staged. Performances select among,

162

reorganize, and make present themes that are implicit in the immediate surround of social life – though these are absent in a literal sense. Reconfiguring the signifieds of background signifiers, performances evoke a new set of more action-specific signifiers in turn.

It is these signifiers that compose a performance's *script*. Social performance cannot be reduced to background culture. Performance is initiated because actors have particular, contingent goals. Scripts are representations, but the reverse is not equally true: background representations are not themselves scripts. It is not "culture" that creates scripts, but pragmatic efforts to project particular cultural meanings in pursuit of practical goals.

Scripts narrate and choreograph conflicts among the sacred, profane, and mundane. An effectively scripted narrative defines compelling protagonists and frightening antagonists and pushes them through a series of emotionally laden, twisting-and-turning encounters. Such agonistic action constitutes a *plot*. Through plotted encounters, social dramas create emotional and moral effects. Their audiences may experience excitement and joy if the plots are romances or comedies, or pity and suffering if they are melodramas or tragedies. If the scripted narrative is effective and if the performance of the plot is powerful, the audience experiences catharsis, which allows new moral judgments to form and new lines of social action to be undertaken in turn.

The scripts of social dramas initially are imagined by would-be authors and agents. They might be written before a performance begins, but they also may be emergent, crystallizing only as the drama unfolds. Here, the dramas that scripts are meant to inspire aim at *audiences* composed of the publics of complex civil societies. The *actors* in these social dramas may be institutional authorities or rebels, activists or couch potatoes, political leaders or foot soldiers in social movements, or the imagined publics of engaged citizens themselves. The motivations and patterns of such actors are affected deeply, though are not controlled, by *directors*. In social dramas, these are the organizers, ideologists, and leaders of collective action (Eyerman and Jamison 1991).

Social-dramatic action needs to be coherently organized, it needs a *mise-en-scène*, literally, putting into the scene. Dramatic enactment also requires control over the means of symbolic production, which suggests a stage, a setting, and certain elementary theatrical props. For social dramas, control over such means points to the need to create platforms for performance in the public imagination and, eventually, to create access to such media of transmission as television, cinema, newspapers, radio, and the Internet.

The elements of performative success and failure

When theatrical dramas are successful, there emerges a kind of fusion between these diverse elements of performance, a coming together of background meaning, actors, props, scripts, direction, and audience. Actors seem really to be their role. Their performances are experienced as convincing, as authentic. Audiences, sometimes literally but always figuratively, forget for the moment that they are in a theater or movie house. The performance has achieved verisimilitude, the aesthetic quality of seeming to be real.

If such triumphant fusion is not easy to produce in the theater, in social performance it is that much more difficult to effect. In small societies with more simplified and integrated social organization, the social-dramatic task is less challenging than in more complex and less integrated ones. Indeed, the frequency with which performative fusion is achieved marks the centrality and effectiveness of ritual in earlier societies. Even in complex societies, however, fusion is still possible, and it frequently is achieved in settings where the elements of performances can be controlled carefully: between the faithful and their priest, rabbi, or mullah; between children and their mothers and fathers; between patients and their doctors and therapists; between motivated employees and inspiring managers; between partisan audiences and artful orators (Grams 2010).

The more complex the society, however, the more often social performances fail to come together in convincing, seemingly authentic ways. The more that institutional and cultural resources become differentiated from one another – the more that political and ideological pluralism allows conflict – the more common performative failure becomes. In complex societies, full-throated social rituals are few and far between.

Long before postmodern philosophers declared the end of metanarratives, the metaphysical logic that established the *telos* of performances in traditional societies began to disappear. As societies become more complex and cultures less metaphysical, the elements of social performance become contingent and more difficult to coordinate and control. Action becomes open-ended, and everything can go awry. Rather than being sympathetically infused with teleological prejudice, social dramas become endemically unconvincing. Actors often seem inauthentic and manipulated, as if they are puppets and not autonomous individuals. Modern audiences tend to see power at work and not to see meaning. They attribute to would-be actors instrumental, not idealistic, motivations.

Performances may fail if any of the elements that compose them are insufficiently realized, or if the relation among these elements is not articulated in a coherent or forceful way. If there is not access to the means of symbolic production, for example, the effectiveness of the other elements goes for naught. Such failure to gain access to contemporary media might be the product of social distance, powerlessness, poverty, or of the unconvincing and unpopular dramatic content of the performance itself.

Even if productions are projected fully onto the public stage, they will fail if the roles and institutions mediating audience interpretation do so in a critical manner. Such interpretive criticism has the effect of separating dramatic intention from dramatic reception. It alienates actors from audience, de-fusing rather than re-fusing the elements of performance. In complex societies, critics, intellectuals, social authorities, and peer groups continuously comment upon the social-dramatic stream, as do the professional journalists who wish to appear merely factually to report upon it. But even if access is gained and if performances are interpreted positively, the thoroughgoing success of a performance can be thwarted if audiences are fragmented. Cultural antagonisms and/or social cleavages can create polarized and conflicting interpretive communities. A drama that is utterly convincing for one audience-public might seem artificial to another. Insofar as group understandings of critical performances diverge, their existential and moral realities become irreconcilable.

Performative failures allow the law of unintended consequences to enter into the cultural sphere. Social dramas produce unintended interpretations; they become performative contradictions in the philosophical sense. Ambiguity replaces clarity. There is a doubleness of text. For the social dramas of complex societies, there seems always to be an absent audience alongside the putative visible one that performers themselves have in mind. The absent audience is likely to understand the performance in a manner that belies its script and the actors' and director's intentions. In this way, the ultimate meaning of a performance is delayed. It is deferred beyond a drama's immediate reception to the audiences waiting "off stage." In complex societies, then, interpretation is marked by *différance* (Derrida 1978).

The performative contradictions of East versus West

In the face of conservative claims about the clash of civilizations, it seems important to begin by emphasizing that, while there are distinctive differences between the great monotheistic religions of the East and West, in broad comparative terms they share the same general symbolic orders to a remarkable degree (see also Alexander 2001; Lapidus 1987; Mirsepassi 2000; Udovitch 1987).

Judaic-Christian, and Islamic religious traditions, which in some significant part form the backdrop for their intercivilizational dynamics, are dualistic and Manichean. They are relatively "this-worldly" and "ascetic" in Weber's (1978) terms, and they contain powerful egalitarian strains. Both have legitimated not only heterodox but also revolutionary movements. Finally, and most tellingly for the present case, each has developed powerful religious legitimation for just, or holy, wars. Drawing from sacred narratives of judgment, each tradition has produced ethical prophecies that legitimate violent means for holy ends, prophecies that culminate in apocalyptic visions of the pathway to paradise.

> Prophetic religion . . . assumes the exclusiveness of a universal god and the moral depravity of unbelievers who are his adversaries and whose untroubled existence arouses his righteous indignation . . . The precursor and probable model for this was the promise of the Hebrew god to his people, as understood and reinterpreted by Muhammad . . . The ancient wars of the Israelite confederacy, waged under the leadership of various saviors operating under the authority Yahweh, were regarded by the tradition as holy wars. This concept of a holy war, i.e., a war in the name of a god, for the special purpose of avenging a sacrilege, which entailed putting the enemy under the ban and destroying him and all his belongings completely, is not unknown in Antiquity, particularly among the Greeks. But what was distinctive about the Hebraic concept is that the people of Yahweh, as his special community, demonstrated and exemplified their god's prestige against their foes. Consequently, when Yahweh became a universal god, Hebrew prophecy and the religion of the Psalmists created a new religious interpretation. The possession of the Promised Land, previously foretold, was supplanted by the farther-reaching promise of the elevation of Israel, as the people of Yahweh, above other nations. In the future all nations would be compelled to serve Yahweh and to lie at the feet of Israel. On this model Muhammad constructed the commandment of the holy war involving the subjugation of the unbelievers to political authority and economic domination of the faithful . . . The religion of the medieval Christian orders of celibate knights, particularly the Templars . . . were first called into being during the Crusades against Islam and . . . corresponded to the Islamic warrior orders. (Weber 1978: 473–5)

The dichotomies informing the complementary Eastern and Western narratives of salvation and damnation can be sketched out

166

Table 8.1 Binary options

Sacred/Friend	Profane/Enemy
Peaceful	Violent
Cooperative	Antagonistic
Honest	Deceitful
Equal	Dominating
Rational	Irrational
Solidarity	Fractious
Ethical	Instrumental
Honorable	Corrupt
Faithful	Cynical

in this very rough way (Table 8.1). If the same semiotic code supplies the signifiers for the sacred political actions in both religious and civilizational traditions, why do groups representing these civilizations stand today in such dangerous conflict? The reason is that, mediated through a series of historical developments, the signifieds of these signifiers have become strikingly, even fatefully, different. The Christian Crusades, the geopolitics of the Mogul and Ottoman Empires, the military triumphs of European empire – through such historical developments as these, the shared signifiers of the great monotheistic religions became connected with concrete signifieds that conveyed not their mutual understanding of the sacred and profane but extraordinary cultural difference and social antagonism. Over the long course of historical time, and with tragic and sometimes terrifying consequences, there gradually emerged the pronounced tendency for the Islamic, Jewish, and Christian religio-political civilizations to embody evil for each other. What has developed is a self-reinforcing system of cultural-cum-social polarization, in which the sacralizing social dramas of one side have been the polluting dramas of the other.

From the mid-twentieth century, this system of performative contradiction has been fueled by such proximate social and political developments as Israeli statehood; the failure of Pan-Arabism and economic modernization in the regions of the Islamic crescent; the increasing relative and often absolute impoverishment of what once was called the third world; the globalization of capital markets and the undermining of national sovereignty; the rise of feminist movements; American displacement of France and Britain as the preeminent capitalist and military power; and the end of the bipolar world and the emergence of America's asymmetrical military, cultural, and economic position.

At every point, these economic and political developments were mediated, channeled, and crystallized by the background codes and narratives that polarized the East and West as cultural-political regions. The religious orientations that Islamic East and the Judeo-Christian West share in the most general comparative terms were so refracted by social history that mutual misunderstanding became the norm. Indeed, what has remained constant through the twists and turns of contingent events is the polarizing cultural logic that forms a background to them. The social performances of one side are misperceived by audiences on the other. Even when Western actors and roles are scripted and played as sincere protagonists, they pass fluidly, artfully, and authentically into the position of antagonists in the scripts that emerge from the perceptions of the "Eastern" side. At the same time, when Islamic scripts portray Eastern actors as protagonists in leading roles, they are easily reinterpreted as antagonistic "others" in the eyes of Western audiences.

There is no better illustration of this performative contradiction than the *jihad*. Created as a violent means for religious-cum-political purification within medieval Islam (Black 2001), the *jihad* was applied to Western occupiers in a later historical time (Kepel 2002). For its Islamic practitioners and key sections of Islamic audiences, this modern *jihad* is viewed as a sacred and highly demanding performance of holy war. For its non-Islamic victims and audience, the performance of *jihad* is interpreted in precisely the opposite manner, as an authentic demonstration of the polluted and demonic qualities of Islam itself.

Highly consequential emplotments of this tragic contrapuntal culture structure emerged from American performances in Afghanistan in the 1980s and the Gulf War and its aftermath in the 1990s. The first Afghan war, despite its apparent triumph for the anti-communist West, marked a failed performance, for it unintentionally produced an anti-Western understanding in a significant segment of its audience. Having helped Islamic insurgents dislodge the Soviet occupation of Afghanistan, a defeat that significantly contributed to the larger project of destabilizing the Communist "evil empire," the United States declared victory and withdrew. This triumphal exit was interpreted as typical Western indifference by the national and religious formations that had framed the anti-Soviet war from their own, radically different point of view. This construction of Jewish-Christian-American infidelity is what generated the first wave of organized anti-American *jihad*, a vicious and determined counter-performance.

168

The interpretation of the Gulf War and its aftermath followed a similar pattern. Presented to Western audiences as a virtuous war of liberation, it served merely to confirm Western deceit and aggression to groups of radical Islamic nationalists. The post-war United Nations (UN) treaty, which allowed Iraq continued sovereignty while sharply curtailing its economic and military freedom, was presented at the time of the war's conclusion as reasonably motivated and humane in its concerns. During the course of the 1990s, however, the treaty provisions – and its steadfast and aggressive American and British guarantors – came to be regarded, first by radical Islamic groups in the region and subsequently by many humanitarian agencies and critical intellectuals around the world, as selfish, militaristic, and even orientalist. Once again, the unintended consequences of performative action had intensified the polarizing understandings of earlier misinterpretations. These audience reactions inspired Islamic radicals to engage in new and even more destructive counter-performances in turn.

> Why are we fighting and opposing you? The answer is very simple . . . Because you attacked us and continue to attacks us . . . You attacked us in Palestine . . . which has sunk under military occupation for more than 80 years . . . overflowing with oppression, tyranny, crimes, killing, expulsion, destruction and devastation . . . The blood pouring out of Palestine must be . . . revenged. [And] you have starved the Muslims of Iraq, where children die every day. It is a wonder that more than 1.5 million Iraqi children have died as a result of your sanctions, and you did not show concern . . . It is commanded by our religion and intellect that the oppressed have a right to return the aggression. Do not await anything from us but Jihad. (bin Laden 2002a)
>
> We kill the kings of the infidels, kings of the crusades, and civilian infidels in exchange for those of our children they kill . . . Our goal is for our nation to unite in the face of the Christian crusade. This is the fiercest battle. Muslims have never faced anything bigger than this. Bush said in his own words: "crusade" . . . This is a recurring war. The original crusade brought Richard [the Lionhearted] from Britain, Louis from France, and Barbarus from Germany. Today the crusading countries rushed as soon as Bush raised the cross. They accepted the rule of the cross. (bin Laden 2002b)

These tragic misperformances recall another war-ending misinterpretation that became, equally unwittingly, a war-starting one. When the triumphant Allies wrote the Treaty of Versailles after World War I, their strategic aim was to secure a long-term international peace. But the treaty negotiations, and the final document, were also scripts that allowed leaders to project performances to their French, American, and British audiences back home. Not surprisingly, German audiences read these performances in a very different manner. Eventually, an immensely talented but deeply malevolent Austrian political actor wrote a new script for holy war and soon after assumed a position to direct Germany's actual performance of it.

Initial success: bin Laden assembles the performative elements of terror

Osama bin Laden was another world-historical actor who would lead another "people" in another anti-Western counter-performance at another time.

> We – with God's help – call on every Muslim who believes in God and wishes to be rewarded to comply with God's order to kill the Americans and plunder their money wherever and whenever they find it. We also call on Muslim *ulema*, leaders, youths, and soldiers to launch the raid on Satan's US troops and the devil's supporters allying with them, and to displace those who are behind them so that they may learn a lesson. The ruling to kill the Americans and their allies – civilians and military – is an individual duty for every Muslim who can do it in any country in which it is possible to do it, in order to liberate the al Aqsa Mosque [in Jerusalem] and the Holy Mosque [in Mecca] from their grip, and in order for their armies to move out of all the lands of Islam, defeated and unable to threaten any Muslim. (1997 CNN interview, excerpts taken from "*Osama bin Laden v. the U.S*: Edicts and Statements," www.pbs.org/frontline, quoted in Bernstein 2002: 90)

Like that other infamous but highly effective demagogue before him, bin Laden responded to the social despair and the moldering anger that marked significant segments of his home audience – in this case an Arab-Islamic, not a German, one. Activist in the anti-Soviet holy war and embittered and impotent observer of the Western occupation of Saudi Arabia during and after the Gulf War, bin Laden proved himself to be enormously effective in staging the next phase of the contrapuntal performance cycle of East versus West. He imagined how a new kind of performance could be staged in the conditions of today. His innovation was to turn terrorism into mass murder and to place this counter-performance on the world stage. Bin Laden not only imagined himself as the protagonist of a massively organized and globally televised *jihad*, but he also had the awful artfulness and the personal resources to actually place himself in the center of the real thing.

Because bin Laden was rich and well connected, he possessed the resources to hire "actors" for a vastly larger terrorist organization than ever had been put together before, and he also had the networks to find possible actors and to interview them before allowing them to join his production teams. But more than resources were involved. Bin Laden was charismatic and creative. He had a real feeling for the story line, the traditional Islamist agonistic that plotted virtuous al-Qaeda heroes fighting for their sacred honor against villainous Americans with money in their hearts and blood on their hands. This cunning director established secret training camps that allowed backstage rehearsals for the public performances to come. In these protected spaces, fresh recruits were coached on how they could assume the parts assigned to them faithfully and convincingly in the al-Qaeda script. When the new "method" could be assumed with utter authenticity, the actor-terrorists were released into "perform-ance teams," which secretly prepared for the full-dress production of martyrdom in Western lands.

> Bin Laden organized a network of about a dozen different training camps . . . Each *mujahid*, or holy warrior, was given a code name so that even his fellow recruits generally did not know his real name . . . The training . . . was accompanied by steady infusions of Islamic fervor, in the form of Koran study, movies, lectures, and pamphlets. There was great stress on the glory of giving one's life for Allah, and the two greatest prohibitions [were] called "love of the world" and "hatred of death." A key slogan was "In time of war there is no death." (Bernstein 2002: 86)

"One of the pieces missing in the reconstruction of the September 11 plot," Bernstein writes (Bernstein 2002: 145), "is the training in hijackings while they were in the United States." Did the terror-performers have "at their disposal mock-ups of passenger aircraft interiors where they could have gone through dress rehearsals?" While "it is possible, that they dispensed with such rehearsals, and simply made their plans on the basis of what they knew of the interi-ors of Boeing 767s from having been passengers on them," Bernstein suggests it "would seem more likely that the hijackers would have preferred to do some serious practice."

The terrorists did have a sheet of final instructions, evidently pre-pared by Mohammed Atta, about how to prepare themselves just before the performance began. The night before, they were to shave their bodies of excess hair and to read *Al Tawba* and *Anfal*, the war chapters in the Koran. The goal was to control the inner self so that it would not interfere with their performative role.

> Remind your soul to listen and obey . . . purify, convince it, make it understand, and incite it . . . and do not fight among yourselves or else

you will fail. And be patient, for God is with the patient. When the confrontation begins, strike like champions who do not want to go back to this world. Shout "Allah'u Akbar" because this strikes fear in the hearts of the nonbelievers. (Bernstein 2002: 173)

But perhaps what most distinguished bin Laden was his ability to command the means of symbolic production. He needed a world-wide stage and means for murder on a scale far larger, and more dramaturgically compelling, than he had been able to acquire before. His demonic genius was to teach his would-be martyrs yet another role – that of student-visitors to America who were eager to learn to fly the big planes. Once the actor-terrorists possessed this skill, they could commandeer passenger jets that already were inside the American staging area. With these props, the martyr-terrorists could attack and try to destroy the symbols of polluted power that were central to the emotional dynamics of their script. If they were fortunate, they also could kill thousands of Americans, and other Westerners, outside the passenger plane. If this occurred, then the bin Laden performance of *jihad* would possess the widest possible public stage.

As the world learned at 9:03 EDT on September 11, 2001, bin Laden's performance of mass terror unfolded with barely a hitch. It created a shocking narrative of gothic horror that unfolded, in agonizing and simultaneous detail, before an audience of hundreds of millions. The terrorist-martyr-actors succeeded in destroying polluted icons of modern American capitalism, the Twin Towers, which evocatively symbolized their atheistic Western enemy. The terrorist performances created not only unprecedented physical destruction and loss of life but also moral humiliation and emotional despair, and they captured the world's media attention for days on end.

In purely sociological terms – which for the sake of analysis must bracket normative considerations – this performance surely marked an extraordinary achievement. So many personnel and so much materiel had to be organized and directed. The scripts had to be refined so continuously. The terrorists' method acting had to be sustained so continuously. So many failures were possible, yet in the end, the play went on.

The audience responds: Interpretations of the terror-performance

But to what end? Did the performance have its intended effect? Was the plot, when enacted, perceived as martyrdom for a just cause?

172

Did the physical destruction lead beyond immediate social instability and chaos to political imbalance and moral delegitimation? Destabilization is both objective and subjective. Emotions are coded and regulated symbolically; the objects of cathexis are not simply felt; they must also, simultaneously, be understood. Because traumas are subject to interpretation, different background understandings led to different reactions and, eventually, to different counter-performances to recover from trauma in turn.

Such considerations point to the fragmentation that marks contemporary societies. If the elements of artful staging are de-fused, and are difficult to bring successfully together, so indeed is the audience. For most public events there are multiple audiences, and their reactions to the same event often are framed by fiercely incompatible scripts. It was the failure to understand the separation of audience from performance – and the fragmentation of these separated audiences into different and often hermetically sealed interpretive spaces – that made the initial success of the terrorist *jihad* so short lived and the response to it only a partial success.

The events on that morning of September 11 played before profoundly different viewing groups. Some Arab-Islamic audiences hailed the performances with great applause. The "Arab street" sometimes danced with joy. Among the networks of some Arab elites, emails of satisfaction and triumph were passed quietly. Among these groups, real performative fusion with terrorist actions occurred in the destruction's immediate wake. Terrorists were perceived as martyrs who had gone on to their heavenly reward. The infidels had been punished, and Allah would treat them, too, in an appropriate way. As the producer and director of this world-historical drama, and as its protagonist-at-a-distance, Osama bin Laden became an object of extraordinarily intense identification. He was lionized as a hero, mythologized in an instant. His likeness was emblazed on T-shirts displayed like totemic images on human bodies. Recordings of his triumphant words were reproduced and continuously replayed on video and compact disk. Among these audiences, the seamless interweaving of script, actors, audience, background representation, means of symbolic production, power and *mise-en-scène* was impressively achieved.

> A few weeks after the attacks, bin Laden was with some of his close aides and a visitor from Saudi Arabia, and, sitting on a rug, relaxing with their backs leaning against the wall behind them, they expressed joy at the extent of the destruction, and they made jokes . . . about the events of September 11.

173

"The TV broadcast the big event," said Sulaiman Abou-Ghaith, a radical Kuwaiti cleric who served as a close adviser to bin Laden. "The scene was showing an Egyptian family sitting in their living room. They exploded with joy. Do you know when there is a soccer game and your team wins? It was the same expression of joy."

"A plane crashing into a tall building was out of anyone's imagination," the visitor from Saudi Arabia put in. "This was a great job" . . . He was Khaled al-Harbi, a veteran of the wars in Afghanistan, Bosnia, and Chechnya who had lost his legs in combat.

"It was 5:30 p.m. our time," bin Laden said. "Immediately, we heard the news that a plane had hit the World Trade Center. We turned the radio station to the news from Washington. The news continued and there was no mention of the attack until the end. At the end of the newscast, they reported that a plane just hit the World Trade Center."

The visiting sheik interrupted to give a kind of religious sanction to the happy news. "Allah be praised," he intoned . . .

Bin Laden continued his account of how he experienced September 11. "After a little while," he said, "they announced that another plane had hit the World Trade Center. The brothers who heard the news were overjoyed by it." (Bernstein 2002: 9–10)[1]

But what about the other audiences?

When *jihad* emerged in medieval Islamic society, its success did not depend on wide audience response. Success required only the performance of assassination itself. Because social structure and culture were simpler and more integrated, the *jihad* message was readable, clearly and directly, from the act. In a complex global society, the performative success of *jihad* was much more difficult to achieve.

At first, it appeared that Western audiences might react in a manner consistent with al-Qaeda's script. As the drama unfolded, American viewers witnessed objective destruction and experienced fears of personal annihilation and of the center giving way. The unimaginable destruction of giant buildings and the vicarious experience of mutilation and violent death were palpable, shocking, and psychologically debilitating. Because Western viewers identified with those who were attacked, they experienced the injuries as if they were attacks on their own buildings, bodies, and minds.

That the jaws of destruction had opened and the final days were at hand were powerful experiences in the immediate aftermath of the terror. Images of just punishment, of hell and damnation, are deep and recurrent themes in the Western imagination, and images of the New York City crash site were framed by aesthetic archetypes of apocalypse that recalled the late medieval paintings of Hieronymus Bosch. Dust blotted out the sun. Day turned to night. People caught on fire, suffocated, and jumped to their death (Bowler 2011). Hysteria and wild screaming were recorded and were transmitted worldwide. Strong men cried; firefighters and guards and policemen were brought to their knees, and they died in abject confusion, gasping for air. In the towers above, rich and powerful men and women waited helplessly, their sophisticated machines useless, and they died in even greater numbers. Unable to evoke an explicitly religious framework, commentators and observers evoked metaphors of the long-feared nightmare of nuclear holocaust to describe the scene, and they soon named the crash site "Ground Zero."

Not only physical but also ontological security was threatened, and there was a specifically American dimension as well. For in the country's collective imagination, America remained a virgin land (Smith 1950), a shining beacon on a protected hill. It also was imagined as a fortress that foreigners would forever be unable to breach. Indeed, the nation's sacred soil had not been stained with American blood since the middle of the nineteenth century.

The innocent honor of this mythical America stood in grave danger of being polluted on this day. Fear stalked the land. Americans were reluctant to venture outside their homes and neighborhoods. There was a real and immediate deflation of generalized social trust. People stopped driving, stayed away from public transportation, and failed to show up for work. The stock market dipped sharply, and deposits were withdrawn from banks. Tourism evaporated, and pleasure traveling disappeared.

These early American reactions, projected worldwide as denouement to the initial performative act, provided some foreign audiences, including radical Islamic ones, with evidence that the terrorist activity had succeeded not only in its immediate but also in its ultimate aims. Justifiable as such initial impressions were, they proved incorrect. The structural conditions for fusion proved impossible to overcome. The fragmentation of media and critics was a social fact; so were the polarized background meanings that structured the audiences for the terrorist performance on a global scale. The contrapuntal logic of East–West confrontation continued, and there emerged counter-readings that eventually generated counter-performances (Hartman 1958).

Bin Laden misperforms: American counter-reading and idealization

What was heroism for one audience was terrorism for the other. In fact, the terrorist pollution and destruction of American core symbols produced, within large segments of the American audience, a one-sided idealization in turn of everything American. This idealization began almost immediately, became stronger in the hours and days after the event, and worked itself out at many different levels of social structure and cultural life. It marked the beginnings of a counter-reading that provided the script for the counter-performances that continue today.

This counter-reading allowed the nightmare story of terrorist destruction to be retold – by critics, commentators, and reporters; by victims, helpers, and sideline observers; and by political, social, and intellectual leaders who were the once and future directors of American actions on the world stage. For themselves and for their audiences of listeners, viewers, and readers, these groups recast the humbling and fearful destruction of America as an ennobling narrative, one that revealed the strength of an ideal American core.[2] The existence of this inner, spiritual core was asserted in a matter-of-fact way, as if it had to do neither with metaphysics nor metaphor but was a matter of self-evident, natural truth. "The fire is still burning, but from it has emerged a stronger spirit," remarked New York mayor Rudy Giuliani when he led a memorial service at the site one month later. Following upon a series of deeply structured symbolic antitheses – ideal and material, soul and body, light and dark, truth and falsehood – Americans described the terrorist destruction as having an effect only on external, physical forms. The ideal inner core of America was still intact, they insisted; indeed, as a result of the effort at destruction, this core actually had grown stronger than ever before. Rather than being threatened or destroyed, the social center was being reconstituted as an ideal and not as a material thing. Because the center of society existed in the imagination, in the nation's soul, it certainly could be rematerialized in the days ahead.

This counter-reading of the terrorist performance took leave from the mundane vagaries of time and place, from the dust, grime, and blood that marked the physical terrorist site. It constituted a new imaginary that created an alternative, a liminal time and space, an existential zone located in the collective consciousness, not in the material world. The new time was symbolized as a new calendrical date, 9/11, a numerical sequence referring literally to an emergency call but whose pragmatic meaning was transformed into an iconic marker of time. After September 11, it was remarked continuously, "Nothing has ever been the same." The new beginning was said to mark the beginning of a new world.[3] Transcendent rather than geographic, this new world would fill in and smooth over the crater threatening the center of American life.

Before 9/11, America had been fractured by social cleavages, by the normal incivilities attendant on social complexity, and even, on occasion, by violent aggressions and hostilities. After 9/11, for a while the national community experienced and interpreted itself as united by feeling, marked by the loving kindness displayed among persons who once only had been friends, and by the civility and solicitude among those who once merely had been strangers. There was an intense generalization of social attention, which shifted away from specificity, concreteness, and idiosyncrasy to abstraction, idealization, and universality.[4] This idealizing emotional and moral framework spread from the physical to the social world, from the individual to the collectivity, from the family to the business community, from the city of New York to the American nation, and from the fate of the American nation to (Western) civilization itself.

Before September 11, the giant Twin Towers that struck upward from the bottom of Manhattan were perceived routinely, were taken for granted as mundane physical objects. If they were noticed at all, it was for their ugliness and vulgarity and for the intrusive and almost aggressive manner in which they towered over lower Manhattan life, overshadowing, it was sometimes said, the light of "Lady Liberty," aka the Statue of Liberty, herself. By the very act of their destruction, however, the towers moved from the mundane and profane to the sacred of symbolic life. They were re-presented as having embodied not capitalism but enterprise; not the bourgeois but the cosmopolitan; not private property but public democracy. They were reconstructed retrospectively as their architects once idealistically had envisioned them, as cool icons of aesthetic modernism, symbols of economic energy that were now deemed to have been compatible fully with the famous statue that represented political freedom in the harbor beyond.

If these physical containers were transformed in the American imagination, so much more so were the maimed and murdered people whom these buildings once contained. Before 9/11, the merchants and traders of Wall Street often had been the objects of envy and resentment, maligned as selfish and indulgent, as a new and unattractively yuppified social class. In America's fiercely fought class wars, no group launched such critical salvos more fiercely than the frequently resentful remnants of America's skilled working class, largely white, ethnic, and male. They themselves also were often objects of popular disdain, ridiculed as macho and racist, as unlettered, beer-drinking, red-necked conservatives too quick to wrap themselves in the American flag. It was this class who composed the larger part of the firefighters and police officers who entered the Twin Towers in the ill-fated efforts to help the elites who worked in the floors above. As they perished, the members of both groups were transformed symbolically. They were made innocent and good, portrayed in a mythical manner that abstracted from their particular qualities of gender, class, race, or ethnicity.

The first level of transfiguration focused on the victims and participants as archetypal individuals *tout court*. In the magazines, televisions, and newspaper elegies composed about them, in the commemorations that unfolded in the weeks and months after the tragic event, the traders and firemen, secretaries and police became the heroic subjects in sentimental, often heart-wrenching stories about their pluck and their determination. Their highly genred (Bakhtin 1986) biographies revealed that the strength, dedication, and kindness of the innocents murdered on 9/11 had allowed each one to build a meaningful, coherent and hope-filled life.

The second level of idealized reconstruction focused on the family. Whatever demographic data might have to say about divorce and loneliness, absent fathers and latch-key children, abandoned wives and extramarital affairs, the now mythically reconstructed individuals who perished on 9/11 were represented as members of warm and loving families. They were devoted husbands and wives, attentive mothers and fathers, loyal children and grandparents. Their familial love was always constant, vivid, and pure.

The third level of symbolic transfiguration concerned the economic elite itself. The highly profitable, often cut-throat, and relentlessly competitive business enterprises that rented space in the Twin Towers were now represented as decent, entirely human enterprises. They made an honest living, and their industry contributed to the bounty of American life. Their employees typically had risen from rags to riches, and they were, by ethnicity, taste, and personal life, no different in any important way than their fellow Americans. On the day after 9/11, CNN interviewed the president of the investment firm Cantor Fitzgerald, all of whose World Trade Center employees had perished. In the course of recounting his company's tragedy, this powerful businessman broke down and wept in a pitiable way. This scene was remarked upon throughout the world. It was the human face of 9/11's American side, a punctum that that the terrorists had targeted actual human life, not the "West" or "capitalism" or some other abstraction of modernity. The punctum also demonstrated that the humanity the terrorists had tried to destroy somehow had managed to survive.

From this transformation of degraded and antagonistic economic classes into idealized images of individual, family, and enterprise, the generalization of solidary feelings expanded like a ripple from a stone thrown into the middle of a tranquil pond. New York City often had been portrayed as a dirty, angry, and competitive place, the epicenter of the cut-throat, impersonal cosmopolitanism that conservative Americans loved to hate. After 9/11, it was presented as a prototypically human place. It was a living organism that had been attacked by virulent foreign bodies, and it was fighting for its life. Residents of small towns sent messages not just of condolence but also of identification. "Arkansas Prays for You" and "Southwest Airlines Loves NYC" were scrawled at the wreckage site. One Midwestern town raised money for a replacement fire engine, and others for new earth-moving machines.

> In Normal, Illinois, three local radio stations set up a tent in front of Schnucks Supermarket on Veterans' Parkway to collective donations in five-gallon water bottles – and the money came in at the rate of $5,000 per hour. (Bernstein 2002: 247–8)

Hundreds of Americans actually traveled to the city and joined volunteer brigades to clean up and to purify the damaged area and to help "survivors," those who had been traumatized by the events. Europeans publicly pronounced their love and affection for this quin-tessentially American city and expressed alarm over its injury. New York City became the center of the ideal core, concentrating within itself the spirit, energy, and openness to difference that made America the "land of the free and the home of the brave."

These gestures of identification toward the center from the peripheries had the reciprocal effect of strengthening national and supranational "Western" solidarity in turn. While it was only one part of New York City that was injured, and only 2,813 particular persons who perished within it, the news headlined an attack on "America," and ordinary citizens everywhere expressed themselves with the plural first-person pronoun "we." In the long aftermath of 9/11, during the period of the new beginning, it was not uncommon for this identification to expand outside of the American nation as well. In the first year of the George W. Bush administration, there had been increasing hostility and separateness between America and Europe. After 9/11, the German prime minister proclaimed, "We are all Americans now." The reciprocal bonds between Europe and the

United States were reasserted idealistically, and the moral debt from World War II was repaid symbolically. The North Atlantic Treaty Organization (NATO) declared its determination to defend America, as if to underscore the bond of extranational, shared civilization itself. Once again Europeans and Americans were united under a great cause to fight for the common good, but this time the unity was wider, for it extended to Germany and Russia and even to Japan.

From counter-script to counter-performance: The "war against terrorism" and beyond

Osama bin Laden's terrorist performance had achieved physical destruction and social instability, and it briefly threatened to disrupt the American nation's political life. But it did not achieve terrorism's most significant goal, which has to do with the moral delegitimation of the regime itself. This performative turn seemed to have taken the director, bin Laden, by surprise, and certainly it must have disappointed him. According to the binaries of his background script, if al-Qaeda were strong and pure, then America was soft and corrupt, its regime democratic only in the formal sense. Convinced of their weak motives, devious relations, and corrupt institutions, bin Laden believed that neither Americans nor their government would be able to respond politically, socially, or morally to his perfectly executed script.

In late October, 2001, in a televised Al-Jazeera interview, bin Laden gestured to the earlier American withdrawal from Somalia – after the notorious "Blackhawk down" incident – as evidence of the nation's weakness in the face of radical Muslim attack.

> We found they had no power worthy of mention. There was a huge aura over America – the United States – that terrified people even before they entered combat. Our brothers . . . tested them, and together with some of the mujahedeen in Somalia, God granted them victory. America exited dragging its tails in failure, defeat, and ruin, caring for nothing. (bin Laden: February 5, 2002)

He pronounced the effects of 9/11 to be just as effective, and much more definitive.

> The events of Tuesday, September the 11th, in New York and Washington are great on all levels. Their repercussions are not over. Although the collapse of the twin towers is huge . . . the events that followed, and I'm not just talking about the economic repercussions, those are continuing,

the events that followed are dangerous and more enormous than the collapse of the towers. The values of this Western civilization under the leadership of America have been destroyed. Those awesome symbolic towers that speak of liberty, human rights, and humanity have been destroyed. They have gone up in smoke . . . I tell you freedom and human rights in America are doomed. The US government will lead the American people and the West in general will enter an unbearable hell and a choking life . . . Just as they've been killing us, we have to kill them so that there will be a balance of terror. This is the first time the balance of terror has been close between the two parties, between Muslims and Americans, in the modern age. (bin Laden: February 5, 2002)

However, the midterm effect of al-Qaeda's performance actually was quite the opposite from what bin Laden predicted and so ardently hoped to achieve. Rather than moral destabilization, there was revivification. Osama bin Laden's terrorism was performed before a fragmented and polarized audience, and it produced a counter-reading to those intended by the terrorist-actors themselves.

This counter-reading led directly to the renewal of national solidarity, and indirectly to a new militarization of America, and to a war that would, for some initial period, destroy al-Qaeda's national-territorial base. The cultural-sociological processes described here were causes to these latter, more material effects. The new solidarity that developed in reaction to 9/11 deepened the divisions that had produced it. The idealization of America and the West was constructed in relation to an equally powerful stigmatization of everything not Western and American. The new national unity produced a new global polarity at the same time. The counter-reading had created an idealized and powerful protagonist, and it emplotted an equally threatening antagonist in turn. Without a powerfully evil opponent, there would be no tension to the plot, and the redemption of the moral actors would not be allowed to realistically unfold. Purification demanded pollution, and salvation required revenge. The discourse of friends and enemies was ready at hand. The terrorists were constructed as bitter and frustrated, as marginal, as weak and cowardly human beings. They were monsters, not men, and their actions had no principled rationale.

Against such sinister creatures the only appropriate response was force, for they could not be reasoned with but only suppressed. "None of us will forget this day," President Bush told the nation on the evening of September 11, "yet we go forward to defend freedom and all that is good and just in the world" (quoted in Woodward

2002: 30). There must be a war against terror. The terrorists were evildoers. "We haven't seen this kind of barbarism in a long period of time," the president later remarked (Woodward 2002: 94). He added, "This crusade, this war on terrorism is going to take a while." But it was not only a matter of recalling from the fog of memory the Christian campaigns against the Muslim usurpers of earlier times. Fiercely virtuous military campaigns had defended Republican regimes against "despotic" invaders from Athens to Florence to the beaches at Normandy (Hanson 2001).

Looking back from ten years after the launching of this military counter-performance, it seems apparent it did not succeed as planned, but actually produced another counter-performance in turn. It is well to recall that even the most successful of the Crusades failed to roll back Islam's energetic expansion, much less its theological-political self-regard. Terrorism produces wars against it, and crusades produce *jihads* in turn. Contingent actions taken in freedom often can reaffirm the binding structures of contrapuntal plot. This logic of performance and counter-performance has not been appreciated fully yet by the leaders of either side.

With the arrival of the "Age of Terror" (Talbot and Chanda 2002), the power to initiate the newest phase in the contrapuntal cycle has moved from West to East. But the *mise-en-scène* has not been altered. Islamic terrorism is a dramatic gesture, the Western response to it a dramatic misunderstanding. Islamic and Western scripts fuel iterative sequences of misperformance.

In the run-up to the second Iraq war, George W. Bush insisted that "events aren't moved by blind chance" but by "the hand of a just and faithful God." "We do not claim to know all the ways of Providence, yet we can trust in them," he declared in his January 2003 State of the Union address, but "this call of history has come to the right country" (Lears 2003). Two weeks later, the spiritual leader of the Palestinian group Hamas, which had earlier initiated the strategy of suicide terrorism in Israel and the West Bank, instructed Muslims around the world to retaliate in the event of an American attack. Describing the imminent invasion as "a crusader's war" against Islam by "the envious West and the US first among them," he insisted that "as they fight us, we have to fight them" (Bennet 2003). The day before the actual conflict began, Iraqi president Saddam Hussein described war with the United States as "the decisive battle between the army of faith, right and justice, and the forces of tyranny and American-Zionist savagery on the other." Declaring himself a "*jihad*ist," he called for a "holy war" that would "wipe out the ranks" of the invading American troops (Tyler 2003).

Unless this cycle of plot and counter-plot, performance and counter-performance is broken, it will undermine the prospects for social stability and international understanding and, for many unfortunate persons, the very right to life.

— 9 —

WAR AND PERFORMANCE: AFGHANISTAN AND IRAQ

"9/11" created not only extraordinary material and human injury but a deeply traumatic wound to the American collective identity. Lingering in the collective consciousness for long afterward, the attack itself marked a palpably new sense of America as a vulnerable nation, as a potential victim. Yet, far from undermining American collective identity, this lingering fear and distinct sense of danger actually enraged and energized it. From the smoldering ashes of destruction there emerged an American counter-performance of strength not weakness, of triumph not trauma (chapter 8). This revivification of "civil communitas" pointed, not to the destruction, but to the vitality of America as a democratic, civil nation.

The movement from trauma to triumph, however, was not only civil in its transforming power; it was also militaristic. It revivified not only civil community but the "community of warriors," the ancient band of brothers, the nation in its primordial and primitive, not modern and democratic guise. This ritual revivification had nothing to do with civility or inclusion and everything to do with the ethic of manly struggle. The roots of this ethic lay outside Christian civilization, emerging from within the republican-warrior cultures of Greece and Roman cultures, whose archetypes have continued to energize, and deplete, Western civilizations today (Carroll 2001; Gibson 1994).

The United States is not only a democratic but a warrior nation. It was founded, and twice refounded, not only by Puritan covenant, Bill of Rights, and Reconstruction-era amendments, but by Indians wars, a long military struggle against Britain, and a much bloodier civil war. In the 150 years since, the American Republic has been engaged in more or less continuous war on behalf of itself and others. In this

Figure 9.1. Front page of *New York Times*, September 12.

republican-warrior nation, we find the language of friend and enemy, not in the civil and Madison but in the Schmittian sense.

America's counter-performance to terror, in other words, was not only about the reconstruction of civil community, with an emphasis on solidarity, autonomy, and equality. It was also about reconstructing the technical and organizational capacity to project military power, and the moral capacity to sustain hierarchy, discipline, command, and control. If we examine the front page of the left-leaning *New York Times* on the morning after the attack, September 12, it is this militarizing frame of aggression and defense that we see widely displayed (Fig. 9.1).

In a front page story entitled "Awaiting the Aftershocks," the legendary *Times* reporter R. W. Apple, who first distinguished himself for critical reporting on the Vietnam war, wrote that the "astonishingly well-coordinated attacks on the World Trade Center" had "plunged the nation into a war-like struggle against an enemy that will be hard to identity with certainty and hard to punish with precision." On its

185

back page, the *Times*'s house conservative, William Safire, entitled his column "New Day of Infamy," metaphorically associating the attacks with President Franklin Roosevelt's iconic characterization of the Japanese attack on Pearl Harbor almost 60 years before.

Defining the attacks of 9/11 in terms of war was the result neither of cabal nor neo-conservative ideology. It was rooted, rather, in the political culture of a republican nation. The counter-signifying effect of 9/11 concerned not only civil communitas, therefore, but also military reconstruction. It triggered the movement from attacked to attacker, from victim to victor, from civilian to soldier.

The invasion of Afghanistan was the first *mise-en-scène* for this triumphant script. As a military performance, it made both metaphoric and metonymic sense. It entered physically and symbolically into the heart of darkness that had endangered the American nation, challenging both the symbolic and physically profane. The skillful military invasion and scattering of the Taliban was meaningfully compelling and pragmatically effective. Launched only weeks after the terrorist attacks, the Afghan invasion fused the separate elements of this American counter-performance into an apparently seamless whole. It was viewed, by American and Western audiences more broadly, as possessing authenticity and verisimilitude. Constituting a solidarizing quasi-ritual, it linked the democrat and warrior, the communitas of civil and military life. This successful performance created a satisfying, if short-lived, triumph, one that seemed to follow from and "correct" the trauma of 9/11.

The Iraq war that followed can be viewed, in performative terms, as a sequel, or even "triqual." Who were the directors of this new performance? Certainly the American president, his staff, his military chiefs, and cabinet ministers. But perhaps they were more the producers, the political sources that facilitated its production. The real directors were less visible, a secretive and determined group of neo-conservative strategists and ideologues. These neoconservatives were at once deeply idealistic about the possibilities of democratic reconstruction globally, and specifically in the Middle East, and deeply cynical about democratic process at home. They were hard-eyed realists who saw themselves through rose-colored glasses as republican warriors, and their opponents, both inside and outside the US, as dangerous and corrupted enemies.

For most of the decade preceding the second Bush presidency, these "Vulcans," as they called themselves, had been itching to invade Iraq and overthrow Saddam Hussein. Now, with the great success of the first and second acts of the counter-performance "From Trauma to

Triumph," these determined ideologues seized their opportunity. To the American people, they presented the Iraq invasion as the drama's third act. An "iteration" of those earlier smash-hit performances, it constituted a telos, a narrative denouement that would bring down the curtain to standing ovations. The revival of America's civil and military communitas would be fully achieved. The arc of counter-signification would be complete.

When social performances end, they constitute collective memories, providing representations that background subsequent performance in turn. This was certainly the case for the Afghan invasion, which was fought, metaphorically and metonymically, with the martyrdoms and triumphs of the up-from-ashes aftermath of 9/11 firmly in mind. The residues of the Afghan success, in turn, left glowing nuggets of collective memory for the would-be Iraqi revival that followed. One big question remained, however. Even if the background representations for this third act were readily available, would the other elements of performance fall into place?

Let us begin with the problems of scripting, which must assemble and foreground codes and narratives, either proscriptively or retroactively, from background representations. To create a hermeneutically effective script is never easy to do. To *persuasively* and not only *physically* fight Saddam – to be allowed and encouraged to start a second Iraq war – a new action-specific script would have to be created, one that could mediate between triumphant background representations and the pragmatics of the here and now. After establishing a coherent interface between realistic exigencies and background symbolic structure, this scripted coding and narrative would have to fold into, or at least seem to complement, the other elements for successful performance that remained to be defined. It would have to help generate authentic acting. It would have to adapt to, and help generate access to and control over, the means of symbolic production. It would have to be open to, as well as defend against, the resources of hovering social powers. It would have to complement the flow of *mise-en-scène*, the unfolding of the invasion and its aftermath on the ground. Last but not least, it would have to calibrate a fit between message and audiences.

Good scripts must be agonistic, coding actors into the binaries of good and evil and narrating a plot that has beguiling beginnings, ambiguous middles, and cathartic ends. Most good scripts also strive for clarity and concision. These hermeneutical requirements point to the first problem that scripting the Iraq invasion encountered on the ground. It was easy to describe Saddam as evil but not to give this evility sufficient weight. Without writing the protagonists as a seriously evil, the script's invasion could not be read as fateful, as adumbrating an imminent and decisive triumph. Only a crusade could sustain a narrative of blood sacrifice in war.

That script writers for the Iraq war faced such an immense hermeneutic challenge goes far to explaining the war's fabricated justifications. One way to thicken Saddam's evility was to connect him to the earlier trauma that had justified the immediately preceding war. Despite the presidential advisors' fervent hopes and queries, however, it was not credible to assert that Saddam actually had helped plan, or even to support, the September 11 attack.

The connection between Saddam and 9/11 would have to be metonymically and metaphorically made. If Saddam could be linked to terrorism, by giving stipends to the families of suicide bombers and or even harboring terrorists on his own national soil, a rhetorical if not empirical association to 9/11 could be constructed. He had, in fact, given money to suicide bombers; allowed a small terrorist group inside his national boundaries; engaged in state terrorism; committed gross human rights violations, ethnic cleansing, and mass murder. Each of these issues was placed on the table by the scripters of "Iraq." Through such metonymic relationships it might be possible to build a metaphorical bridge to 9/11. This would make it easier to draw powerful moral sustenance from the binary representations of the originating trauma. If the evility of the Iraq antagonist was deepened, the invasion could be narrated in a salvationary way.

Even these imaginative constructions, however, did not meet the symbolic requirements of the day. Americans were well misled, a majority believing the fictive linkages to be undeniable fact. The serial relationship between Saddam's actions in Iraq and 9/11 at home, however, was too extended. The danger remained too far away. The victims of Saddam's terrorist efforts were of little interest to most Western audiences. Such narrowness of empathic imagination suggests moral failure; it also had significant sociological effect. For Western audiences, Saddam was evil, but ten years after the Gulf War he did not seem seriously or world-historically evil, a threat to the moral and physical existence of life in the West.

The serial relation would have to become fused. To be truly evil, Saddam needed to be linked to a world-historical crime. This semiotic demand led to the assertion that Saddam possessed, had used, and would use again weapons of mass destruction, the famously eponymous WMDs, capitalized and acronymized, that were scripted lavishly and spoken in hushed tones. If such weapons did exist, and

188

about that there was said to be certainty, and if we lived in an age of global transportation and transmission, which was undeniable, then it was only a matter of time before these weapons of horror would strike at Americans, and, before that, at Israelis and possibly Europeans too. To write WMDs into the script was to evoke the previous century's most apocalyptic events. Chemical weapons had terrorized tens of thousands of soldiers during World War I, and nuclear weapons had killed hundreds of thousands at the end of World War II. WMDs and their possible victims also recalled another "mass," the mass murder of the Jews that became the Holocaust, the terrifying symbol of evil that continually threatened to darken modernity's good name.

It was for these reasons of symbolic logic that WMDs become central to the Iraqi invasion script. But if this script now worked aesthetically, could it be made to walk and talk, to work pragmatically as well? Could the script be put into practice, such that it would produce performances with which audiences could identify and stand up and applaud? To create such dramaturgical fusion, audiences must be convinced that performances have verisimilitude, that they are authentic and true.

It was just this necessity that led to the play within the play. The WMD-centered script was to be pre-tested in an out-of-town performance. The actor was American Secretary of State Colin Powell. The stage was the emergency meeting of the UN Security Council. The time was early February, 2003.

Social performances are historically, not only geographically, layered. Secretary Powell's appearance was recognized as an iteration, both by his production team and its incipient critics, of an earlier iconic moment during another national crisis. Adlai Stevenson, John Kennedy's American ambassador to the United Nations and a hero of the democratic left, had turned in a bravado performance at an emergency meeting of the UN Security Council during the Cuban missile crisis, nearly four decades before.

President Bush and his aides had chosen Secretary of State Colin Powell because he, too, was popular with the liberal left, despite his Republican affiliation. He was reputed to be honest and bold, and he was thought to be politically independent. Alone among the president's men, Powell's performative utterances would not immediately be framed in a partisan way. The American and global audience would likely hear him out. Looking relaxed and sure of himself, and making ample help of visual aids, Secretary Powell seized the podium and dramatically put the administration's big lies into the global civil sphere. When it was over, he felt that he had given "the perform-ance of his life." Many segments of his audience, particularly the American, seemed to agree. Polling support showed a bump.

The success of this global aesthetic performance was not preor-dained. Its fusion had to be achieved; it was not ascribed. That it was successful transformed the performance from dress rehearsal into prolog. What quickly followed, the dramatic opening scene of the Iraq invasion, was characterized in terms of another aesthetic term – of sublime "shock and awe." Yet, while success came easily, it was too immaculate. For in the days immediately leading up to the invasion, and in those that quickly followed, the dramaturgical justifications for blood sacrifice ran into trouble.

Effective scripting depends on agonism. The tension between sacred and profane must be sustained, so that the zigzag reversals that make plots interesting can lead to cathartic resolution. This agonism was undermined by two events on the ground, contingent and unscripted happenings that threatened the hegemonic script. The first was Saddam's agreement to cooperate with, rather than to confront, the new Security Council resolutions, allowing weapons inspectors relatively free access to look around. They traveled through Iraq investigating putative weapons sites. Of course, the meaning and motivation for Saddam's accession were ambiguous, and the effec-tiveness of the inspection process far from transparent, but taken together they manifestly weakened the cut of the antagonist's evility, and threatened to undermine the tense agonism being constructed by the war-making script.

Eventually, these inspectors, headed by a grave and stolid Swedish diplomat, asked the UN for more time, in order to be rational and fair. By opposing this request, the US and UK, and their allies in the developing war coalition, publicly and dramatically broke with the democratic procedural process of the Security Council. This cast a bad light, and even possibly a polluting shadow, on those who would be the war's moral protagonists, foreshadowing their own potential for evility in turn.

These unscripted, symbolically realigning events led to the break-up of the Western democratic alliance. The American-led military party adopted a go-it-alone attitude, a self-described "coalition of the willing" that, despite its civil-sounding label, also connoted gangs or posses. This split in the Western alliance made it that much more dif-ficult to frame the resort to violence in a consensual and democratic way. It increased the distance between the civil and military narra-tives that swirled around the initial days of the Iraq war.

From the invasion's earliest moments, then, there developed, among significant American and Western audiences, a counter-coding and counter-narration opposing the script projected by the governments of America and its allies. In this emerging counter-script, it would be the American President Bush who was inscribed as a symbol of arbitrary authority and violence, not Saddam. It would be Bush who projected a dangerous and polluting aura, whose honesty and sincerity were doubted, whose motives were projected as irrational, and whose actions generated fear.

Coalition military and civilian leaders had predicted that the performance of "Iraqi Freedom" would not only be successful in instrumental terms – routing the Iraq army – but theatrically as well. Audiences of Iraqi citizens would welcome the soldiers as liberators, with flowers in their hands, and the subsequent installation of democracy would justify America's warrior myth in civil terms.

This did not occur. After the dispersal of Saddam and his army, conspicuous groups of Iraqis began publicly looting their national treasures, not only destroying their own patrimony but carrying away vital icons marking the very beginnings of civilization. Because American soldiers looked the other way, refusing to block this profanation, the civil side of the democratic-warrior balance was destabilized. More doubt was cast on the master narrative of liberation that was to legitimate the military founding of civil society in the Middle East.

Soon the narrative of military triumph itself was subject to challenge. Coalition control became undermined by growing insurgency, countering both the pragmatic effectiveness and the moral integrity of the American counter-performance against terror. The multiplicity of social power poses immense challenges to performative success. In the aftermath of the invasion, American forces failed to monopolize the means of violence. The invading coalition army was too small, the established Iraqi armed forces were disbanded, and the most experienced members of the Iraqi nation's administrative apparatus were purged in the campaign against the Baathist party. America allowed, in effect, the creation of counter-powers, an underground leadership, administrative staff, and armed insurgency that further undermined not only the effectiveness of American and British military force but chances for its sympathetic framing and interpretation by Iraqi audiences.

Tone-deaf American political authorities also failed to find ways to bridge the yawning problems of sectarian majority rule. As it became increasingly clear that the Shiite Muslims exercised effective cultural control, the connections between American occupying forces and both Iraqi and American domestic audiences became ever more attenuated, or de-fused. Global audiences were fragmented as well. The early pro- and anti-America splits within Western audiences deepened throughout the post-invasion period. Events seemed to confirm the initially skeptical counter-narratives of influential intellectuals and political elites in such nations as Germany, France, Italy, and Spain. These and other critical "reviews" of the unfolding military intervention constructed barriers between European publics and coalition actions that proved difficult to breach. These barriers did not prevent the coalition from waging war; they undermined its symbolic power for legitimate war-making.

The resulting instability and chaos, and the resurgence of anti-American feelings, effected an extraordinary rhetoric transformation in the critical scripting of war. The American army gradually but unmistakably shifted from "liberator" to "occupier," from the democratic to the anti-democratic side. This new labeling was deployed as much by American reporters as by others. This symbolic transformation crystallized and exacerbated the shifting fortunes of America's symbolic justification for war.

As the WMDs failed to appear in the days, then weeks and months after the invasion, the anti-democratic construction of American action became more deeply entrenched, for the language of deceit and political manipulation became harder to avoid. The revelations of systematic torture at Abu Ghraib, publicity about secret CIA kidnappings and renditions, the US Supreme Court's ringing declaration that holding enemy aliens without trial and representation was illegal, the exposure of NSA domestic spying without prior warrant – these revelations further diminished America's status of democratic protagonist.

While the signifiers of the discourse of American civil society remained powerful, the ability of the discourse to successfully represent this discourse in the social signifieds of the war project had failed. The stage of "Operation Iraqi Freedom" was being evacuated. The Americans in Iraq were increasingly constructed as colonial oppressors who would have to exit stage right if Iraqis were, in fact, ever to become free. Yet the Iraqis themselves seemed less and less likely to be constructed as having the capacity for freedom, as sectarian militia and death squads took murderous aim, not only at Americans but at one another.

The American "surge" helped stabilize the American military occupation of Iraq, and the "Sunni uprising," which emerged alongside it, went some way to ameliorating Shia sectarian rule. What these late adjustments did not do, however, was to restore to the military invasion an aura of performative success.

Conclusion

One reason for America's performative failure was the difficulty of formulating an effective script, one that could mediate between the background traumas and triumphs and the actual exigencies of geopolitical realities. It must also be attributed to the difficulties of making the script walk and talk on the ground, to the unexpected actions of Iraqi citizens and insurgents, the incompetent and often undemocratic actions of American officials in Iraq and at home, the plurality of social powers, and the fragmentation of audiences in the US and abroad.

In the arc that stretches from the sacred restorative communitas of 9/11, through the bitter days of military and ideological polarization of 2002–6, and on to the political paralysis and sporadic violence that marks the soon to be post-occupation of today, we observe not only the defeat of a great nation's military project but also its demoralization. In performative terms, we see symbolic inversion and evacuation, a drama whose unfolding was blocked, and whose meaning still seems at once elusive and dangerously incomplete.

As the American war party was pushed from the sacred to the profane, the very symbolic identity of the enemy wobbled and became diffuse. The figure of Saddam shifted from a vainglorious and threatening dictator, to a hermit-trickster hiding in a hole, to dazed and unkempt prisoner, and then to raving defendant, before finally coming to rest as the first hectoring, then hectored, then seemingly dignified victim of a botched if still morally justified execution. In the course of this signifying process, the iconic "Saddam" as evil slipped away, and a more comic and even pathetic figure appeared.

The good and evil positions as originally plotted disappeared, but the soon to be empty stage will not quickly become the setting for a morally satisfying triumph. No sacred and compelling narrative has emerged from the insurgent side. Forty years ago, in an earlier military debacle, the apparently humanistic and compelling narratives of socialism and national liberation made America's enemies – Ho Chi Min, the Viet Cong, and the National Liberation Front – seem attractive to significant audiences and elite critics both at home and abroad. By contrast, even among the Iraq war's fiercest opponents, there was

193

little enthusiasm for the sectarian ideologies, political leaders and organization, much less the military tactics of the insurgency. Nor is there any admiration for the leadership cliques that remained in control of Iraq after the insurgency died.

Yet, without a sacred place of one's own to stand, it is difficult to represent evil. If America has been murderous and invasive without good reason or just cause, how can we condemn those who have opposed the invasion, or those who, no matter how ambivalent about democracy, have emerged to take their place? Some critics have called the Iraq war a tragedy, others a stupid and unforgivable mistake. It is now beyond good and evil. Neither sacred nor profane, it has become mundane.

INTELLECTUALS AND PUBLIC PERFORMANCE

According to philosophical convention, the public is a space separated from the immediate, particularistic demands, and also the resources, of organizations. It is a space outside of them – in which people can, indeed are compelled to, exercise their reason, as Kant said, or, in Habermas' terms, engage in unfettered critical discourse. The public is also the imagined and widely inclusive community that is implied and constructed by such putative reasoners and discoursers, a "civil sphere" evoked by critics and sometimes loyalists as a counterpoint to demands of the market, the state, religion, and family.[1]

Intellectuals are actors who can exercise judgment because they themselves are free-floating, independent of particular commitments. They are defined as those motivated by such general categories as justice and truth. They make statements on behalf of humanity, in order to serve Rousseau's general will, the broad sense of which everyday actors, because they are prone to bias or irrationality, are not themselves consciously aware. Theoretically then, "intellectuals" and "public" are concepts that go hand in hand. This is also true sociologically and historically. The emergence of the public sphere corresponds with the rise of intellectuals.

Ancient Greece was where the polis first emerged and from which the term "public" first came into being. The polis was literally a separate sphere of activity, peopled by every adult male who was not a foreigner or a slave. It was held to constitute the "community" of the city-state, whose activity was discourse, reasoning, rhetoric, argument, and, of course, voting and, via executive delegation, governing.

Once an actual place, since its demise the polis has become myth, a regulating idea. At the center of this myth has been an intellectual, Socrates. Socrates was a real person, but we know him only through

Plato's construction. As we learn about him in the dialogs, Socrates is the man of truth, who speaks from total disinterest, as an individual with no attachments of a particularistic sort – friendship, oikos, city-patriotism, passion. He is the objective truth teller. He embodies, as such, the ethics of the public sphere. He died because he refused to stop speaking the truth against power, to buckle down to the particular will in a time of war. The story about the death of Socrates has always been at the heart of what the ideals of the public, and the obligations of an intellectual, should be.

This "republican" tradition, which has exercised such extraordinary power over the last 2500 years, was virtually ignored by sociology's foundational historical and comparative thinker, Max Weber.

Yet, Weber was himself deeply interested in the origins and influence of public intellectuals. What might the relation between Weber's theory of religious rationality and the Socratic tradition be? Weber can be seen as providing a broad religious-cum-cultural understanding of why the West has been so responsive to the myth of public intellectuals and rational-critical judgment. It has been so because of the new role of prophecy, which emerged with ancient Judaism and was institutionalized first in Christianity and later, and much more emphatically, in Protestantism.

The prophets were, in Weber's scheme, the religious equivalents of intellectuals. While, in purported contrast with public intellectuals, they were motivated by an a priori system of beliefs, the abstracted and transcendental status of this belief system allowed them independence and critical distance from the more particularistic institutions, organizations, and other belief sets of their day. Eisenstadt demonstrated this connection when he made use of Weber's comparative theory to explain the historical rise of the intellectuals in the different civilizations of the Axial Age (Eisenstadt 1982).[2]

Weber and Eisenstadt are right: the modern public intellectual is also a prophet. The performance of "intellectual" has depended, since the Christian and Roman mixing of the Jewish and Greek, on the background script of prophecy, especially the thundering Old Testament kind. But this background culture structure is not enough. The role of public intellectual must also be performed (Eyerman 2011). To be a public intellectual is a matter of making, of performing, and of convincing others of the same. As Austin would have said, the linguistic term "public intellectual" is not just constative, but connotative and subjunctive. Being a public intellectual is not only locutionary, a matter of linguistic definition, but illocutionary and perlocutionary, a matter of doing thing with words. It is a performative, not just a constative. It is not just a matter of role taking but of role making.

A good example of this distinction can be found in the life of the French sociologist Pierre Bourdieu. Throughout most of his career, Bourdieu was content to be a sociologist-intellectual, pursuing the truth through empirical and theoretical studies. Of course, the normative reference for this scientific work was the civil sphere, and the French audience for Bourdieu's studies extended into the non-academic civil-public, but Bourdieu did not become a public intellectual until, in the last decade of his life, he published *La Misère du Monde*, made regular appearances on French television, and ostentatiously associated with *Le Monde Diplomatique* and the "Gauchist" movement that opposed the French Socialist Party and its supposedly "neo-liberal" policies.

So being a public intellectual is not just a matter of telling the truth and of being separate and free-floating, of truly representing the universal. It is a matter of performing as if one were all these things. Being a public intellectual is symbolic action, a matter of becoming what Emerson called a "representative man." To become exemplary in this manner is to dramatically embody the myth of universalism, the binary code of public versus private, and the narrative of progressive triumph.

This is not, of course, how Plato wished to understand Socrates, and certainly it does not accord with Socratic myth. According to Plato, Socrates hated "rhetoric." In the *Gorgias*, Socrates rails against rhetoricians as the equivalents of what we would now call publication flacks or spin doctors. He maintains that philosophers speak truth, that only they have the courage to face facts, and that their influence rests entirely upon their ability to present rational and logical deductions and empirical inductions based on observations. As Detective Joe Friday used to say on the American television drama *Dragnet*, "I want just the facts, ma'am, nothing but the facts."

Plato distrusted fiction and hated mimesis, yet did not Socrates himself have a "style"? Was he himself not dramatic and persuasive? On his daily trips throughout the Athenian marketplace, did he not want to grab and hold the attention of his fellow citizens, and to draw an audience around him, and was he not surrounded by a supporting cast? Performance was there at the very origins of the public intellectual. The teachers and schools of rhetoric emerged in Athens at the very same time as the new philosophers of truth. Their aim was to allow speakers in the polis to be more persuasive, and thus more effective, to supply them with the performative capacity to increase their illocutionary and perlocutionary force.

How much more performative has been the status "public intellectual" in the millennia since the Greeks. As mythical figures, Socrates and the Old Testament prophets are the principal protagonists in a narrative script that has displayed an extraordinary reproductive power. In this script, the ancient republic is presented as a golden age, in relation to which public intellectuals measure the decline of the civil-public sphere in their own, modern days.

The Socratic sense of truth-telling as purely constative – as non-performative rational judgment – is a form of philosophical false consciousness which has created problems of self-understanding for modern public intellectuals, and, in some instances, for their ability to have public effect. It is often suggested that the rational presentation of objective and unbiased knowledge can, and should, be the basis for effective entry into the public sphere. Nothing could be further from the truth. Public intellectuals need to connect with, and speak on behalf of, the great narrative myths of our time, to sing about the possible triumph of progress, to strike the chords of national, regional, and ideological myths about equality and democracy. They must strive to become symbolic icons who can embody rationality and universalism in the present day.[3]

In relation to the civil-public sphere, the role of the public intellectual is to offer not only the hope but also the road map to institutionalizing its ideals. Now, it might be said that ever since their reception, these ideals have been in trouble. They were undermined in ancient Greece, in the Roman republic, in the Renaissance city-states. Even as the civil-public sphere first became institutionalized in a national form, by law and democratic procedure, it was accosted on every side, by markets and classes, parties, states, families, religions, regional chauvinism, ethnic and racial ties. To sustain even the semblance of a differentiated and voluntary association of human cooperation and solidarity has been no easy thing. To maintain formal democracies, let alone social democracies, has been perilous, and this is only to speak of conditions inside the nation-state. It has been utterly impossible between them.

Such difficulties, and their fateful and often fatal consequences, have created audiences eager for public-intellectual performance. Demanding that the fragmented solidarity of the civil sphere be repaired, public intellectuals defend the integrity of, and outline the possibilities for, a more civil society. Their performances have two parts. The first identifies "destructive intrusions" to the civil ideal.

The second recommends how the rents in the fabric of civil solidarity can be repaired.

Walzer (1965) describes the post-Marion exiles, the Puritans, as the first public intellectuals of the revolutionary tradition. Inheritors of Weber's prophets, they also helped create empirical science, were strong believers in truth-telling, and intensely committed to democratic and participatory politics. They framed the English revolution in terms of demands for a more level society, denouncing "Popist" hierarchies, magic and mystery, and what public intellectuals today might call "bullshit" of all kinds – except, of course, their own. In Puritan literature these dangers were described as destructive intrusions to civil-cum-religious solidarity.

The first liberal democratic theory, such as Locke's, came out of this Puritan tradition, and the English and Scottish democratic theorists of civil society informed what later became French Enlightenment thought. The *philosophes* were the first group of secular public intellectuals in the revolutionary tradition, presenting empirical truth as highly corrosive of corrupt kinships, social divisions, and dogma. In the name of rationality they performed denunciation, and created at least the ideological conditions for the first secular and violent social revolution, which began in France in 1789.

By the 1840s, the revolutionary prophecy carried by public intellectuals became translated into the idioms of socialism, symbolized and stimulated by the publication of *The Communist Manifesto*. The fundamental reference of this version of the prophecy remained the same. It was to abolish unequal social divisions, on the one hand, and repressive domination, on the other, so as to stitch back together a more thoroughgoing solidarity. According to this socialist version, such a natural and spontaneous association could be achieved only if economic life were freed from the destructive intrusion of the market.

This originating moment of anti-capitalist public intellectual performance emerged from both the Socratic and biblical traditions (Alexander 2010c). The "young Hegelians" from whom Marx emerged drew on their master's belief in a god-like and immanent reason which, while historicizing Kant, was also steeped in spiritual understandings of a life-altering other-worldly force. The émigré communist workers who commissioned Marx and Engels to write their *Manifesto* in London were themselves a chiliastic religious brotherhood, rooted in a version of primitive Christianity. In their eloquent and stirring manifesto, Marx and Engels combined all this with the highest truth-telling social science of their time, British political economy.

The iconic figure "revolutionary public intellectual" became a myth, and it powerfully buffeted Western societies well into late days of the last century. The new performative role became reconfigured in other religio-cultural orders that had also emerged from the Axial Age. The revolutionary public intellectual became a hero with a thousand faces. He became Mao Tse Tung, the Leninist neo-Confucian scholar who emerged as the great prophet of the middle kingdom and exercised near god-like performative authority. He became Franz Fanon, the prophet, philosopher, and therapist of civil repair in its anticolonial form. Fanon's belief in the transformative power of revolutionary violence to repair psyche and society was rooted not only in his experience as a subaltern psychiatrist but also in the teachings of Sartre, one of the most esoteric of the free-floating and universalizing intellectuals of the century we have only recently left behind (Baert 2011).

From Mao and Fanon were derived the whole repertory of "third world revolutionaries," the hero prophets from Che Guevera to Subcomandante Marcos. Marcos, the populist leader of Mexico's Zapatista rebellion, was outed as having been a privileged philosophy graduate student at UNAM, which explains his confident claims on secular truth. While Marcos' commitment to the civil repair of Mexico was genuine, so was the Subcomandante's performative sense. This pipe-smoking, mask-wearing, manifesto-writing public intellectual is a familiar role. Osama bin Laden presents the most recent incarnation of this revolutionary tradition. His aim was to repair the solidarity, not of the ancient Greek Republic but of the ancient Islamic one. Not only is the terrorism of Al Queda highly dramaturgical, but the organization provides videotapes and recordings performing denunciation, a whole series of choreographed performances of revolutionary Islamicism since their entry onto the global stage on September 11, 2001.

The public-intellectual performance of civil repair does not have only to be revolutionary. It is more democratic, if not nearly so exciting, when it is reformist. One thinks here of such public intellectuals as Bentham and Mill in nineteenth-century Britain, and later of the Fabian Society. Such reformist figures and organizations denounce the corruption, repressions, and exclusions of modern society and through their evocative and impassioned road maps, lay claim to knowledge about how to repair it. John Maynard Keynes was the most influential reforming public intellectual of the twentieth century. His performance combined brilliant truth-telling with passionate commitment to solidarity and its repair, and the high dudgeon of moral denunciation with ethereal participation in an idealized aesthetic world far removed from everyday modern life. Keynes condemned capitalists for their demonic and irrational "animal spirits," but he fervently believed in the singular power of capitalist economies to provide the material means that were necessary to facilitate the good life.

If time and space permitted, I would explore other sub-genres of the public intellectual role. Radical right-wing revolutionaries have been immensely influential public intellectuals, although the *gemeinshaftlich* solidarities they would restore are definitely not of the civil type. In the West today neo-conservatives are the most influential public intellectuals of all. Denounced by their opponents as anti-civil egoists, they are not, in fact, concerned only with wealth and power, but also with civil repair in their own key. Just as those on the Left, neo-conservative intellectuals derive their performative power and authority from their defense of the civil sphere and their promise to repair it. They frame the threat to civil solidarity as emanating, not from the market, but from the state and, indeed, from liberal and secular intellectuals themselves. Following such thinkers as Ludwig von Wiese, Milton Freedman, and Ayn Rand, neo-cons see markets as all about freedom and reciprocity, as civil societies in miniature. Other more traditional conservative public intellectuals, in the spirit of Burke and Oakeshott, assert that traditional authority is essential if trust is to be restored to civil life.

Nor are the genres of public intellectual performance exclusively political. There is a psychoanalytic tradition of therapist as public teacher that orients itself to the interactional level of civil society. From Freud and Jung to Erik Erikson and Jacques Lacan, these therapist-prophets have sought to restore the subjective capacity for feeling, balance, confidence, and rationality. Through their intellectual performances as public therapists, they too have tried to save civilization.

Public intellectuals are not as free-floating and universalizing as they, or we, think they are or would like to be. The civil sphere is instantiated in real time and space, and it is concerned as much with exclusion as inclusion. Civil discourse is binary, promoting not only liberty but also repression. As iconic figures of the civil sphere, public intellectuals have reflected its imbeddedness in race, nation, religion, ethnicity, gender, sex, and civilization. Their cries for civil repair have not only extended solidarity by humanizing others, and thus allowing emancipation. These cries have also constituted rhetorics of demonization, constructing certain groups as unworthy of inclusion into civil society and thus as candidates for annihilation.

I do not advance this slightly heretical, and perhaps even perverse, argument as itself an objective and free-floating proposition. Rather, I am putting into a general sociological form the actual language of public intellectuals themselves, who are forever denouncing one another, and the putative groups and interests intellectuals are said to represent. They paint their opponents as uncivil, and thus as unattractive, so as to undermine their effectiveness in the performances of public life. Napoleon did this famously for the French revolutionaries and radical men of letters, calling them not philosophers or intellectuals but ideologues, chastising them for promoting dogma rather than truth, and accusing them of thinking not about the public but about themselves. Since that time, to call somebody an ideologue has been to accuse them of particularistic self-interest, and to strip from them their publicness.

The denunciation of the public intellectual as neither universal nor truthful but as particularistic, self-interested, and dogmatic is a universal trope that can take many different forms. The Marxist left denounced civil reformers as middle class and bourgeois, as merely coopting the indignation of the lower classes, and often condemned one another as trying to rise to rulership themselves (Konrad and Szelenyi 1979). Conservatives and reformers, for their part, have "exposed" revolutionary public intellectuals as actually concerned with class or party rather than with the civic body as such, and as insensitive to the corrosive effects of violence upon their utopia of civil society.

The most sweeping and effective contemporary deconstruction of public intellectuals has been the postmodern. Radicals, reformers, and conservatives alike have been condemned as modernists, and thus, whether knowingly or unknowingly, restricted by whiteness, maleness, homophobia, orientalism, and, above all, by their own commitment to universalizing rationality (Seidman 1994). Presenting modernism as narrow, violent, and anti-civil, postmodern public intellectuals make the claim that flexibility, humor, and a sensitivity to the particular and concrete can restore the trust and reciprocity upon which civil community depends.

The self-proclaimed "new cosmopolitans" might perhaps be said to represent public intellectuals of a post-postmodernist kind. Speaking on behalf of an imminent global civil sphere, Ulrich Beck accuses all social science hitherto of methodological nationalism, evoking a newly energized discourse of civil idealism on a worldwide scale. Other global public intellectuals, such as David Held and Mary Kaldor, develop road maps for global civil repair of a more practical but just as anti-nation state. The performance of these new cosmopolitans is closely related to the public intellectuals of the new Europe, whose civil and Socratic public aspirations have been sharply highlighted by the recent counter-movement of anti-constitutional backlash. But the dialectic turns. Volker Heins (2005) accuses Habermas and other avowedly cosmopolitan European public intellectuals of "orientalizing America," of engaging in a particularistic discourse that divides and ranks the world's civil societies and privileges Europe as more worthy and pure.

Despite these rather sobering qualifications, public intellectuals are among the most important carrier groups for the discourse of civil society, whose ideals and partial institutionalizations are the closest human societies have yet come to making the universal concrete. Civil repair is a project, and public intellectuals participate in it in a critical, if often highly ambiguous, way.

ICONIC POWER AND PERFORMATIVITY: THE ROLE OF THE CRITIC

Materialism is a mundane mode of understanding, one that indulges the self-evident common sense of a rationalized, de-magicalized modernity. No doubt the most sophisticated manner in which the self-consciousness of modern mundaneity has been applied to materiality is the commodity theory of Marx (2001 [1867]). Energized morally by icono*clasm*, this radical critic of icon*icism* produced a brilliant but deeply misleading empirical theory of modern social life. Marx believed that market processes strip material objects of their value – both use value (their practical or true value, as dictated by design, shape, and form) and moral value (their status as product of social labor). Insofar as material objects are so commodified, in Marx's view, they can be viewed only abstractly rather than in concrete terms; they are seen merely as exchange value and measured by money. Emptied of meaning, material objects become simply things. Any commodity is the same as any other commodity that can be traded at the same price, no matter how differently they seem in their appearance.

At the opposite end of the modern social theory of material objects stands Durkheim's late theory of the elementary, totemic forms of religious life. Durkheim (1966 [1912]) insists that material objects actually make tangible the moral values of society. Because moral values are specific and distinctive, totemic objects are concrete and distinctive in form. They are collective representations that carry social force, communicate sacred and profane meanings, and generate intense emotional identifications through ritualistic practices centering on their material form. Refining this originary understanding via structuralism and semiotics, such figures as Barthes, Eco, and Harré describe material objects are referents, or signifieds, whose meanings are established not by themselves but by their relation to invisible signifiers. We do not see or experience an actual material object as such, but see them as signs, signifier and signified combined.

Neither Marx (at all) nor Durkheim and the semioticians (only slightly) shed light on the artistic design of material objects, the formal properties of material surface that allow aesthetic experience. This feeling for form was first explained, in modern thinking, by eighteenth-century aesthetic philosophies of beautiful and sublime and more recently by Heidegger-inspired writings about presence effects versus meaning effects, for example in the writing of Hans Ulrich Gumbrecht (2006).

My own contribution to this debate has been to suggest that if there is to be a cultural sociology of material objects, then the aesthetic and the moral approaches to material stuff must be combined (Alexander 2008a, 2008b). The aesthetic can be thought of as surface form, the moral conceived as depth meaning. Surface and depth together create the basis for a modern theory of iconic consciousness. Constructing the material surface creates an aesthetic experience that works on the senses. The nature of this sense experience depends on the structure of form – in terms of visual sense, for example, on textures, colors, lines, curves. Sculpted and drawn forms are successful, according to the standards of classical aesthetic philosophy, if they are able to create sensations of the beautiful and the sublime. (Postmodern theory, a la Danto, would disagree, emphasizing the aesthetic significance of banality and ugliness, but that's another story.) Beneath the aesthetic surface there exists social meaning, the depth of material objects. The discursive and moral meaning of material objects comes not from aesthetic surface but from society, from somewhere outside the objects themselves.

The first thing that is remarkable about surface and depth is that they are invisible to ordinary lay consciousness. To everyday social actors, the world seems to be populated not by aesthetically formed surfaces and culturally constructed depths, but simply by animate and inanimate things. The second remarkable fact is that, even when observers are aware of the aesthetic surface and moral depth, these two independently constructed and distinctive domains invariably seem to be thoroughly and completely intertwined. On the one hand, a particular aesthetic form seems to "be" the meaning of the material thing, to naturally and perfectly express it; on the other hand, some particular social meaning seems intrinsically to demand some specific articulation of the beautiful or sublime. Everyday consciousness is reified; it seamlessly naturalizes arbitrary meaning structures even as it essentializes historically contingent aesthetic forms.

Let me give an example of how this works from Kant's pre-critical *Observations on the Feeling of the Beautiful and Sublime*. Kant waxes eloquently about how women's moral qualities *allow* them to be "known by the mark of the beautiful" – "her figure in general *is* finer, her features more delicate and gentler, and her mien more engaging and more expressive" (Kant 1960 [1764]: 76, italics added). Kant treats the aesthetic surfaces of women, in other words, as reflections of ingrained moral qualities; historically contingent judgments of gender appearance are naturalized as objective forms corresponding with social and moral difference. Women, he writes, naturally "prefer the beautiful to the useful." They are beautiful because from "very early they have a modest manner about themselves," knowing "how to give themselves a fine demeanor . . . at an age when our well-bred male youth is still unruly, clumsy, and confused" (p. 77). Affirming that "the moral composition makes itself discernible in the mien or facial features," Kant believes that a woman "whose features show qualities of beauty *is* agreeable," for "in her face she portrays a tender feeling and a benevolent heart" (p. 87, original italics). That women are thought to be beautiful is due neither to aesthetic convention nor social practice. They are beautiful, because they are, well, women!

Performance and iconicity

In this chapter, my interest is not *whether* iconic consciousness exists. For the sake of this discussion, I assume iconic objects can exert a powerful social force. My interest, rather, is *how* iconic power varies. Yes, material stuff matters, both morally (depth) and aesthetically (surface), but iconic objects do not matter equally. They vary in their impact, their power rising and falling in historical time and, within the same historical period, distributed differently not only across individuals but among the demographics of segmented and fragmented societies.

I propose to understand this variation through the idea of performativity. One might think of an icon as a performer, sending off signals according to how it is designed. The effects of these signals, their signaling power, cannot be measured, however, simply by the intentions of an object's designer, even if it has one. There is the matter of reception, of audience impact. Between projected meanings and audience response are a series of mediations. In addition to its design, projecting iconic power depends, for example, on access to the means of symbolic production. You need a stage for the designed product, lighting and photography to portray it. You need technical and artistic skills to put the iconic object "into the scene" (*mise-en-scène*). Iconicity also depends on power. These include the more obvious powers of production and distribution: you need a dealer, an agent, a gallery, a factory. But iconic effect is also mediated by "hermeneutical power," the understandings and evaluations offered by independent interpretation. Critics exercise interpretive power in a big way, getting in between the designs of iconic objects and their reception.

Iconic objects produced by high art and popular culture send off potential meanings and experiences, often by design. Whether audiences – other designers and artists, or members of the lay publics whether connoisseur or commodity consumer – register these iconic impressions, indeed whether they are affected by these material performances at all, is an open question. The answer depends, to some significant degree, on how critics evaluate an object's aesthetic excellence and communicative success. In the research upon which I report very selectively here, I have collected from the pages of the *New York Times* – the most influential single popular medium in the United States – recent reviews of architecture, paintings, music, automobiles, dresses, and graphic logo designs. I analyze these reviews, not simply as *reflections* of iconic power but, more importantly, as *recipes* for understanding how iconic power comes about. My research explores the positive and negative mediation of popular criticism, illuminating how public rhetoricians and their putative audiences actually talk about an icon's surface and depth.

The *New York Times* meets Louis Kahn

Sometimes critics distance their audience from an icon's potential power, negatively evaluating the designer, painter, or composer, proclaiming the icon a "false idol" whose aesthetic surface is ugly, stupid, boring, clichéd, or banal, or whose moral depth is confused, profane, polluted, or simply obfuscated by the aesthetic failures of the surface. Often, however, the opposite is the case. In this regard, let us consider the architecture critic of the *New York Times*, Nicolai Ouroussoff. To examine Ouroussoff's reviews is to encounter an immensely influential critic propelling, undermining, explaining, and exploring iconic power. Occupying a relatively autonomous position in the performative production of iconicity, Ouroussoff mediates the performance process by which architectural icons are made, distributed, evaluated, received, and sometimes revitalized and enhanced.

Our type case for this discussion will be Ouroussoff's front page review in the Arts Section of the *Times* on December 11, 2006. Its headline is "Restoring Kahn's Gallery and Reclaiming a Corner of Architectural History, at Yale." In what follows, I will suggest that this review instructs us on how to become fused with the first great material sign that Louis Kahn – a revered American architect from mid-century – ever produced. Writing ostensibly from a critical distance, Ouroussoff's writing closes the distance to become part of the process of creating iconic power. Fifty years after the building was designed and built, and long after Kahn himself had departed from this earth, Ouroussoff teams up with Kahn, revving up iconic consciousness for Yale's restoration of his earliest big project. Ouroussoff contributes to Kahn's performative success, even as he purports to provide a rational and objective appraisal.

Powerful icons combine the generic (they typify) and the unique (they singularize). Ouroussoff writes this combination into the surface of the Kahn building and also into its depth. "The restoration of the Yale Art Gallery," he announces, "reawakens one of America's great architectural beauties." It is "like the return of a long-long friend." Ouroussoff communicates here a sense of arch-type: the Kahn Gallery is an ur-example of "modern architecture." Yet, at the same time, the critic insists that Kahn's Gallery is special, its surface an idiosyncratic artistic object. Absolutely singular, Kahn single-handedly created a uniquely anti-Corbusier style. Ouroussoff's case for the singularity of the archetype's constructed surface is thickened by continuous evocation of its "Yale" depth. The elite Ivy League university is everywhere visible in the background of this review, contributing its own cultural power as a singular yet simultaneously iconic arch-type. The Kahn building is presented as just the kind of magnificent surface structure that a college as glorious as Yale would have.

Great icons salvage mundane material objects from the realm of mere banality, making them beautiful and sacred and counter-posing them not only to the ugly but to the morally profane. Ouroussoff continually frames the Art Gallery's aesthetic surface via the traditional criteria of beauty. He offers frank proclamations of aesthetic delight and evokes the philosophical criterion of beauty as the principal object of design.

These exclamations about the triumph of surface beauty are faithfully linked to an insistence on the Yale Art Gallery's sacred depth. It is because Kahn succeeds in creating an extraordinarily beautiful surface, Ouroussoff implies, that he has been able to create a deeply spiritual site for transcendental experience. References to divinity abound. Ouroussoff exclaims that the restoration allows Kahn to be "put back on the pedestal he so richly deserves." Sacred things great and people – the critic freely dispenses with the adjective "great" – must be separated from the mundane, given higher and more elevated status. Kahn is not only great but a "genius," which means that he is not only generically sacred but also unique. And just as totems procreate, producing other sacred objects, so Kahn possesses fecundity. He is said to have produced *many* "great masterpieces." Ouroussoff weaves Kahn a mythical narrative. A supernatural figure, Kahn is part of history, wrapped in folkloric stories, biographies, movies, and art books. Restoring his building's iconicity has a metaphysical quality. Ouroussoff tells a story about recovering a "long lost friend," about awakening "beauties from a slumber." This is a story about discovering buried treasure; of bringing something dead back to life. Restoration has breathed life into a long "dead" relic of modernity. Ouroussoff narrates the past, present, and future of iconic temporality. Once great, his Art Gallery was abused and fell into oblivion, but it is now restored to its original glory. The icon's narrative arc takes on a teleological form. It becomes pivotal to the mythical story of modernity. The first great work of an architectural genius, its brilliance foreshadowed future landmarks, and its own beauty can now be discovered again.

The Art Gallery's surface is described in visual terms that reveal the "elements of genius." Ouroussoff writes fluidly and passionately about the "bold geometric forms, the sharp lines, the sensitive use of light, the tactile love of his materials." Revitalized, the Yale Art Gallery is "sleek," its sensuous surface fully possessing the aesthetic power to suck us in. Yet, even as the Gallery construction "stresses materials and surfaces," Ouroussoff reminds us that it reaches below mere surface, "projecting an air of mystery." Gallery surface draws us into a Gallery depth. "The project should also be understood," Ouroussoff instructs, "as part of a larger effort to reclaim a corner of the Yale campus." Architectural surface connects us to Yale sacred ground. Citing "the incorporation of an old rough-hewn stone retaining wall," Ouroussoff explains that Kahn used the wall "to frame his outdoor courtyard [and] to lock the building into its historic surroundings." The depth of the Gallery's aesthetic surface is linked to these historical surroundings, for Yale is not just a great university but an historical container for the most sacred art of early modern and modern times. In this manner, the aesthetic power of Kahn's modernist building is intertwined with classical and romantic artistic forms: "Paintings [that] range from early Italian Renaissance to contemporary are displayed on partitions supported on steel legs that break the rooms down into a series of small informal spaces," and "paintings by Monet, Renoir and Pissarro hang in big gilded frames along the concrete-block wall that runs the length of the main façade."

Discussing the decades of obfuscating accretions to the Kahn building that now stand corrected, Ouroussoff condemns them as grossly insensitive, not only as ugly aesthetically but offensive morally. Here again the binary of sacred/banal is continually evoked. This is manifest first in Ouroussoff's mythical narrative about recovering spiritual depth. It is only because "years of callous alterations have been reversed" that the sacral elements of the iconic building can be restored "in all their glory." So also is this binary central to explaining the iconic power of the restored Gallery's surface form. Time and again light is evoked as a material representation of divine sacrality. It is central to the restoration of iconic surface, in part because it is visually alluring, in part because it evokes an ethereal sacred depth. Reporting that "the west façade has been rebuilt," Ouroussoff explains that "its glass and steel frame" – banal and mundane in themselves – now "regains its original lightness." Pointing to another of Kahn's aesthetic innovations obscured by banal historical accretion – "a sunken exterior court that was senselessly roofed over" – Ouroussoff reports that this courtyard "has been restored, allowing light to spill down once more into the lower galleries." In reporting on the Art Gallery's interior court, Ouroussoff's narrative of aesthetic conversion is much the same: "The entire space is animated by [Kahn's] masterly handling of light . . . A narrow vertical slot of glass overlooking the entrance court . . . allows a stream of light to wash down a back wall."

The aesthetic power of the Gallery's surface, like the moral power of its depth, is sustained by splitting meaning categories into sharp binaries. Ouroussoff sets light off against shadow, smooth against sharp, thick against thin, angle against curve. He reports, for example, that "the elegance of that west wall, gently set back from the street, contrasts with the forceful concrete-block façade of the main entrance, an opaque expressionless screen." Elegant is to concrete block as gentle is to forceful as transparent screen is to opaque – [Elegant: concrete-block :: gentle : forceful :: screen : opaque]. We are drawn into the iconic power of the revitalized Gallery, the critic suggests, because "the stunning variety of the light and the tension between the forms and materials – the delicacy of the partitions . . . versus the brute weight of the concrete – keep us alert. Everything here is warmly alive." This creates iconic power: "Mysticism over purity. Obliqueness over transparency. Historical nuance over an abstract utopia."

Having explained the binary construction of the iconic power of the Gallery's exterior, Ouroussoff leads the reader inside the building,

210

Table 11.1   The binary discourse of iconic power

Profane	*Sacred*
Kitsch	Art
Utilitarian	Aesthetic
Negative	Positive
Jumbled	Clear
Confused	Transparent
Muddy	Careful
Slipshod	Thoughtful
Heavy	Light
Clumsy	Fluid
Cringe-inducing	Epiphanic
Artificial	Authentic
Doctrinaire	Liberating
Engineered	Inspired
Efficient/hurried	Patient contemplation
Weak	Strong/bold
Cautious	Courageous
Parochial	Universal
Superficial	Deep
Banal	Lofty
Manipulative	Principled
Conformist	Creative
Reeking	Purity
Compromise	Conviction

to the sensuously exalting contact with the sacred center, which is also rendered in a polarizing way. "Inside the building," the critic reports, the sense of restraint "gives way to an intoxicating blend of muscularity and delicacy." Surface sublimity leads powerfully to meaningful depth: "The deep triangulated beams of the ceilings, with their deep shadows, lend the room a mystical air; the stark silo-like concrete cylinder housing the staircase reaffirms the galleries" status as a sacred space." But "the true revelation occurs when you step into the galleries." Those who can take this step will experience objectification, and, as their subjectivity becomes concrete, they will experience transcendence as well: "The potent thrust of the concrete-beam ceiling draws you into them as if you were being lured into a sacred tomb. You gaze up in awe, and then turn to the paintings." Table 11.1 illustrates the binaries Ouroussoff employs to describe, and bring into being for the reading audience, the restored Gallery's aesthetic and moral power.

211

Ouroussoff's passionate account of the Kahn renovation adumbrates another revelation, the imminent unveiling of the Paul Rudolph designed Art and Architecture building just down the street. According to the *Times* critic, the Rudolph building, a controversial monument of "Brutalism," has also been polluted to the point of banality. Subjected to "physical abuse" and "gutted by fire," the 1960s building has endured "a series of unforgivable alterations" that have made its true sacrality invisible and, instead, suggested its profanation: "Skylights and windows were covered over, transforming the interiors into dark, cavelike spaces." The aesthetic-sacred has been defiled by mundane utilitarianism: "Additional studio floors were crammed, so that the towering vertical spaces that made up the core studios became cramped and gloomy." The result has been that the aesthetic "clarity" of Rudolph's original design has been lost.

The restoration undertaken by Charles Gwathmey, who had been a student at Yale Architecture when Rudolph was Dean, will allow the misunderstood Brutalist building's iconic power finally to shine through. In so doing, it will recreate a contagious interaction with the restored sacrality of the Kahn building next door. Rudolph had intended to create this concatenation but did not pull it off – at least in the minds of earlier critics and lay audiences. Restored, Rudolph's aesthetic surface will finally expose the building's daring and courageous moral depth, and connect it fluidly to the Kahn next door. "Its glass façade will regain its original transparency, echoing Kahn's glass façade across the street." The banal utilitarianism will be eliminated and Rudolph's sublimity restored: "The additional floors will be ripped out, opening up the old stark vertical spaces that lent the studios their grandeur." Sacred light will be let back in: "Light wells that were closed up will be replaced, allowing daylight to stream down the back of the library wall." The sensuous and meaningful will now be available, and iconic consciousness restored: "When finished, the building should feel as audacious as it did four decades ago, a delicious counterpart to Kahn's restrained elegance."

Naturalizing iconic power: The disappearing critic

In conclusion, let us return to iconic consciousness as reification. Iconic power depends on the seamless intertwining of surface aesthetic and depth meaning, such that an actor experiences sensuous surface and understands discursive meaning at the same time. Yet, in

212

spite of an icon's social power, or more precisely because of it, social actors themselves are not reflexive about this process. As far as they are concerned, they feel themselves interacting with real, animate or inanimate, things.

My discussion of Nicolai Ouroussoff's writings suggests how criticism can contribute to such naturalization of iconic consciousness. Critics report on architecture's aesthetic success, stating this objectively, as a truth. They employ the language of description: this façade works because it is beautiful; that one doesn't because it's ugly or banal. The critic's claim is that the plastic achievement – this column, that façade, this internal stairway – "is" good, that it functions aesthetically, in contrast to another plastic feature innovation "is" bad, and "fails" the aesthetic test. Critics, in other words, do not own up to their subjectivity, much less to the interpretive power of their aesthetic judgment.

Whether this is modesty or false consciousness, critical performance not only creates interpretations of an icon for an audience but creates an audience for the icon. Critics provide public judgments before lay members of the public, and even other artists, have themselves been able to experience a work. The effect, in a large and complex society, is not just to offer an evaluation but to create a context for its reception. Critics tell people what to look for and how to feel, and they often do so in a personal, not a distanced way. Far from being objective, and thus merely informative, Ouroussoff presents his review as an account of his personal experience. He describes the sensuous impact of the object on his own senses, and its depth meaning for him. It is a breath-intaking record of an intimate encounter, an exhilarating first-person report on the critic's journey to the center of a sacred thing.

Through the critical text an audience first experiences the iconic power or weakness of an aesthetic object. The reader is primed; the critic instructs. The critic can distance the reader from a material form, de-fusing rather than re-fusing, by describing his own sense of being distant when encountering it himself. The critic can bring into being a hesitant and withholding audience, making it difficult for readers to give themselves over to the object, in the unlikely case they should now actually make the trip to encounter it face to face. Reading a critical review, we are wary and suspicious of the object; we are skeptical and raise our guard, most likely staying away. A glowing review has the opposite effect. We are halfway seduced already and waiting to fall in love. We want to be fused, to be taken by the experience, to fall into the object.

That Ouroussoff is constructing us as an audience, that he is instructing us so as to facilitate our fusion, is not at all explicit. It is not something that the critic would admit, and it is not something about which the reader, the person at the receiving end of this performative process, would be aware. This lack of awareness reflects the nature of iconic consciousness itself, and the success of the critic's role in causing an icon to perform powerfully enough to make it happen. The icon is absorptive. Feeding upon our need for transitional objects, it allows us to subjectify material reality and to materialize ourselves inside it in turn. As we read Ouroussoff's review, we are encouraged to imagine imminent experiences of absorption and projection, to participate vicariously in Ouroussoff's journey. We experience iconic consciousness at one remove, a second-order arousal. The review is presented as if it were communicating aesthetic judgments (which it is); yet these judgments are also simultaneously presented as immediate and personal reactions of a person to whose social power we, as interested readers, are inclined to submit.

The critic speaks

In spring 2008 I invited Nicolai Ouroussoff to my undergraduate seminar on iconic consciousness in New Haven, and we engaged with Yale students in a spirited discussion of what it takes and what it means to be an architectural critic for the nation's most influential popular mass medium. Ouroussoff declares that the principal requirement is having a "feeling for the building as object," but, asked to reflect on how he employs this feeling in his capacity as influential critic, he betrays some confusion and concern. About the interpretive power he wields, he replies, "I don't think about it. It'd be a killer if I did," he explains, exclaiming "I don't have power!" As evidence, he offers the fact that "I rarely can actually kill a project." Reminding him the query concerns interpretive, not material power, the critic evokes the idea of objective aesthetic truth: "If you're getting closer to some kind of truth, then you [do] have power. If you're not, you don't have any."

Ouroussoff's reply illuminates something profound about just how hermeneutical power mediates performativity. To deny his power, the critic presents himself less an interpreter than an accurate reader, an observer of objective form, a kind of scientist of the aesthetic life. On the one hand, he implicitly acknowledges possessing power; on the other hand he denies it. He, as a subject, has no independent leverage. What actually possesses power is truth. Because aesthetic judgment is objective, it is truth that has power. One is a good reviewer, perhaps even a highly influential one, only to the degree that one's writing reveals objective truth. Ouroussoff asserts, in fact, that the nature of architectural truth has been discovered; it revolves around the nature of forms. We have a "growing understanding about how bodies move through space," he explains. Citing decades of architectural writing and psychology, he asserts that we now understand how people "experience their material environment." So, Ouroussoff does not see himself as guiding people to an opinion, but as educating them about the nature of aesthetic truth. If people actually go and see the building he has written about, they will agree with his review. Their reaction will be as influenced as his criticism by the revelation of an icon's objective power, or the lack of it.

Not because of his influence, but because they will be able to confirm with their own eyes aesthetic truth. Faced with this assertion of aesthetic objectivity, I ask Ouroussoff why, then, are his reviews written with evocative language? Why bother to write so expressively, rather than simply suggest in an accurate manner the information at hand? At this point in the conversation, the critic confesses to being a writer and not only an author, in Barthes' sense. Reviews, for him, are about "feeling," not only about information. He wants to communicate the "experience" of "how you move through the space," of "how the narrative develops as you move through the building." He describes his review as a first-person narrative that aims to transmit the experience of seeing, making an analogy between his own literary creativity and the architect's plastic power: "You do through the writing what the architect has done through his building." Taking the reader through the building, you "use language to try to convey the sense of space, rhythm, motion." Just as today's architects "try to create an innocence" about forms and shapes, so Ouroussoff wants his readers to experience architectural objects in a fresh way. He offers an example. If you drive under one of the complex and curved overpasses of a Los Angeles freeway, you might experience it as ugly, filled with darkness, garbage, and potential crime. From the perspective of the architectural critic, "you need to get people to break through this 'learned reaction' – to see these spaces for what they are," to allow "emotional resonance." You need words for that, not just pictures.

So the review is itself performative, a literary exercise that aims to recreate the feeling of plastic art. If Ouroussoff's own aesthetic performance succeeds, it will create fusion between his critical text and *Times* readers and, at the same time, he will have drawn the reader's emotional-cum-symbolic identification toward the plastic object. He recalls for the assembled students a valuable piece of advice he himself had received as a young critic. "Don't be afraid to fall in love" with a work of art, an older critic had advised him, and he confesses that today, as an architecture reviewer, "I want to fall in love with the building" and "I feel a sense of tragic disappointment if I don't." What frustrates him most? "When I can't get people to see the things I see in a building. When they are blind."

Criticism and the de-fusion of iconic power

Iconic power is typically not mediated by critics in such an explicit manner. It often builds up by invisible accretions, without any relation to an organized social power that plans and engineers its production and distribution, or to interpretive powers that subject its success and worthiness to "review." Consider the iconic power of trees and sky and light, home furnishings, one's own hair, body, and clothing, or – for the most part – one's gender, race, and sexuality. That the presentation of an icon is not explicitly mediated by organized criticism, however, does not mean that its power is not subject to performative mediation. Iconicity is a process, not an objective fact, and it is subject to powerful social mediation. Iconicity has a temporal arc. To explore the "aura" of an icon is also to explore its "half life." Iconic power may continue to spiral and radiate long after critical mediation. Icons can perform without apparent aid of other powers because, once launched, they have power independent of the processes that performatively produced them.

In traditional societies, iconic objects are tightly intertwined with sacred scripts, their producers with their consumers, and there are no critics. In complex, modern, and (even more so) in postmodern societies, the elements of iconic performance have become separated and de-fused. Thinking about them is often concentrated and separated. Production is in one place, design another, and display, advertising, and publicity are all somewhere else. Absorption by the viewer – which may be consumption, adulation, or appreciation depending on the social arena – is so separated from these other elements that it is often not available for public scrutiny, and seems entirely contingent and arbitrary besides. It is because of this de-fusion that a fascinating new element has become central to iconic performance – the critic.

NOTES

Chapter 1

1 For example, while I agree with Sewell's (1992) metatheoretical formulation that text, situation, and agency all shape social life, discussion about this interplay must be much more specific and nuanced, and show how these elements actually interact. The generality of Sewell's formulation disguises the tension between the different formulations of structure and agency he brings together. Any framework that "combines" Giddens with Bourdieu, and the two with Sahlins and Geertz, without providing a new explanatory model, has great difficulties. Emirbayer's (Emirbayer and Mische 1998) metatheoretical discussions are more coherent, and much more closely approximate the direction we take cultural pragmatics here, but they perform a much more thoroughgoing critique of culturalism than of pragmatics. Emirbayer's reluctance to develop a correspondingly forceful criticism of pragmatism – from the perspective of culture structure and citational meaning-making – makes his model vulnerable to the reinsertion of the structure–agency dualism.

2 Saussure's *Course in General Linguistics* is a reconstruction of lectures he delivered at the University of Geneva between 1906 and 1911. First published in book form in 1913, the lectures appeared in an English translation in 1959.

3 The attribution of inauthenticity to a performance in public discourse often demonstrates a particular logic: that which is accused of being inauthentic and fake is represented as either threatening a just social order or as (seductively) trapping people in an unjust one.

4 "Textocentric" academics (Conquergood 2002: 151), who practice a Geertzian approach to studying social life, are included in the group of ignorant members of the dominant culture.

5 "[Judith] Butler turns to Turner – *with a twist* . . . [She] twists Turner's theory of ritual into a theory of normative performance," McKenzie criticizes (in Phelan 1993: 222–3).

6 Where in her earlier and most influential contributions to performance theory Judith Butler (1990) presented resistance to gender stereotyping in an exaggeratedly agent-centered manner, she has tried to escape from such an exclusively

217

agent-centered understanding of "resistance" in her later essays (e.g., Butler 1993b), emphasizing the kind of citational qualities of performance we are pointing to here.

Chapter 2

1 Because Durkheim is the founder of virtually every strong program for cultural analysis in the human sciences, it is particularly unfortunate that he equated socially meaningful symbolic action with ritual, rather than conceptualizing ritual as one moment along a continuum of social performance that ranges from fused to defused. One result has been the very broad usage of "ritual" as a synonym for symbolic action (e.g., Goffman 1967; Collins 2004), a usage that camouflages the contingency of symbolic action. Another result has been the restriction of symbolic action to highly integrated and repetitive, i.e., "ritualized," situations, a restriction that conceptualizes cultural, strategic, and materialistic "practices" as taking up the rest of the action space. In his "religious sociology" of aboriginal societies, Durkheim wished to establish the basic elements of a cultural sociology of contemporary life. While he succeeded in laying the foundations for such a theory, he failed to sufficiently differentiate, in an analytical manner, the conditions for symbolic action in simpler and more complex societies. He could not have fully succeeded in his ambition, then, without the kind of differentiated and variable theory of the social conditions for symbolic activity I am presenting here. For a critical examination of Durkheim's late cultural theory from this perspective of performance, see Smith and Alexander 2005: 25–31.

2 Normative theorizing about the deliberative aspects of democracy has been allergic to its aesthetic and symbolic dimensions, implicitly equating the latter with anti-democratic, irrationalist commitments. The cultural pragmatics of social performance can provide an important corrective. For their part, Marxian hegemony and Foucaultian power-knowledge perspectives fail to conceptualize the myriad of contingencies that successful symbolic reproduction entails. It is very difficult to hyphenate power with knowledge and to gain the fusion that is indicated by an audience's inability to perceptually differentiate these two dimensions.

3 The relative autonomy of the "actor" element in contemporary social drama was demonstrated in a tragic and world-historical manner by US Secretary of State Colin Powell, whose televised speech to the United Nations Security Council on February 5, 2003, provided the crucial legitimation that allowed America and its allies to launch the Iraq war. By that late date, billions of dollars had already been spent on preparation, American military forces were primed and ready, and the most powerful military and political leaders in the world's most powerful nation were intent on launching the invasion. By their own accounts, however, they felt that they could not do so unless the war was legitimated on the global public stage. This legitimation depended on making the case that Saddam Hussein possessed weapons of mass destruction (WMDs) and that their deployment was imminent. After several failed efforts to prepare for such a performance, those who were directing it decided that only one man could play the critical role. In the following account, the veteran reporter Bob Woodward continually makes resort to performative concepts,

including rehearsal, preparation, background scripts, symbolic polarization, actor motivation and skillfulness, *mise-en-scène*, audience perspective, critics, and audience response.

[President George] Bush and [National Security Advisor Condoleezza] Rice had asked the CIA to put together the best information in a written document – the "slam dunk" case [for WMDs] that [CIA Director George] Tenet had promised . . . The president was determined to hand the evidence over to experienced lawyers who could use it to make the best possible case. The document was given to . . . Scooter Libby . . . On Saturday, January 25, Libby gave a lengthy presentation in the Situation Room . . . Holding a thick sheaf of paper, Libby outlined the latest version of the case against Saddam . . . The most important response came from [former presidential assistant] Karen Hughes. As a communications exercise, she said, it didn't work . . . This was a communications problem, not a legal one . . . So who then should present the public case? . . . Powell was the logical choice . . . To have maximum credibility, it would be best to go counter to type and everyone knew that Powell was soft on Iraq [and] when Powell was prepared, he was very persuasive . . . "I want you to do it," Bush told the secretary of state. "You have the credibility to do it." Powell was flattered to be asked to do what no one else could. Rice and Hughes told Powell that he should get three days for the presentation to the Security Council . . . "No way," Powell said. "I'm doing it once." Okay, [then] it might be three or four hours long. "No, it won't," Powell insisted. "You can't hold these guys for three to four hours." They would fall asleep . . . Powell won agreement that the length and content would be his decision . . . Public expectation was building on Powell's presentation. Newspaper stories and cable television were running with it hard: Will Powell deliver a knockout blow? What does he have? What secrets will finally be let out of the box? Will Saddam be exposed? Will Powell have an Adlai Stevenson moment? Will Saddam fold? Will Powell fold? Powell was well aware that the credibility of the United States, of the president, and his own, were going to be in the Security Council room that day . . . After the final rehearsal in Washington, Tenet announced that he thought their case was ironclad . . . "You're coming with me," Powell said. He wanted Tenet sitting behind him at the UN as a visible, on-camera validation of the presentation, as if the CIA director were saying each word himself. Tenet was not the only prop. Powell had a sound and light show, audios and visuals to be presented on large hanging monitors in the Security Council chamber. He even had a teaspoon of simulated anthrax in a small vial to wave around. Millions around the world watched and listened on live television . . . Dressed in a dark suit and red tie, hands clasped on his desk, Powell began cautiously . . . He had decided to add his personal interpretation of the intercepts [of Iraqi military conversations] to his rehearsed script, taking them substantially further and casting them in the most negative light . . . He had learned in the Army that meaning had to be explained in clear English . . . The secretary's presentation took 76 minutes [but] the mixture of understatement, overstatement, and personal passion made for riveting television. Mary McGrory, the renowned liberal columnist for the *Washington Post*,

and a Bush critic, wrote in the lead column for the next day's op-ed page
... "I can only say that he persuaded me, and I was as tough as France to
convince ... I'm not ready for war yet. But Colin Powell has convinced
me that it might be the only way to stop a fiend, and that if we do go, there
is reason." (Woodward 2004: 288–312)

4 Twentieth-century linguistic theory – which was central in creating social
understandings of discourse – was marked by a struggle between structuralism
and pragmatics. The present theoretical effort can be understood as a sociological extension, and reformulation, of the series of fundamentally significant
philosophical-linguistic efforts to transcend this divide, e.g., Bakhtin's (1986)
concepts of dialog and speech genre, Jakobson's dynamic synchrony (1990b:
64) and code/message schema (1987: 66), and Morris's (1938) syntactic-
semantic-pragmatic model. I am also following upon, while challenging
and revising, significant synthetic efforts in sociological theory, e.g., Swidler
(1986), Sewell (1992), and most especially Emirbayer and Mische (1998).
As these latter efforts suggest, twentieth-century sociological theory was
marked by a sharp tension between pragmatic and structural approaches,
against which some of my own earlier theoretical efforts were directed as well
(Alexander 1998, 1987b, 1987c, 1982–1983).

Chapter 4

1 Alexis de Tocqueville introduces this idea of self-interest "rightly understood"
in *Democracy in America* (vols. I and II, New York: Library of America,
2004 [1835, 1840], book 2, chapter 8). He does so to distinguish narrow
and egoistic interest ("*l'intérêt*") from a more solidaristic kind ("*l'intérêt bien
entendu*"). With this latter conception Tocqueville indicates "the disinterested,
spontaneous impulses that are part of man's nature" (p. 611), as compared
with the more consciously calculated and selfish estimates of material well-
being that propel the capitalist marketplace, and also frame the approach
to action in many political and economic theories today. Self-interest rightly
understood, Tocqueville writes, suggests motives and relations that "are disciplined, temperate, moderate, prudent, and self-controlled" (p. 612), which
rather precisely describes the civil-rationality of the contemporary voter as
he or she is discursively constructed today. Tocqueville credits "mores" – the
accepted English translation of "*les meurs*" – as the social force that allows
democratic citizens to understand their own interest more broadly, and he
defines mores in a cultural manner, as "habits, opinions, usages, beliefs"
(p. 356). The most recent English translation of *Democracy in America*, excel-
lent in other respects, translates "*l'intérêt bien entendu*" as "self-interest properly understood," unfortunately shifting the English rendition of a concept
that has become a classic theoretical term in democratic theory.
2 For demagicalization, see Weber, "Introduction" and part II, section IV in
Weber, *The Protestant Ethic and the Spirit of Capitalism*, New York: Scribner,
1927 [1904–05]; for aura and mechanical reproduction, Walter Benjamin,
"The Work of Art in the Age of Mechanical Reproduction," pp. 211–44 in
Benjamin, *Illuminations*, New York: Harcourt, Brace, 1968; for alienation,
Marx, "Economic and Philosophical Manuscripts," pp. 61–219 in *Karl Marx:*

Early Writings, T. B. Bottomore, ed., New York: McGraw-Hill, 1963 [1844]; for "all that is holy," Marx and Engels, op. cit; for superstructures, Marx, *The German Ideology*, Moscow: International Publishers, 1970 [1846]; for meaning as dependent variable in the sociology of culture, see Alexander and Philip Smith, "The Strong Program in Cultural Sociology: Elements of a Structural Hermeneutics," pp. 11–26 in Alexander, *The Meanings of Social Life: A Cultural Sociology*, New York: Oxford University Press, 2003.

3 Alexander and Smith, op. cit., and Alexander and Smith, "The Strong Program: Mission, Origins, Achievements and Prospects," in John Hall, Laura Grindstaff, Ming-Cheng Lo, eds., *Handbook of Cultural Sociology*, London: Routledge, 2010; more generally, Alexander, *The Meanings of Social Life*, loc. cit., passim; Durkheim, *Elementary Forms*, loc. cit., p. 1.

4 For Birmingham, Stuart Hall et al., *Policing the Crisis*, London: Macmillan, 1978; for governmentality, Graham Burchell et al., eds., *The Foucault Effect: Studies in Governmentality*, Chicago: University of Chicago Press, 1991; for isomorphism, John Meyer and Brian Rowan, "Institutionalized Organizations: Formal Structure as Myth and Ceremony," *American Journal of Sociology* 83 (1977): 340–63; for cultural capital, Pierre Bourdieu, *Distinction: A Social Critique of the Judgment of Taste*, Cambridge, MA: Harvard University Press, 1984; Murray Edelman, *The Symbolic Uses of Politics*, Champaign, IL: University of Illinois Press, 1964.

5 For narratives, see Hayden White, *The Content of the Form*, Baltimore, MD: Johns Hopkins University Press, 1987 and Barthes, "Introduction to the Structural Analysis of Narratives," in Barthes, *Image-Music-Text*, New York: Hill and Wang, 1977; for the entwinement of narratives and the discourse of civil society, see Ronald Jacobs, *Race, Media, and the Crisis of Civil Society: From Watts to Rodney King*, New York: Cambridge University Press, 2000, and Philip Smith, *Why War? The Cultural Logic of Suez, the Gulf War, and Iraq*. Chicago: University of Chicago Press, 2005; for heroes, see Thomas Carlyle, *On Heroes, Hero Worship, and the Heroic in History*, Berkeley, CA: University of California Press, 1993 [1841]; Joseph Campbell, *The Hero with a Thousand Faces*, Princeton, NJ: Princeton University Press, 1949; John Carroll, *The Western Dreaming: How the Western World Is Dying for Want of a Story*, Sydney: Harper Collins, 2001; and Bernhard Giesen, *Triumph and Trauma*, Boulder, CO: Paradigm Publishers, 2004.

Chapter 5

1 Haugaard (1998: 167–8) has also connected performativity to power: "Structural constraint works on the level of infelicity. When an actor intends to reproduce structures or meaning but other actors treat the intended meaning as infelicitous, there is a failure in structural reproduction . . . If others are willing to grant the same meaning to an act of commanding as is intended by the speaker, then . . . the command is reproduced. If, on the other hand, the act of commanding meets a response of infelicity then it is not a command . . . Except for direct coercion, it is always the attitude of the second actor B who determines the success of an exercise of power . . . The person extending power is always potentially open to infelicitous reactions which represent the structural limits of their power. On the other hand, by performing well or gaining

trust, it is possible to redefine a position and, in so doing, create new power resources."

Chapter 7

1 I draw here from Alexander (2006a) *The Civil Sphere*, chapter 5.

Chapter 8

1 The *New York Times* reporter Richard Bernstein comments here on – and draws from – videotape discovered by American forces in Afghanistan in the months after 9/11. The tape allowed Western audiences to become privy to bin Laden's own response to the 9/11 terrorist performance and to his close associates' comments about reactions to the broadcast among Islamicists from other Arab nations.
2 These recastings were not reported as constructions but were presented as actual accounts, as objective descriptions and objective rememberings. This ambiguity, how the implicit social role of journalism in such liminal situations contradicts its explicit professional ethics, is revealed nicely in the Forward written by the executive editor of the *New York Times*, Howell Raines, to *Out of the Blue: The Story of September 11, 2001: From Jihad to Ground Zero*, authored by a *Times* journalist and based on the staff's reporting of the previous year.

> As daily journalists, of course, we do not set about our work with the idea of being teachers or moral historians. We are engaged in an intellectual enterprise built around bringing quality information to an engaged and demanding readership. Sometimes that means writing what some have called the first rough draft of history. Sometimes it also means constructing a memorial to those whose courage and sacrifice we have recorded or – to speak more precisely – erecting a foundation of information upon which our readers can construct their own historical overviews, their own memorials to those who are lost and to the struggle to preserve democratic values. (Bernstein 2002: x)

3 For a discussion of "new beginning" as a metaphorical construction that allows consensual commitment and social reform, see Edles's (1998) reconstruction of this image as one of the core representations that allowed the Spanish transition to democracy in post-Franco Spain.
4 Thousands of examples of such generalization and abstraction can be culled from the communicative media in the days, weeks, and months that followed 9/11. The nuanced ways in which this idealization functioned as a medium for identification and solidary-extension would be well worth the effort at hermeneutic reconstruction. A single quotation, merely as illustration, will here suffice. As the one-year anniversary of the tragedy approached, a flood of books appeared, written by some of the same journalists who initially had reported the events in the daily news media. The generalization and memorialization that formed the contents of these books then were condensed further

222

and were broadcast to a much larger audience by the short book reviews published in the daily media in turn. Under the headline "On a Hijacked Airliner, Moments of Moral Clarity," the following paragraph appeared in a review of a book-length account of the passengers on United Flight 98, who evidently were able to overwhelm the hijackers and to prevent a fourth terrorist conflagration.

> Heroism is rarely the province of kings. This certainly emerged as a lesson in the many acts of courage we saw on Sept. 11, and it is a sustaining message within the story of the men and women who helped bring down United Flight 98 in the woods of Pennsylvania that day, on the one hijacking mission that failed to strike an intended target. The passengers and crew members were "ordinary" men and women who remind us again that no one, in fact, is ordinary; they saved innumerable other lives and contributed to our sense in the midst of that tragedy that as capable as we humans are of destruction, we are even more reliably capable of love, dedication, and sacrifice. (*New York Times,* August 29, 2002: E5)

Chapter 10

1 Despite this convention, I am not entirely happy with the "public" as a sociological-cum-philosophical category, but will generally employ the hyphenated term "civil-public" in the following discourse about public intellectuals. See *The Civil Sphere,* Oxford University Press, 2006, for an explanation.

2 As Weber did not himself connect his religious sociology to the origins of philosophy and reason in the Greek public sphere, he betrays his own ambivalence about the democratic tradition. He saw the prophets as the first demagogues and equated modern mass democracy with plebiscitary caesarism – far from the Socratic ideal.

3 This is a major problem in Michael Burawoy's (2005) understanding of public intellectuals, which is informed, and deformed, by the Enlightenment, or "modernist," idea of intellectuals as legislators, as truth carriers of expert knowledge. As Bauman has suggested, there is at the core of such a perspective a rather "vanguardist" idea of a closed scientific system. While Burawoy's embrace of such an image of the public sociologist is well-intended and public spirited, taken literally his particular approach carries some of the elitist dangers that bedeviled left-wing and right-wing revolutionary and liberal social engineering movements in the twentieth century. (For a strong elaboration of this criticism, see Martinelli 2008.)

REFERENCES

Abrahams, R. D. (1995) Forward to the Aldine Paperback Edition. In Victor Turner, *The Ritual Process: Structure and Anti-structure*. Aldine, New York.

Alexander, J. C. (1981) The Mass News Media in Systemic, Historical and Comparative Perspective. In E. Katz & T. Szecsko (eds.), *Mass Media and Social Change*. Sage, London, pp. 17–51.

Alexander, J. C. (1982–1983) *Theoretical Logic in Sociology*. University of California Press, Berkeley, CA.

Alexander, J. C. (1987a) *Twenty Lectures: Sociological Theory Since World War II*. Columbia University Press, New York.

Alexander, J. C. (1987b) Constructing Scandal. *New Republic* 3777, June 8, pp. 18–20.

Alexander, J. C. (1987c) Action and its Environments. In J. C. Alexander, B. Giesen, R. Munch & N. Smelser, (eds.), *The Micro–Macro Link*. University of California Press, Berkeley, CA, pp. 289–318.

Alexander, J. C. (1988a) Action and its Environments. In *Action and its Environments: Toward a New Synthesis*. Columbia University Press, New York.

Alexander, J. C. (ed.) (1988b) *Durkheimian Sociology: Cultural Studies*. Cambridge University Press, Cambridge, UK.

Alexander, J. C. (1992) Citizen and Enemy as Symbolic Classification: On the Polarizing Discourse of Civil Society. In M. Fournier & M. Lamont (eds.), *Cultivating Differences: Symbolic Boundaries and the Making of Inequality*. Chicago University Press, Chicago, IL, pp. 289–308.

Alexander, J. C. (1994) Modern, Ante, Post, and Neo: How Social Theories Have Tried to Understand the "New World" of "Our Time." *Zeitschrift fur Soziologie* 23(3): 165–97.

Alexander, J. C. (1996) Cultural Sociology or Sociology of Culture? *Culture* 10(3–4), 1–5.

Alexander, J. C. (1998) After Neofunctionalism: Action, Culture, and Civil Society. In *Neofunctionalism and After*. Blackwell, Malden, MA, pp. 210–33.

Alexander, J. C. (2002) Citizen and Enemy as Symbolic Classification: On the Polarizing Discourse of Civil Society. In M. Lamont & M. Fournier (eds.),

Cultivating Differences: Symbolic Boundaries and the Making of Inequality. University of Chicago Press, Chicago, IL, pp. 289–308.

Alexander, J. C. (2003a) On the Social Construction of Moral Universals: The "Holocaust" from War Crime to Trauma Drama. In *The Meanings of Social Life: A Cultural Sociology.* Oxford University Press, New York, pp. 27–84.

Alexander, J. C. (2003b) *The Meanings of Social Life: A Cultural Sociology.* Oxford University Press, New York.

Alexander, J. C. (2003c) Watergate as Democratic Ritual. In *The Meanings of Social Life: A Cultural Sociology.* Oxford University Press, New York, pp. 155–78.

Alexander, J. C. (2003d) Modern, Ante, Post, and Neo: How Intellectuals Explain "Our Time." In *The Meanings of Social Life: A Cultural Sociology.* Oxford University Press, New York, pp. 193–228.

Alexander, J. C. (2004) From the Depths of Despair: Performance and Counter-Performance on September 11th. *Sociological Theory* 21(1), 88–105.

Alexander, J. C. (2006a) *The Civil Sphere.* Oxford University Press, New York.

Alexander, J. C. (2006b) Cultural Pragmatics: Social Performance between Ritual and Strategy. In J. C. Alexander, B. Giesen & J. Mast (eds.), *Social Performance: Symbolic Action, Cultural Pragmatics, and Ritual.* Cambridge University Press, New York, pp. 29–90.

Alexander, J. C. (2008a) Iconic Consciousness in Art and Life: Beginning with Giacometti's "Standing Woman." *Theory, Culture & Society* 25(3), 1–19.

Alexander, J. C. (2008b) Iconic Consciousness: The Material Feeling of Meaning. *Environment and Planning D: Society and Space* 26(5), 782–94.

Alexander, J. C. (2009) *Remembering the Holocaust: A Debate.* Oxford University Press, Oxford and New York.

Alexander, J. C. (2010a) *The Performance of Politics: Obama's Victory and the Democratic Struggle for Power.* Oxford University Press, New York.

Alexander, J. C. (2010b) The Celebrity Icon. *Cultural Sociology* 4(3), 1–14.

Alexander, J. C. (2010c) Power, Politics, and the Civil Sphere. In K. Leight & C. Jenkins (eds.), *Handbook of Politics: State and Society in Global Perspective.* Springer, New York, pp. 111–26.

Alexander, J. C. (2010d [1982]) Marxism and the Spirit of Socialism: Cultural Origins of Anti-capitalism. *Thesis Eleven* 100, 84–105.

Alexander, J. C. & Colomy, P. A. (eds.) (1990) *Differentiation Theory and Social Change.* Columbia University Press, New York.

Alexander, J. C. & Dromi, S. (2011) Trauma Construction and Moral Restriction: The Ambiguity of the Holocaust in Israel. In R. Eyerman, J. C. Alexander & E. B. Breese (eds.), *Narrating Trauma: On the Impact of Collective Suffering.* Paradigm Publishers, Boulder, CO.

Alexander, J. C. & Sherwood S. (2002) "Mythic Gestures": Robert N. Bellah and Cultural Sociology. In R. Madsen, W. M. Sullivan, A. Swidler & S. M. Tipton (eds.), *Meaning and Modernity: Religion, Polity, and Self.* University of California Press, Berkeley, CA, pp. 1–14.

Alexander, J. C. & Smith, P. (1993) The Discourse of American Civil Society: A New Approach for Cultural Studies. *Theory and Society* 22(2), 151–207.

Alexander, J. C. & Smith, P. (1998) Cultural Sociology or Sociology of Culture? Towards a Strong Program for Sociology's Second Wind. *Sociologieet Societes* 30(1), 107–16.

Alexander, J. C. & Smith, P. (2003) The Strong Program in Cultural Sociology: Elements of a Structural Hermeneutics. In J. C. Alexander, *The Meanings*

225

of Social Life: A Cultural Sociology. Oxford University Press, New York, pp. 11–26.

Alexander, J. C. & Smith, P. (2010) The Strong Program: Origins, Achievements and Prospects. In J. Hall, L. Grindstaff & M. Lo (eds.), *Handbook of Cultural Sociology.* Routledge, New York.

Alexander, K. (2001) Was it Inevitable? Islam Through History. In J. F. Hoge Jr. & G. Rose (eds.), *How Did This Happen? Terrorism and the New War.* Public Affairs, New York, pp. 53–70.

Alexander, J. C., Giesen, B. & Mast, J. (eds.) (2006) *Social Performance: Symbolic Action, Cultural Performance, and Ritual.* Cambridge University Press, New York.

Apter, D. E. & Saich, T. (1994) *Revolutionary Discourse in Mao's Republic.* Harvard University Press, Cambridge, MA.

Arendt, H. (1951) *The Origins of Totalitarianism.* Harcourt, Brace, New York.

Arendt, H. (1958) *The Human Condition.* University of Chicago Press, Chicago, IL.

Aristotle (1987) *Poetics.* Hackett, Indianapolis, IN.

Assmann, J. (2002) *The Mind of Egypt: History and Meaning in the Time of the Pharaohs.* Metropolitan, New York.

Aston, E. & Savona, G. (1991) *Theatre as Sign-System: A Semiotics of Text and Performance.* Routledge, London.

Auslander, P. (1997) *From Acting to Performance: Essays in Modernism and Postmodernism.* Routledge, London.

Auslander, P. (1999) *Liveness: Performance in a Mediatized Culture.* Routledge, London.

Austin, J. L. (1957) *How to Do Things with Words.* Harvard University Press, Cambridge, MA.

Baert, P. (2011) The Power Struggles of French Intellectuals: A case study in the sociology of ideas and the study of cultural trauma. *European Journal of Social Theory* 4.

Bakhtin, M. (1986) *Speech Genres and Other Late Essays.* University of Texas Press, Austin, TX.

Barber, B. (1983) *The Logic and Limits of Trust.* Rutgers University Press, New Brunswick, NJ.

Barthes, R. (1972a [1957]) The World of Wrestling. In R. Barthes, *Mythologies.* Hill & Wang, New York, pp. 15–25.

Barthes, R. (1972b [1957]) *Mythologies.* Hill & Wang, New York.

Barthes, R. (1977) Introduction to the Structural Analysis of Narratives. In *Image-Music-Text.* Hill & Wang, New York.

Bataille, G. (1985) *Literature and Evil.* Marion Boyard, London.

Baudrillard, J. (1983) *In the Shadow of the Silent Majorities, or, The End of the Social, and Other Essays.* Semiotext(e), New York.

Bauman, R. (1989) Performance. In E. Barnouw (ed.), *International Encyclopedia of Communications.* Oxford University Press, New York.

Bauman, Z. (1993) *Postmodern Ethics.* Blackwell, Cambridge, MA.

Bell, D. (1963) Interpretation of American Politics. In D. Bell (ed.), *The Radical Right.* Doubleday, New York, pp. 47–74.

Bellah, R. N. (1970) Religious Evolution. In *Beyond Belief: Essays on Religion in a Post-Traditional World.* Harper & Row, New York, pp. 20–51.

Bendix, R. (1964) *Nation Building and Citizenship.* John Riley, New York.

Benhabib, S. (1996) *The Reluctant Modernism of Hannah Arendt*. Sage, London.

Benjamin, W. (1968 [1936]) The Work of Art in the Age of Mechanical Reproduction. In W. Benjamin, *Illuminations*. Schocken Books, New York, pp. 217–52.

Bennet, J. (2003) Hamas Leader Tells Muslims to Retaliate if US Attacks. *New York Times*, February 8, p. 9.

Berezin, M. (1991) The Organization of Political Ideology: Culture, State, and Theater in Fascist Italy. *American Sociological Review* 56 (October), 639–51.

Berezin, M. (1994) Cultural Form and Political Meaning: State Subsidized Theater, Ideology, and the Language of Style in Fascist Italy. *American Journal of Sociology* 99(5), 1237–86.

Berezin, M. (1997) *Making the Fascist Self: The Political Culture of Interwar Italy*. Cornell University Press, Ithaca, NY.

Bernstein, R. (2002) *Out of the Blue: The Story of September 11, 2001, from Jihad to Ground Zero*. Times Books, New York.

Bhabha, H. K. (1994) *Location of Culture*. Routledge, New York.

bin Laden, O. (2002a) Bin Laden's Letter to America. *Guardian.co.uk*. November 24, 2002.

bin Laden, O. (2002b) Transcript of Bin Laden's October [2001] Interview. *CNN.com* February 5, 2002. [CNN translation]

Birnbaum, N. (1955) Monarchies and Sociologists: A Reply to Professor Shils and Mr. Young. *Sociological Review* 3, 5–23.

Black, A. (2001) *The History of Islamic Political Thought*. Routledge, New York.

Boorstin, D. (1961) *The Image: or, What happened to the American Dream*. Atheneum, New York.

Boulton, M. (1960) *The Anatomy of Drama*. Routledge & Kegan Paul, London.

Bourdieu, P. (1984) *Distinction: A Social Critique of the Judgment of Taste*. Harvard University Press, Cambridge, MA.

Bourdieu, P. (1990 [1968]) Artistic Taste and Cultural Capital. In J. C. Alexander & S. Seidman (eds.), *Culture and Society: Contemporary Debates*. Cambridge University Press, New York, pp. 205–16.

Bowler, W. (2011) Seeing Tragedy: The News Image of September 11. In J. C. Alexander, D. Bartmanski & B. Giesen (eds.), *Iconic Power: Materiality and meaning in Social Life*. Palgrave, New York.

Brecht, B. (1964) *Brecht on Brecht*. Methuen, London.

Broder, J. M. (2008) Obama, adopting economic theme, criticizes McCain. *New York Times*, June 10.

Brook, P. (1969) *The Empty Space*. Avon, New York.

Brooks, P. (1976) *The Melodramatic Imagination: Balzac, Henry James, Melodrama, and the Mode of Excess*. Yale University Press, New Haven, CT.

Brooks, C. & Manza, J. (1997) The Social and Ideological Bases of Middle-Class Political Realignment in the United States, 1972–1992. *American Sociological Review* 61 (April), 191–208.

Brucker, G. A. (1969) *Renaissance Florence*. John Wiley & Sons, New York.

Bumiller, E. (2003) Keepers of Bush Image Lift Stagecraft to New Heights. *New York Times*, May 16, p. A1.

Burawoy, M. (2005) 2004 American Sociological Association Presidential Address: For Public Sociology. *British Journal of Sociology* 56(2), 259–94.

Burchell, G., Gordon, C. & Miller, P. (eds.) (1991) *The Foucault Effect: Studies in Governmentality*. University of Chicago Press, Chicago, IL.

Burke, E. (1987 [1790]) *Reflections on the Revolution in France*. Hackett, Indianapolis, IN.

Burke, K. (1957 [1941]) *The Philosophy of Literary Form: Studies in Symbolic Action*. Vintage, New York.

Burke, K. (1959) On Catharsis, or Resolution, with a Postscript. *The Kenyon Review* 21, 337–75.

Burke, K. (1965) Dramatism. *Encyclopedia of the Social Sciences* 7, 445–451.

Butler, J. (1990) *Gender Trouble: Feminism and the Subversion of Identity*. Routledge, New York.

Butler, J. (1993a) *Bodies that Matter: On the Discursive Limits of "Sex."* Routledge, New York.

Butler, J. (1993b) Critically Queer. *GLQ* 1(1), 17–32.

Butler, J. (1999) *Gender Trouble: Feminism and the Subversion of Identity*, 10th anniversary edition. Routledge, New York.

Campbell, J. (1949) *The Hero with a Thousand Faces*. Princeton University Press, Princeton, NJ.

Carlson, M. (1996) *Performance: A Critical Introduction*. Routledge, London.

Carlson, M. (2001) *The Haunted Stage: The Theatre as Memory Machine*. University of Michigan Press, Ann Arbor, MI.

Carlyle, T. (1993 [1841]) *On Heroes, Hero Worship, and the Heroic in History*. University of California Press, Berkeley.

Carroll, J. (2001) *The Western Dreaming: How the Western World Is Dying for Want of a Story*. Harper Collins, Sydney.

Champagne, D. (1992) *Social Order and Political Change: Constitutional Governments Among the Cherokee, the Choctaw, the Chickasaw, and the Creek*. Stanford University Press, Stanford, CA.

Chan, E. (1999) Structural and Symbolic Centers: Center Displacement in the 1989 Chinese Student Movement. In M. Berezin & J. C. Alexander (eds.), *Democratic Culture: Ethnos and Demos in Global Perspective*, special issue of *International Sociology* 14(3), 337–54.

Chinoy, H. K. (1963) The Emergence of the Director. In T. Cole & H. K. Chinoy (eds.), *Directors on Directing*. Bobbs-Merrill, Indianapolis, IN.

Clifford, J. (1986) On Ethnographic Allegory. In *Writing Culture: The Poetics and Politics of Ethnography*. University of California Press, Berkeley, CA, pp. 98–121.

Clifford, J. (1988) *The Predicament of Culture: Twentieth-Century Ethnographer, Literature, and Art*. Harvard University Press, Cambridge, MA.

Collins, R. (2004) *Interaction Ritual Chains*. Cambridge University Press, New York.

Conquergood, D. (1992) Performance Theory, Hmong Shamans, and Cultural Politics. In J. G. Reinelt & J. R. Roach (eds.), *Critical Theory and Performance*. University of Michigan Press, Ann Arbor, MI, pp. 41–64.

Conquergood, D. (1995) On Caravans and Carnivals: Performance Studies in Motion. *Drama Review* 39(4), 137–42.

Conquergood, D. (2002) Performance Studies: Interventions and Radical Research. *Drama Review* 46(2), 145–56.

Copeau, J. (1955 [1923]) *Notes surle Me'tier de Comedien*. Michel Brient, Paris.

Copeland, R. (1990) The Presence of Mediation. *TDR: Journal of Performance Studies* 34(4), 28–44.

228

Cornog, E. (2004) *The Power and the Story: How the Crafted Presidential Narrative Has Determined Political Success from George Washington to George W. Bush.* Penguin, New York, p. 5.

Crick, B. (1962) *In Defense of Politics.* Penguin Books, London.

Crotty, W. J. (2009) Electing Obama: The 2008 Presidential Campaign. In W. J. Crotty (ed.), *Winning the Presidency 2008.* Paradigm Publishers, Boulder, CO, pp. 20–47.

Csikszentmihalyi, M. (1975) *Beyond Boredom and Anxiety.* Jossey-Bass, San Francisco, CA.

Dahl, R. (1961) *Who Governs? Democracy and Power in an American City.* Yale University Press, New Haven, CT.

Dayan, D. & Katz, E. (1992) *Media Events: The Live Broadcasting of History.* Harvard University Press, Cambridge, MA.

Derrida, J. (1978) *Writing and Difference.* University of Chicago Press, Chicago, IL.

Derrida, J. (1982a [1972]) Signature Event Context. In *Margins of Philosophy.* University of Chicago Press, Chicago, IL.

Derrida, J. (1982b) Différance. In *Margins of Philosophy.* University of Chicago Press, Chicago, IL.

Derrida, J. (1988) *Limited Inc.* Northwestern University Press, Evanston, IL.

Derrida, J. (1991) Différance. In P. Kamuf (ed.), *A Derrida Reader: Between the Blinds.* Columbia University Press, New York, pp. 59–79.

Dewey, J. (1966 [1916]) *Democracy and Education.* Free Press, New York, p. 87.

Diamond, E. (ed.) (1996) *Performance and Cultural Politics.* Routledge, New York.

Diderot, D. (1957 [1830]) *The Paradox of Acting.* Hill & Wang, New York.

Dilthey, W. (1976) The Construction of the Historical World in the Human Studies. In H. P. Rickman (ed.), *Selected Writings.* Cambridge University Press. Cambridge, UK, pp. 168–245.

Douglas, M. (1967) *Purity and Danger: An Analysis of Concepts of Pollution and Taboo.* Praeger, New York.

Downs, A. (1957) *An Economic Theory of Democracy.* Harper & Row, New York, p. 36.

Durkheim, E. (1957) *Professional Ethics and Civic Morals.* Routledge & Kegan Paul, London.

Durkheim, E. (1996 [1912]) *The Elementary Forms of Religious Life.* Free Press, New York.

Edelman, M. (1964) *The Symbolic Uses of Politics.* University of Illinois Press, Champaign, IL.

Edles, L. D. (1998) *Symbol and Ritual in the New Spain: The Transition to Democracy after Franco.* Cambridge University Press, Cambridge, UK.

Eisenstadt, S. N. (1963) *The Political System of Empires.* Free Press, New York.

Eisenstadt, S. N. (1982) The Axial Age: The Emergence of Transcendental Visions and the Rise of Clerics. *European Journal of Sociology* 23, 294–314.

Eley, G. (1992) Nations, Publics, and Political Cultures: Placing Habermas in the Nineteenth Century. In C. Calhoun (ed.), *Habermas and the Public Sphere.* MIT Press, Cambridge, MA, pp. 289–339.

Emirbayer, M. & Goodwin, J. (1996) Symbols, Positions, Objects: Toward a New Theory of Revolutions and Collective Action. *History and Theory* 35(3), 358–74.

229

Emirbayer, M. & Mische, A. (1998) What Is Agency? *American Journal of Sociology* 103, 962–1023.

Evans-Pritchard, E. E. (1940) *The Nuer: A Description of the Modes of Livelihood and Political Institutions of a Nilotic People.* Oxford University Press, London.

Eyerman, R. (2006) Performing Opposition or, How Social Movements Move. In J. C. Alexander, B. Giesen & J. Mast. (eds.), *Social Performance: Symbolic Action, Cultural Pragmatics, and Ritual.* Cambridge University Press, New York, pp. 193–217.

Eyerman, R. (forthcoming) Intellectuals and Cultural Trauma. *European Journal of Social Theory* 4.

Eyerman, R. & Jamison, A. (1991) *Social Movements: A Cognitive Approach.* Polity, London.

Ferrara, A. (2001) The Evil That Men Do. In M. P. Lara (ed.), *Rethinking Evil.* University of California Press, Berkeley, CA.

Flesch, R. (1946) *The Art of Plain Talk.* Harper & Brothers, New York.

Foucault, M. (1970) *Discipline and Punish: The Birth of the Prison.* Vintage, New York.

Foucault, M. (1972) *Archeology of Knowledge.* Pantheon Books, New York.

Frankfort, H. (1948) *Ancient Egyptian Religion.* Harper & Row, New York.

Fraser, N. (1992) Rethinking the Public Sphere: A Contribution to the Critique of Actually Existing Democracy. In C. Calhoun (ed.), *Habermas and the Public Sphere.* MIT Press, Cambridge, MA, pp. 109–42.

Freud, S. (1950 [1900]) *The Interpretation of Dreams.* George Allen & Unwin, London.

Fried, M. H. (1971) On the Evolution of Social Stratification and the State. In S. N. Eisenstadt (ed.), *Political Sociology.* Basic Books, New York, pp. 101–4.

Friedland, R. & Alford, R. R. (1991) Bring Society Back In: Symbols, Practices, and Institutional Contradictions. In W. W. Powell & P. J. DiMaggio. (eds.), *The New Institutionalism in Organizational Analysis.* University of Chicago Press, Chicago, IL, pp. 232–63.

Friedland, R. & Mohr, J. (eds.) (2004) *Matters of Culture: Cultural Sociology in Practice.* Cambridge University Press, Cambridge, UK.

Frischmann, D. H. (1994) New Mayan Theatre in Chiapas: Anthropology, Literacy and Social Drama. In D. Taylor & J. Villegas (eds.), *Negotiating Performance: Gender, Sexuality and Theatricality in Latin/o America.* Duke University Press, Durham, NC.

Furet, F. (1981) *Interpreting the French Revolution.* Cambridge University Press, Cambridge, UK.

Garfinkel, H. (1967) *Studies in Ethnomethodology.* Prentice Hall, Englewood Cliffs, NJ.

Geertz, C. (1973a) Ideology as a Cultural System. In *The Interpretation of Cultures.* Basic Books, New York.

Geertz, C. (1973b) Deep Play: Notes on the Balinese Cockfight. In *The Interpretation of Cultures.* Basic Books, New York.

Geertz, C. (1973c) Thick Description: Toward an Interpretive Theory of Culture. In *The Interpretation of Cultures.* Basic Books, New York.

Geertz, C. (1973d) *The Interpretation of Cultures.* Basic Books, New York.

Geertz, C. (1980) *Negara: The Theatre State in Nineteenth Century Bali.* Princeton University Press, Princeton, NJ.

Gerth, H. H. & Mills, C. W. (1964) *Character and Social Structure: The Psychology of Social Institutions.* Harcourt, Brace, & World, New York.

Gibson, J. W. (1994) *Warrior Dreams: Paramilitary Culture in Post-War America.* Hill & Wang, New York.

Giesen, B. (1998) *Intellectuals and the Nation: Collective Identity in a German Axial Age.* Cambridge University Press, New York.

Giesen, B. (2004) *Triumph and Trauma.* Paradigm Publishers, Boulder, CO.

Giesen, B. (2006) Performing the Sacred: A Durkheimian Perspective on the Performative Turn in the Social Sciences. In J. C. Alexander, B. Giesen & J. Mast (eds.), *Social Performance: Symbolic Action, Cultural Pragmatics, and Ritual.* Cambridge University Press, New York.

Goffman, E. (1956) *The Presentation of Self in Everyday Life.* Doubleday, New York.

Goffman, E. (1967) *Interaction Ritual.* Pantheon, New York.

Goffman, E. (1974) *Frame Analysis.* Harper & Row, New York.

Goodman, T (2007) Setting the Stage for a "New" South Africa: A Cultural Approach to the Truth & Reconciliation Commission. PhD Thesis, Yale University.

Goody, J. (1986) *The Logic of Writing and the Organization of Society.* Cambridge University Press, Cambridge, UK.

Gouldner, A. (1965) *Enter Plato: Classical Greece and the Origins of Social Theory.* Routledge & Kegan Paul, London.

Grams, D. (2010) Freedom and Cultural Consciousness: Black Working Class Parades in Post-Katrina New Orleans, unpublished manuscript.

Gramsci, A. (1971) *Selections from the Prison Notebooks.* International Publishers, New York, pp. 12–13, 234, 263, 268.

Green, D., Palmquist, B. & Schickler, E. (2002) *Partisan Hearts and Minds: Political Parties and the Social Identities of Voters.* Yale University Press, New Haven, CT.

Greenberg, D. (2004) *Nixon's Shadow: History of an Image.* Norton, New York.

Greenblatt, S. (1980) *Renaissance Self-Fashioning: From More to Shakespeare.* University of Chicago Press, Chicago, IL.

Gumbrecht, H. (2006) Aesthetic Experience in Everyday Worlds: Reclaiming an Unredeemed Utopian Motif. *New Literary History* 37(2), 299–318.

Habermas, J. (1984) *The Theory of Communicative Action.* Beacon Press, Boston, MA.

Habermas, J. (1989 [1962]) *The Structural Transformation of the Public Sphere.* MIT Press, Cambridge, MA.

Habermas, J. (1993) *Justification and Application: Remarks on Discourse Ethics.* MIT Press, Cambridge, MA.

Hagstrom, W. (1965) *The Scientific Community.* Free Press, New York.

Halberstam, D. (1999) *The Children.* Fawcett, New York.

Hall, S., Critcher, C., Jefferson, T. & Clarke, J. N.(1978) *Policing the Crisis: Mugging, the State and Law and Order.* Macmillan, London.

Hall, S. (1980) Encoding/Decoding. In S. Hall, D. Hobson, A. Lowe & P. Willis (eds.), *Culture, Media, Language.* Hutchinson, London, pp. 128–38.

Hall, S. & Jefferson, T. (eds.) (1976) *Resistance Through Rituals: Youth Subcultures in Post-War Britain.* Hutchinson, London.

Hanson, V. D. (2001) *Carnage and Culture: Landmark Battles in the Rise of Western Power.* Doubleday, New York.

Hardison, O. B. (1965) *Christian Rite and Christian Drama in the Middle Ages.* Johns Hopkins Press, Baltimore, MD.

Hartman, G. (1958) Milton's Counterplot. *Journal of English Literary History* 25(1), 1–12.

Hartnoll, P. (1968) *A Concise History of the Theatre.* Thames & Hudson, London.

Harwood, J. (2008a) The caucus – democratic primary fight is like no other, ever. *New York Times,* June 2, Section A.

Harwood, J. (2008b) Flip flops are looking like a hot summer trend. *New York Times,* June 23, Section A.

Haugaard, M. (1998) *The Constitution of Power: A Theoretical Analysis of Power, Knowledge and Structure.* Manchester University Press, Manchester, UK.

Hays, S. (1994) Structure and Agency and the Sticky Problem of Culture. *Sociological Theory* 12(1), 57–72.

Healy, P. (2008) Target: Barack Obama. Strategy: what day is it? *New York Times,* July 4.

Heins, V. (2005) Orientalising America? Continental Intellectuals and the Search for Europe's Identity. *Millennium: Journal of International Studies* 34(2), 433–48.

Hobbes, T. (1651) *Leviathan: The Matter, Form and Power of a Common Wealth Ecclesiastical and Civil.*

Hobsbawm, E. J. (1959) *Social Bandits and Primitive Rebels.* Free Press, Glencoe, IL.

Horkheimer, M. &. Adorno, T. W. (1972) *Dialectic of Enlightenment.* Continuum Publishing, New York.

Huizinga, J. (1950 [1938]) *Homo Ludens: A Study of the Play Element in Culture.* Beacon Press, Boston, MA.

Hunt, D. (1997) *Screening the Los Angeles "Riots."* Cambridge University Press, New York.

Hunt, L. (1984) *Politics, Culture, and Class in the French Revolution.* University of California Press, Berkeley, CA.

Hymes, D. (1964) *Language in Culture and Society.* Harper & Row, New York.

Iser, W. (1980) Interaction Between Text and Reader. In S. R. Suleiman & I. Crosman (eds.), *The Reader in the Text: Essays on Audience and Interpretation.* Princeton University Press, Princeton, NJ, pp. 106–19.

Jacobs, R. (1996) Civil Society and Crisis: Culture, Discourse, and the Rodney King Beating. *American Journal of Sociology* 101, 1238–72.

Jacobs, R. (2000) *Race, Media, and the Crisis of Civil Society.* Cambridge University Press, Cambridge, UK.

Jaeger, W. (1945) *Paideia: The Ideals of Greek Culture,* vol. 1. Oxford University Press, Oxford, UK.

Jakobson, R. (1987) Linguistics and Poetics. In R. Jakobson (ed.), *Language and Literature.* Harvard University Press, Cambridge, MA, pp. 62–94.

Jakobson, R. (1990a) *On Language.* Harvard University Press, Cambridge, MA.

Jakobson, R. (1990b) My Favorite Topics. In *On Language.* Harvard University Press, Cambridge, MA, pp. 61–6.

Jameson, F. (1991) *The Postmodern Condition, or, The Cultural Logic of Late Capitalism.* Duke University Press, Durham, NC.

232

Jamieson, K. H. & Waldman, P. (2001) *Electing the President, 2000: The Insiders' View*. University of Pennsylvania Press, Philadelphia, PA, p. 2.

Kane, A. (1991) Cultural Analysis in Historical Sociology: The Analytic and Concrete Forms of the Autonomy of Culture. *Sociological Theory* 9, 53–69.

Kane, A. (1997) Theorizing Meaning Construction in Social Movements: Symbolic Structures and Interpretation during the Irish Land War, 1879–1882. *Sociological Theory* 15, 249–76.

Kant, I. (1960 [1764]) *Observation on the Feeling of the Beautiful and the Sublime*. University of California Press, Berkeley, CA.

Kantorowicz, E. H. (1957) *The King's Two Bodies: A Study of Medieval Political Theology*. Princeton University Press, Princeton, NJ.

Kemp, B. J. (1989) *Ancient Egypt*. Routledge, London.

Kepel, G. (2002) *Jihad: The Trail of Political Islam*. Harvard University Press, Cambridge, MA.

Konrad, G. & Szelenyi, I. (1979) *Intellectuals on the Road to Class Power*. Harcourt, Brace, Jovanovich, New York.

Kovaleski, S. (2008) Obama's organizing years, guiding others and finding himself. *New York Times*, July 7, p. A1.

Kristol, W. (2008) cited in A campaign we can believe in? *New York Times*. June 9, Section A.

Ku, A. (1999) *Narrative, Politics, and the Public Sphere*. Ashgate, Aldershot, UK.

Labaree, B. W. (1979) *The Boston Tea Party*. Northeastern University Press, Boston, MA.

Lamont, M. (1992) *Money, Manners, and Morals: The Culture of the French and American Upper-Middle Class*. University of Chicago Press, Chicago, IL.

Landes, J. (1988) *Women and the Public Sphere in the Age of the French Revolution*. Cornell University Press, Ithaca, NY.

Lang, G. E. & Lang, K. (1968) *Politics and Television*. Quadrangle Books, Chicago, IL.

Lang, G. E. & Lang, K. (1983) *The Battle for Public Opinion: The President, the Press, and the Polls During Watergate*. Columbia University Press, New York.

Lapidus, I. M. (1987) Islam and Modernity. In S. N. Eisenstadt (ed.), *Patterns of Modernity: Vol. 2, Beyond the West*. Francis Pinter, London, pp. 65–88.

Lash, S. & Urry, J. (1994) *Economies of Signs and Space*. Sage, London.

Laswell, H. D. (1936) *Politics: Who Gets What, When, How*. McGraw-Hill, New York.

Leach, E. R. (1972) Ritualization in Man in Relation to Conceptual and Social Development. In W. A. Lessa & E. Z. Vogt (eds.), *Reader in Comparative Religion: An Anthropological Approach*, 3rd edition. Harper & Row, New York, pp. 333–337.

Lears, J. (2003) How a War Became a Crusade. *New York Times*. March 11, p. 25.

Leenhardt, J. (1980) Toward a Sociology of Reading. In S. R. Suleiman & I. Crosman (eds.), *The Reader in the Text: Essays on Audience Interpretation*. Princeton University Press, Princeton, NJ, pp. 205–24.

Levy-Bruhl, L. (1923) *Primitive Mentality*. Macmillan, London.

Levi-Strauss, C. (1963) The Sorcerer and His Magic. In *Structural Anthropology*. Basic Books, New York, pp. 167–85.

Levi-Strauss, C. (1967) *The Savage Mind*. University of Chicago Press, Chicago.

Levi-Strauss, C. (1973 [1955]) *Tristes Tropiques*. Athenaeum, New York.

Liebes, T. (1992a) Decoding TV News: The Political Discourse of Israeli Hawks and Doves. *Theory and Society* 21, 357–81.

Liebes, T. (1992b) Our War/Their War: Comparing the Intifadeh and the Gulf War on US and Israeli Television. *Critical Studies in Mass Communication* 9, 44–55.

Liebes, T. & Katz, E. (1990) *The Export of Meaning: Cross-Cultural Readings of "Dallas."* Oxford University Press, Oxford, UK.

Lilla, M. (2011) The Beck of Revelation, New York Review of Books, December 9, http://www.nybooks.com/articles/archives/2010/dec/09/beck-revelation (Accessed on June 27, 2011).

Lim, E. T. (2008) *The Anti-Intellectual Presidency: The Decline of Presidential Rhetoric from George Washington to George W. Bush.* Oxford University Press, New York.

Lipset, S. M. (1981 [1960]) Elections: The Expression of the Democratic Class Struggle. In *Political Man: The Social Bases of Politics.* Johns Hopkins University Press, Baltimore, MD, pp. 230–78.

Locke, J. (1694) *The Second Treatise on Government: An Essay Concerning the True Original, Extent, and End of Civil Government.*

Luhmann, N. (1995) *Social Systems.* Stanford University Press, Stanford, CA.

Lukes, S. J. (1977) Political Ritual and Social Integration. In *Essays in Social Theory.* Columbia, New York, pp. 52–73.

Luo, M. & Zeleny, J. (2008) Obama, in shift, says he'll reject public financing. *New York Times,* June 20, Section A.

MacAloon, J. (1984) Introduction: Cultural Performances, Culture Theory. In *Rite, Drama, Festival, Spectacle: Rehearsals Toward a Theory of Cultural Performance.* Institute for the Study of Human Issues, Philadelphia, PA, pp. 1–18.

McCarthy, M. (1974) *The Masks of State: Watergate Portraits.* Harcourt, Brace, Jovanovich, New York.

McConachie, B. A. (1992) Historicizing the Relations of Theatrical Production. In J. G. Reinelt & J. R. Roach, *Critical Theory and Performance.* University of Michigan Press, Ann Arbor, MI, pp. 168–78.

McCormick, L. (2009) Higher, Faster, Louder: Representations of the International Music Competition. *Cultural Sociology* 3(1), 5–30.

McKenzie, J. (2001) *Perform or Else: From Discipline to Performance.* Routledge, New York.

McKenzie, J. (1998) Gender Trouble: (the) Butler Did It. In P. Phelan & J. Lane (eds.), *The Ends of Performance.* New York University Press, New York,, pp. 217–35.

Mann, M. (1986) *The Sources of Social Power, Vol. 1.* Cambridge University Press, New York.

Mannheim, K. (1971 [1927]) Conservative Thought. In K. H. Wolff (ed.), *From Karl Mannheim.* Oxford University Press, New York.

Margolick, D. (2000) *Strange Fruit: Billie Holiday, Café Society, and an Early Cry for Civil Rights.* Running Press, Philadelphia, PA.

Martinelli, A. (2008) Sociology in Political Practice and Public Discourse. *Current Sociology* 56(3), 361–70.

Marvin, C. & Ingle, D. W. (1999) *Blood Sacrifice and the Nation: Totem Rituals and the American Flag.* Cambridge University Press, New York.

Marx, K. (1962 [1852]) The Eighteenth Brumaire of Louis Bonaparte. In *Karl*

Marx and Frederick Engels: Selected Works, Vol. 1. Foreign Languages Publishing House, Moscow, pp. 246–360.

Marx, K. (1963 [1844]) Economic and Philosophical Manuscripts. In T. B. Bottomore (ed.), *Karl Marx, Early Writings*. McGraw-Hill, New York, pp. 61–219.

Marx, K. (1970 [1846]) *The German Ideology*. International Publishers, Moscow.

Marx, K. (1972) Theses on Feuerbach. In R. Tucker (ed.), *The Marx-Engels Reader*, 2nd edition. W. W. Norton & Co., New York, pp. 143–145.

Marx, K. (2001 [1867]) Commodities. In K. Marx, *Capital, Vol. 1*. BGR: ElecBook, London, pp. 1–53.

Marx, K. & Engels, F. (1962 [1848]). Manifesto of the Communist Party. In *Karl Marx and Frederick Engels: Selected Works, Vol. 1*. International Publishers, Moscow, pp. 18–48.

Mast, J. (2003) How to Do Things with Cultural Pragmatics: A Case Study in Brief. *Theory* (Spring), 8–10.

Mast, J. (2006) The Cultural Pragmatics of Event-ness: The Clinton/Lewinsky Affair. In J. C. Alexander, B. Giesen & J. Mast (eds.), *Social Performance: Symbolic Action, Cultural Pragmatics, and Ritual*. Cambridge University Press, New York, pp. 115–45.

Mast, J. (forthcoming) Cultural Pragmatics and the Structure and Flow of Democratic Politics. In J. C. Alexander, R. Jacobs and P. Smith (eds.) *Handbook of Cultural Sociology*. Oxford, New York.

Mauss, M. (1979) *Seasonal Variations of the Eskimo: A Study in Social Morphology*. Routledge & Kegan Paul, London.

Mayhew, L. (1997) *The New Public: Professional Communication and the Means of Social Influence*. Cambridge University Press, New York.

Mead, G. H. (1964) *Mind, Self, and Society*. University of Chicago Press, Chicago, IL.

Meyer, J. & Rowan, B. (1977) Institutionalized Organizations: Formal Structure as Myth and Ceremony. *American Journal of Sociology* 83, 340–63.

Michels, R. (1962 [1911]) *Political Parties: A Sociological Study of the Oligarchical Tendencies of Modern Democracy*. Free Press, New York.

Miller, D. (1987) *Material Culture and Mass Consumption*. Blackwell, Oxford.

Mills, C. W. (1956). *The Power Elite*. Oxford, New York.

Mirsepassi, A. (2000) *Intellectual Discourse and the Politics of Modernization: Negotiating Modernity in Iran*. Cambridge University Press, Cambridge, UK.

Moore, S. F. & Myerhoff, B. G. (eds.) (1975) *Symbols and Politics in Communal Ideology*. Cornell University Press, Ithaca, NY.

Moore, S. F. & Myerhoff, B. G. (eds.) (1977) *Secular Ritual*. Van Gorcum, Amsterdam, Holland.

Moreno, J. L. (1975) Spontaneity and Catharsis. In J. Fox (ed.), *The Essential Moreno: Writing on Psychodrama, Group Method, and Spontaneity*. Springer, New York, pp. 39–59.

Morris, A. (1984) *The Origins of the Civil Rights Movement: Black Communities Organizing for Change*. Free Press, New York.

Morris, A. (2007) Naked Power and the Civil Sphere. *Sociological Quarterly* 48(4), 629–40.

Morris, C. W. (1938) *Foundations of the Theory of Signs*. University of Chicago Press, Chicago, IL.

Myerhoff, B. (1978) *Number Our Days*. Dutton, New York.

Nagourney, A. & Lebiovich, M. (2008) Clinton ends campaign with clear call to elect Obama. *New York Times*, June 8, p. A1.

Nietzsche, F. (1956 [1872]) The Birth of Tragedy. In F. Nietzsche, *The Birth of Tragedy and the Genealogy of Morals*. Anchor Books, New York, pp. 1–146.

Nochlin, L. (1993) *Realism*. Viking, New York.

Nolan, P. & Lenski, G. (1995) *Human Societies: An Introduction to Macrosociology*. McGraw-Hill, New York.

Noonan, P. (1998) *On Speaking Well*. Harper, New York.

Oakeshott, M. (1981 [1962]) Rationalism in Politics. In *Rationalism in Politics and Other Essays*. Methuen, New York, pp. 1–36.

O'Keefe, G. J. & Mendelsohn, H. (1974) Voter Selectivity, Partisanship, and the Challenge of Watergate. *Communication Research* 1(4), 345–67.

Osborne, J. W. (1970) *The Silent Revolution: The Industrial Revolution in England as a Source of Cultural Change*. Scribners, New York.

Parsons, T. (1967) On the Concept of Political Power. In T. Parsons (ed.), *Sociological Theory and Modern Society*. Free Press, New York, pp. 286–99.

Pavis, P. (1988) From Text to Performance. In M. Issacharoff & R. F. Jones, *Performing Texts*. University of Pennsylvania Press, Philadelphia, PA, pp. 86–100.

Peters, J. S. (2000) *Theatre of the Book, 1480–1880: Print, Text, and Performance in Europe*. Oxford University Press, New York.

Phelan, P. (1993) *Unmarked: The Politics of Performance*. Routledge, New York.

Plato (1965) *The Republic of Plato*. Translated by F. MacDonald Cornford. Oxford University Press, New York, Part I, Chapter 3, p. 18.

Plato (1980) *Gorgias*. Translated by W. Hamilton. Penguin, London.

Powell, M. (2008a) Barack Obama: calm in the swirl of history. *New York Times*, June 4, p. A1.

Powell, M. (2008b) Obama, awaiting a new title, carefully hones his partisan image. *New York Times*, June 3, p. A18.

Powell, M. (2008c) For Obama, a pragmatist's shift toward the center. *New York Times*, June 27.

Powell, M. & Zeleny, J. (2008) Obama fuels pullout debate with remarks. *New York Times*, July 4.

Rambo, E. & Chan, E. (1990) Text, Structure, and Action in Cultural Sociology. *Theory and Society* 19, 635–48.

Rappaport, R. (1968) *Pigs for the Ancestors*. Yale University Press, New Haven, CT.

Rauer, V. (2006) Symbols in Action: Willy Brandt's Kneefall at the Warsaw Memorial. In J. C. Alexander, B. Giesen & J. Mast (eds.), *Social Performance: Symbolic Action, Cultural Performance, and Ritual*. Cambridge University Press, New York, pp. 257–83.

Reiss, T. J. (1971) *Toward Dramatic Illusion: Theatrical Technique and Meaning from Hardy to Horace*. Yale University Press, New Haven, CT.

Rey, A. (ed.) (2006) *Le Robert Micro: Dictionnaire d'apprentissage de la langue française*. Dictionnaires. Le Robert, Paris.

Ricoeur, P. (1971) The Model of the Text: Meaningful Action Considered as a Text. *Social Research* 38, 529–62.

Ricoeur, P. (1976) *Interpretation Theory: Discourse and the Surplus of Meaning.* Texas Christian University Press, Fort Worth, TX.

Ringmar, E. (1996) *Identity, Interest, and Action: A Cultural Explanation of Sweden's Intervention in the Thirty Years War.* Cambridge University Press, New York.

Roach, J.(1993) *The Player's Passion: Studies in the Science of Acting.* University of Michigan Press, Ann Arbor, MI.

Roach, J. (1996) *Cities of the Dead: Circum-Atlantic Performance.* Columbia University Press, New York.

Roach, J. (2000) Cutting Loose: Burying the "First Man of Jazz." In R. Harvey & E. Kaplan (eds.), *Joyous Wakes, Dignified Dying: Issues in Death and Dying.* Humanities Institute of the State University of New York at Stony Brook, pp. 3–14.

Roach, J. (2007) *It.* University of Michigan Press, Ann Arbor, MI.

Rorty, R. (ed.) (1967) *The Linguistic Turn: Essays in Philosophical Method.* University of Chicago Press, Chicago, IL.

Roth, G. (1963) *The Social Democrats in Imperial Germany.* Bedminster Press, New York.

Rouse, J. (1992) Textuality and Authority in Theater and Drama: Some Contemporary Possibilities. In J. G. Reinelt & J. Roach (eds.), *Critical Theory and Performance.* University of Michigan Press, Ann Arbor, MI, pp. 146–58.

Rutenberg, J. (2008) Friendly campaigning, only not so much. *New York Times,* July 12, Section A.

Rutenberg, J. & Zeleny, J.(2008) Obama's campaign tightens control of image and access. *New York Times,* June 19, p. A1.

Sahlins, M. (1981) *Historical Metaphors and Mythical Realities: Structure in the Early History of the Sandwich Islands Kingdom.* University of Michigan Press, Ann Arbor, MI.

Sahlins, M. (1972) *Stone Age Economics.* Aldine de Gruyter, New York.

Sahlins, M. (1976) *Culture and Practical Reason.* Chicago University Press, Chicago, IL.

Saussure, F. (1966 [1916]) *Course in General Linguistics.* McGraw Hill, New York.

Saussure, F. (1985) The Linguistic Sign. In R. E. Innis (ed.), *Semiotics: An Introductory Anthology.* University Press, Bloomington: IN, pp. 28–46.

Schachermeyr, F. (1971[1953]) The Genesis of the Greek Polis. In S. N. Eisenstadt (ed.), *Political Sociology.* Basic Books, New York, pp. 195–202.

Schechner, R. (1976) From Ritual to Theatre and Back. In R. Schechner & M. Schuman (eds.), *Ritual, Play, and Performance: Readings in the Social Sciences/Theatre.* Seabury Press, New York, pp. 196–230.

Schechner, R. (1977a) *Ritual, Play, and Social Drama.* Seabury Press, New York.

Schechner, R. (1977b) *Essays on Performance Theory 1970–1976.* Drama Book Specialists, New York.

Schechner, R. (1981) Performers and Spectators Transported and Transformed. *Kenyon Review* 3, 83–113.

Schechner, R. (1985) *Between Theatre and Anthropology.* University of Pennsylvania Press, Philadelphia, PA.

Schechner, R. (1987) Victor Turner's Last Adventure. In V. Turner, *The Anthropology of Performance.* PAJ Publications, New York, pp. 7–20.

Schechner, R. (1988) *Performance Theory.* Routledge, New York.

Schechner, R. (1998) What is Performance Studies Anyway? In P. Phelan & J. Lane (eds.), *The Ends of Performance*. New York University Press, New York, pp. 357–362.

Schechner, R. (2002) *Performance Studies: An Introduction*. Routledge, New York.

Schegloff, E. A. (1987) Between Macro and Micro: Contexts and Other Connections. In J. C. Alexander, B. Giesen, R. Munch & N. Smelser (eds.), *The Micro–Macro Link*. University of California Press, Berkeley, CA, pp. 207–34.

Schmidt, I. (in progress) When Good Ballots Go Bad: Voting Ritual (and its Failure) in the United States. PhD dissertation, Yale University.

Schudson, M. (1981) *Discovering the News*. Basic Books, New York.

Schudson, M. (1992a) Was There Ever a Public Sphere: If So, When? Reflections on the American Case. In C. Calhoun (ed.), *Habermas and the Public Sphere*. MIT Press, Cambridge, MA, pp. 143–64.

Schudson, M. (1992b) *Watergate in American Memory*. Basic Books, New York.

Schudson, M. (1998) *The Good Citizen: A History of American Civic Life*. Free Press, New York.

Scott, M. B. & Lyman, S. M. (1968) Accounts. *American Sociological Review* 33(Feb.), 46–62.

Searle, J. (1961) *Speech Acts: An Essay in the Philosophy of Language*. Cambridge University Press, Cambridge, UK.

Seidman, S. (1994) *Contested Knowledge: Social Theory in the Post-Modern Era*. Basil Blackwell, Oxford, UK.

Selznick, P. (1951) Institutional Vulnerability in Mass Society. *American Journal of Sociology* 56, 320–31.

Selznick, P. (1952) *The Organizational Weapon*. McGraw-Hill, New York.

Service, E. R. (1962) *Primitive Social Organization: An Evolutionary Perspective*. Random House, New York.

Service, E. R. (1979) *The Hunters*, 2nd edition. Prentice Hall, Englewood Cliffs. NJ.

Sewell, W. Jr. (1980) *Work and Revolution in France: The Language of Labor from the Old Regime to 1848*. Cambridge University Press, New York.

Sewell, W. Jr. (1985) Ideologies and Social Revolutions: Reflections on the French Case. *Journal of Modern History* 57, 57–85.

Sewell, W. Jr. (1992) A Theory of Structure: Duality, Agency, and Transformation. *American Journal of Sociology* 98(1), 1–29.

Sherwood, S. (1994) Narrating the Social: Postmodernism and the Drama of Democracy. *Journal of Narrative and Life History* 4, 69–88.

Shils, E. & Young, M. (1953) The Meaning of the Coronation. *Sociological Review* 1, 63–81.

Shoshan, A. ben (2010) *What Happened to the Israeli Left? Zionism, Democracy and the Construction of Israeli National Identity*. Senior Essay, Yale University.

Simmel, G. (1968) The Dramatic Actor and Reality. In G. Simmel, *The Conflict in Modern Culture and Other Essays*. Teachers College Press, New York, pp. 91–98.

Singer, M. (1959) *Traditional India: Structure and Change*. American Folklore Society, Philadelphia, PA.

Slater, P. (1966) *Microcosm*. John Wiley, New York.

Smelser, N. J. (1959) *Social Change in the Industrial Revolution*. Free Press, New York.

Smith, H. N. (1950) *Virgin Land: The American West as Symbol and Myth*. Harvard University Press, Cambridge, MA.

Smith, P. (1998) The New American Cultural Sociology. In P. Smith (ed.), *The New American Cultural Sociology*. Cambridge University Press, Cambridge, UK, pp. 1–14.

Smith, P. (2005) *Why War? The Cultural Logic of Suez, the Gulf War, and Iraq*. University of Chicago Press, Chicago, IL.

Smith, P. & Alexander, J. (2005) Introduction: The New Durkheim. In J. C. Alexander & P. Smith, *The Cambridge Companion to Durkheim*. Cambridge University Press, Cambridge, UK, pp. 1–40.

Snow, D. A., Rochford, E. B., Worden, S. K. & Benford, R. D. (1986) Frame Alignment Processes, Micromobilization and Movement Participation. *American Sociological Review* 51, 464–81.

Somers, M. R. (1995) Narrating and Naturalizing Civil Society and Citizenship Theory: The Place of Political Culture and the Public Sphere. *Sociological Theory* 13, 229–274.

Spencer, W. B. & Gillen, F. J. (1927) *The Arunta, 2 vols*. Macmillan, London.

Spillman, L. (1997) *Nation and Commemoration: Creating National Identities in the United States and Australia*. Cambridge University Press, Cambridge, UK

Stanislavski, C. (1989 [1934]) *An Actor Prepares*. Theatre Arts Books, New York.

Stanner, W. E. H. (1972) The Dreaming. In W. Lessa & E. Vogt, *Reader in Comparative Religion*. Row, Peterson, Evanston, IL, pp. 269–77.

Stelter, B. & Rutenberg, J. (2008) Obama's speech is a TV hit, with reviewers and commentators alike. *New York Times*, August 29, p. A14.

Swidler, A. (1986) Culture in Action: Symbols and Strategies. *American Sociological Review* 51(3), 273–86.

Sztompka, P. (1999) *Trust: A Sociological Theory*. Cambridge University Press, New York.

Talbot, S. & Chanda, N. (eds.) (2002) *The Age of Terror: America and the World after September 11*. Basic Books, New York.

Taylor, C. (1989) *Sources of the Self: The Making of Modern Identity*. Harvard University Press, Cambridge, MA.

Taylor, D. (1995) Performing Gender: Las Madres de la Plaza de Mayo. In D. Taylor & J. Villegas (eds.), *Negotiating Performance: Gender, Sexuality, and Theatricality in Latin/o American*. Duke University Press, Durham, NC, pp. 275–305.

Taylor, D. (1997) *Disappearing Acts: Spectacles of Gender and Nationalism in Argentina's "Dirty War."* Duke University Press, Durham, NC.

Thompson, K. (1990). Secularization and Sacralization. In J. C. Alexander & P. Sztompka (eds.), *Rethinking Progress: Movements, Forces, and Ideas at the end of the 20th Century*. Unwin Hyman, Boston, MA, pp. 161–81.

Thrift, N. (1999) The Place of Complexity. *Theory, Culture & Society* 16(3), 31–70.

Tocqueville, A. de (2004 [1835, 1840]) *Democracy in America*, vols. I & II. Library of America, New York.

REFERENCES

Todd, C. & Gawiser, S. (2009) *How Barack Obama Won: A State-by-State Guide to the Historic 2008 Presidential Election*. Vintage, New York, p. 16.

Trinh, T. M. (1989) *Woman, Native, Other: Writing Postcoloniality and Feminism*. Indiana University Press, Bloomington, IN.

Turner, J. H. (2002) *Face to Face: Toward a Sociological Theory of Interpersonal Behavior*. Stanford University Press, Stanford, CA.

Turner, V. (1969) *The Ritual Process: Structure and Anti-structure*. Aldine De Gruyter, New York.

Turner, V. (1974a) *Dramas, Fields, and Metaphors: Symbolic Action in Human Society*. Cornell University Press, Ithaca, NY.

Turner, V. (1974b) Religious Paradigms and Political Action: Thomas Becket at the Council of Northampton. In *Dramas, Fields, and Metaphors*. Cornell University Press, Ithaca, NY, pp. 60–97.

Turner, V. (1977) Symbols in African Ritual. In J. L. Dolgin, D. S. Kemnitzer & D. M. Schneider (eds.), *Symbolic Anthropology: A Reader in the Study of Symbols and Meanings*. Columbia University Press, New York, pp. 183–94.

Turner, V. (1982) *From Ritual to Theatre: The Human Seriousness of Play*. PAJ Press, Baltimore, MD.

Turner, V. (1987) *The Anthropology of Performance*. PAJ Publications, New York.

Tyler, P. (2003) War Imminent as Hussein Rejects Ultimatum. *New York Times*, March 19, pp. 1, 9.

Udovitch, A. L. (1987) The Constitution of the Traditional Islamic Marketplace: Islamic Law and the Social Context of Exchange. In S. N. Eisenstadt (ed.), *Patterns of Modernity, Vol. 2, Beyond the West*. Francis Pinter, London, pp. 150–71.

Veltrusky, J. (1964) Man and Object in the Theater. In P. L. Garvin (ed.), *A Prague School Reader on Esthetics, Literary Structure, and Style*. Georgetown University Press, Washington, DC, pp. 83–91.

Verdery, K. (1991) *National Ideology under Socialism*. University of California Press, Berkeley, CA.

Von Hoffman, N. (1978) *Make-Believe Presidents: Illusions of Power from McKinley to Carter*. Pantheon, New York.

Wagner-Pacifici, R. (1986) *The Moro Morality Play: Terrorism as Social Drama*. University of Chicago Press, Chicago, IL.

Wagner-Pacifici, R. (1994) *Discourse and Destruction: The City of Philadelphia versus MOVE*. University of Chicago Press, Chicago, IL.

Wagner-Pacifici, R. (2000) *Theorizing the Standoff: Contingency in Action*. Cambridge University Press, Cambridge, UK.

Walzer, M. (1965) *The Revolution of the Saints*. Harvard University Press, Cambridge, MA.

Warner, W. L. (1959) *The Living and the Dead: A Study of the Symbolic Life of Americans*. Yale University Press, New Haven, CT.

Weber, M. (1927 [1904–05]) Introduction, and Part II, Section IV. In *The Protestant Ethic and the Spirit of Capitalism*. Scribner, New York.

Weber, M. (1978 [1956]) *Economy and Society*. University of California Press, Berkeley, CA.

White, H. (1987) *The Content of the Form*. Johns Hopkins University Press, Baltimore, MD.

White, J. K. (2009) A Transforming Election: How Barack Obama Changed American Politics. In W. J. Crotty (ed.), *Winning the Presidency 2008.* Paradigm Publishers, Boulder, CO, p. 204.

Wittgenstein, L. (1953) *Philosophical Investigations.* Macmillan, London.

Woodward, B. (2002) *Bush at War.* Simon & Schuster, New York.

Woodward, B. (2004) *Plan of Attack.* Simon & Schuster, New York.

Zelizer, B. (1998) *Remembering to Forget: Holocaust Memory Through the Camera's Eye.* University of Chicago Press, Chicago, IL.

Zelizer, V. (1985) *Pricing the Priceless Child: The Changing Social Value of Children.* Basic Books, New York.

INDEX

Made in the USA
Monee, IL
01 September 2023

41969043R00142